DATA DATA
EVERYWHERE

DATA DATA EVERYWHERE

Access and Accountability?

Edited by
Colleen M. Flood

Queen's Policy Studies Series
School of Policy Studies, Queen's University
McGill-Queen's University Press
Montreal & Kingston • London • Ithaca

SCHOOL OF
Policy Studies

Publications Unit
Robert Sutherland Hall
138 Union Street
Kingston, ON, Canada
K7L 3N6
www.queensu.ca/sps/

The preferred citation for this book is:
Flood, C.M., ed. 2011. *Data Data Everywhere: Access and Accountability?* Montreal and Kingston: Queen's Policy Studies Series, McGill-Queen's University Press.

Library and Archives Canada Cataloguing in Publication

Data data everywhere : access and accountability? / edited by Colleen M. Flood.

Co-published by: School of Policy Studies, Queen's University.
Includes bibliographical references and index.
ISBN 978-1-55339-236-1 (pbk.)

1. Medical records—Access control—Canada. 2. Privacy, Right of—Canada. 3. Health—Research—Canada. I. Flood, Colleen M. (Colleen Marion), 1966- II. Queen's University (Kingston, Ont.). School of Policy Studies

R864.D38 2011   651.5'042610971   C2010-901841-9

CONTENTS

UNIQUELY CANADIAN APPROACHES TO DATA LINKAGE

WHAT MAKES US SICK? WHAT MAKES US BETTER?
DATA AND DISEASES

WALKING THE TALK: A ROADMAP FOR ACTION
AND EXCELLENCE

ACKNOWLEDGEMENTS

This volume grew out of a Health Information Summit, held in Toronto on 20–21 October 2008, which brought together over 250 stakeholders from across Canada and abroad. This event was made possible through the financial support of several CIHR institutes: the Institute of Health Services and Policy Research; the Institute of Population and Public Health; the Institute of Infection and Immunity; the Institute of Genetics; the Institute of Musculoskeletal Health and Arthritis; the Institute of Nutrition, Metabolism and Diabetes; the Institute of Aboriginal People's Health; and the Institute of Circulatory and Respiratory Health. In addition the summit was sponsored by Statistics Canada, the Canadian Health Services Research Foundation, the Canadian Institute for Health Information, and Canada Health Infoway.

I would also like to acknowledge the invaluable assistance provided by my colleagues on the event's Steering Committee: Tony Chin, Dale McMurchy, Richard Alvarez, Penny Ballem, Reiner Banken, Ross Hodgins, Peter Liu, David Loukidelis, Pat Martens, Kim McGrail, Annette Trimbee, Fiona Webster, Don Willison, Michael Wolfson, Bobbe Wood, and Glenda Yeates. The event would not have been possible without the deft organizational skills of Tony Chin, Sally Clelford, and Stephanie Soo.

Thanks also to Jennifer Dolling and Amy Stein, my research assistants, and to Valerie Jarus and Mark Howes at the School of Policy Studies, Queen's University, and Ellie Barton for the patience and dedication they have shown in bringing this volume to press. Charlyn Black and Kim McGrail kindly allowed me to use the title *Data Data Everywhere*, which they had coined for a report on similar issues. Thanks also to Brad Abernethy for his patience and fortitude in helping create a common grammar and style across the various contributions.

I would like to conclude with special thanks to two people. First to Dale McMurchy, who provided endless hours of advice on the issues and potential speakers and contributors, and filled in for me to wrap up the conference when ill health kept me from the podium. Finally, thanks to Bryan Thomas, research associate at the Faculty of Law, University of Toronto, for his superb research, organizational support, and editorial advice.

SEARCHING FOR A SWEET SPOT: HOW DO WE TRADE OFF RESEARCH BENEFITS WITH HEALTH INFORMATION PRIVACY CONCERNS?

COLLEEN M. FLOOD AND BRYAN THOMAS

THE STAKES

At a cost of $192 billion per year, if our health-care system were a country, it would rank just above Pakistan in terms of 2009 GDP.[1] Canada's health-care system is an industry equivalent to *three* Microsoft corporations.[2] With many provincial governments now spending nearly 50 percent of their total budgets on health care, it is hard to overstate the importance of information to the effective management and delivery of health care across Canada. But despite this, and a revolution in personal communication devices and modern information technology, Canada has been painstakingly slow at capitalizing on the potential to "electronically capture information as it is created and subsequently reuse that information at negligible incremental cost."[3] Given the scale of Canada's health-care system and the magnitude of existing quality and safety concerns—a conservative estimate suggests 16,500 Canadians die each year in hospital as a result of preventable medical errors[4]—this state of affairs is simply unacceptable.

Without high-quality information, governments do not know to the fullest extent possible the health and cost consequences of their various policy choices, and so are more prone to stakeholder lobbying and to

Data Data Everywhere: Access and Accountability? ed. C.M. Flood. Montreal and Kingston: Queen's Policy Studies Series, McGill-Queen's University Press. © 2011 The School of Policy Studies, Queen's University at Kingston. All rights reserved.

making decisions based on anecdote rather than evidence. Without high-quality information, physicians, nurses, and other health-care providers are robbed of the opportunity to have the fullest information possible to better treat their patients. Finally, without high-quality information, patients themselves are systematically denied the opportunity to monitor the quality of care they receive, to give feedback to providers, and to better manage their own care. In short, we are compromising the quality of patient care and not achieving our potential in improving the health of Canadians.

WHAT WE ADDRESS IN THIS BOOK

Generating more and more data is not the goal; rather, data need to be transformed into reliable evidence. This volume brings together diverse perspectives on the "secondary" use of Canadians' personal health information for the purposes of research and quality improvement. Caring directly for the patient is of course the "primary" use of personal health information, but once collected for this purpose, it may be employed for a variety of "secondary" uses such as improving quality and safety within a hospital or long-term care home; improving the treatment of a specific disease; conducting epidemiological research into the causes of disease across a population; undertaking public health research to determine where investments in disease prevention are most needed; making budgetary decisions about where to target scarce resources across the health system; better managing wait times, and so on. If secondary data are not processed into reliable evidence for the purposes of research and improving health-care quality, we risk "drowning in information and starving for knowledge."[5]

In this volume a diverse group of scholars and decision-makers tackle the challenges and opportunities that exist to harness data, particularly for its secondary use, to improve Canada's health-care system and the health of Canadians whilst protecting the privacy of personal health information. The chapters are clustered into five sections. The first section sets the stage; contributors provide definitions and outline the major issues relating to the protection of personal health information, challenges and opportunities inherent in various technological solutions, and the ethical, legal, and regulatory issues pertaining to secondary use of data. The second section presents a kaleidoscope of different views on how best to balance the health and economic benefits of enabling the use of data for research and quality improvement versus the desire to keep personal health information strictly protected. Canada has, despite the absence of a national strategy, made some enormous strides in data linkage, particularly through provincially sponsored data centres, and these are described and discussed in the third section. Contributors discuss in section four a range of benefits to be had in disease prevention and control from the better employment of secondary data. The final section proposes frameworks for producing policy that better balances the benefits of research and quality improvement against privacy rights and concerns.

It is worth acknowledging, here at the outset, that the distinction between primary and secondary use is not crystal clear. As former Canadian Medical Association president Robert Ouellet notes in his contribution to this volume, it is hard to delineate a patient's "circle of care" with great precision. "Arguably," he writes, "housekeepers/cleaners, dietitians, clergy, social workers, nurses, aides, and doctors all play a part in an individual's health care." One might ask why medical researchers or health services managers—whose work ultimately has an important impact on patient care—should be deemed to fall outside this already expansive circle. In sharp contrast to Dr. Ouellet's claim that "secondary use of electronically stored personal health information has little to do with the immediate care of the patient," contributor Alan Katz urges us to resist any suggestion that secondary use of health information is less *important* than primary use. In our view, the difference is only that secondary usage *may* have a less direct impact upon a particular patient's care. Information gleaned from encounters with other similar patients in similar circumstances is the means by which to provide evidence to inform the treatment of any given patient now. In the larger scheme of things, both primary and secondary usages of health information are vitally important to ensuring high quality, accessible, and affordable health care for each and every patient. We agree with Katz that primary and secondary use should be considered points along a spectrum of information use rather than as distinct categories.

CANADA'S RELATIVELY POOR PERFORMANCE

An important part of the context for this book is the extent to which Canada has lagged behind internationally in implementing electronic information technologies in health care and establishing policy that balances privacy concerns with the need to facilitate use of data for research and quality improvement.[6] The OECD's 2010 economic survey on Canada notes that "in the longer run the soundness of Canada's public finances will likely be largely determined by the decisions regarding the healthcare system" and that "information-technology applications in health care (notably electronic health patient records) should be accelerated, though ways will have to be found to deal with legitimate concerns about patient privacy as some other OECD countries have successfully done."[7] Governments at both the federal and provincial levels appear to have been aware of the need for action for more than a decade.[8] The federal government's strategy to date, under the rubric of Canada Health Infoway, has been heavily focused on the rollout of Electronic Health Records (EHRs) at an institutional level (e.g., in and between hospitals) and is now only slowly moving toward the development of EHRs at the level of primary care.

Again from a comparative perspective we lag far behind—the Commonwealth Fund's 2010 Annual Country Profiles gauge IT within health systems by looking at the proportion of primary care physicians using electronic medical records. Canada, at 37 percent uptake, trails far behind the Netherlands at 99 percent, New Zealand at 97 percent, Norway at 97 percent, the United Kingdom at 96 percent, Australia at 95 percent, Sweden at 94 percent, Italy at 94 percent, Germany at 72 percent, France at 68 percent, and even the United States at 46 percent.[9] To get a quick sense of what Canadians are missing in this regard, consider for example that patients belonging to the US managed-care organization Kaiser Permanente have, for several years,[10] had access to a system called *HealthConnectOnline*, which records allergies, immunizations, future appointments, diagnoses, lab results, and instructions from past visits; the service also allows patients to reorder prescriptions, book appointments, and communicate electronically with health professionals.[11] From a cost and health-outcome perspective, there are significant gains to be made through better management of patients with chronic disease or multiple comorbidities. Moreover, due to lack of integrated information, many Canadian patients do not experience a smooth continuum of care but instead fall through the cracks of our system, causing not only personal distress but also problems in safety and quality. Failing to utilize information to better manage the system does not just waste money, it kills people—Canadians are second only to US patients in the likelihood of experiencing medical, medication, or lab errors.[12]

And at the same time as Canada has been relatively slow to implement EHRs, it has also, as both Willison et al. and Lewis note, paid insufficient attention to ensuring that health information gathered through electronic processes can be subsequently employed for research, quality improvement, and policy-making.[13] Putting off decisions about the secondary use of data may come at a high cost, if it means that EHRs are not built from the ground up with secondary uses in mind—for research and quality improvement, and for policy-making.

Why has Canada moved at a relatively glacial pace when it comes to embracing the possibilities for use of information for research, quality improvement, and better policy-making? There are a number of possible reasons and, as Lewis tersely notes, some are more valid justifications than others. For instance, Lewis, in the final chapter in this book, argues that provider and governmental resistance to the release of more information about their performance may be gussied up in the guise of privacy protection, and thus we need to be alert to a convergence of interests supporting more privacy than is truly necessary. At its nub, the policy trade-off that has to be made is between an individual's potential interest in controlling his or her own personal health information versus the benefits that can accrue from the employment of that data in research, quality improvement, and policy-making. What we sometimes see are warring camps—those in favour of privacy versus those in favour of research, quality improvement, and improving the overall health of the Canadian population. In truth, both are important, and mechanisms are needed to protect and enhance privacy whilst facilitating as much use of data as is feasible for the greater public benefit.

JURISDICTIONAL ISSUES

In terms of those real impediments that Lewis agrees we need to address, complexities arise because, as Kosseim writes, the policy dilemma "at the crossroads of data protection and health research is forcibly multijurisdictional." Under the *Constitution Act*,[14] health care falls under provincial jurisdiction, with the federal government exerting some pressure for national standards through its taxing and spending powers. The political hurdles on the way to establishing a pan-Canadian health information system have been considerable, as a result.[15] The splitting of constitutional responsibility for health care also exacerbates accountability problems, in that the Canadian public is not sure what level of government to hold accountable for a system that does not function nearly as well as it should given the resources invested. Related to this is the possibility that governments are not particularly supportive of the use of data for secondary purposes, particularly research, for fear that such research will reveal failings on the part of governments to adequately manage their respective health-care systems. There has to be a culture change whereby governments are persuaded that research evidence is, on balance, empowering rather than disempowering and, importantly, citizens are persuaded that their privacy rights are sufficiently protected. As Tamblyn notes, in the latter regard researchers must make greater and more sophisticated efforts to communicate to the public what measures they take to protect individual privacy, and what the benefits of secondary use of data are for patients and their families.

A second jurisdictional issue is that the handling of personal health information falls under the purview of both provincial privacy laws (which vary from province to province), federal privacy laws (the *Personal Information Protection and Electronic Documents Act*, or *PIPEDA*), and numerous professional codes of conduct. This overlapping patchwork of laws and regulations has led to uncertainty, which has slowed the development of EHRs[16] and has had a chilling effect on the secondary use of data for research and quality improvement purposes. As Willison, Gibson, and McGrail put it in their chapter: "Nobody wants to be on the wrong side of the law, so initial policy interpretations of the legal requirements have tended to err on the side of restricting access." Gershon and Tu explain how an overly conservative interpretation of existing privacy legislation has significantly hampered observational research in recent years. On a more optimistic note, Kosseim argues that many Canadian provinces have only recently enacted privacy legislation, and there is hope that the uncertainty may be resolved in time. In reviewing their respective legislation, there will be ongoing opportunities for provinces to fine-tune and clarify the operation of privacy protections. It is critical that governing legislation articulates as a core principle the importance of harnessing the benefits flowing from secondary use of data for research and quality improvement and that privacy, whilst important, be balanced against this larger community interest.

PATIENT CONSENT AND TRUST

In addition to the political and technological hurdles just mentioned, there are of course real ethical challenges that must be addressed when contemplating the secondary use of personal health information. These ethical dilemmas are discussed from diverse perspectives throughout this volume. Of central concern here is the patient's right to privacy. Informed consent is the paramount principle in modern medical ethics, and consent requirements extend to the secondary use of patients' personal health information. In carrying out their work, health-care providers are privy to some of the most sensitive details of our personal lives, including mental health issues, drug and alcohol addiction, sexually transmitted infections, and so on. The practice of quality medicine requires a relationship of trust between patients and health-care providers. It is no surprise, then, that the physicians' duty of confidentiality to patients was recognized as far back as the Hippocratic Oath,[17] and has been recognized as a *legal* obligation by the Supreme Court of Canada.[18] As Ouellet and Armstrong note in their respective contributions, where trust erodes, patients may be reluctant to disclose information to their physicians. While EHRs may facilitate the legitimate sharing of health information, they do create a risk that future privacy breaches could be more extensive and harder to contain: recall, a major selling point of EHRs is that they bring together patient information garnered from multiple caregivers. As well, modern testing methods and diagnostic techniques reveal personal information of a sort that was previously unavailable, compounding patient anxieties about privacy. Polls by the Canadian Medical Association show that a considerable number of Canadians admit to withholding information from their health-care providers, for fear it may fall into the wrong hands. Having said that, polls indicate that the vast majority of Canadians are in favour of the use of EHRs, and support the secondary use of patient information in health research, provided identifying information is removed.[19] Canadians need to know that their personal information will be subject to robust privacy protections *and* that their experiences with the health-care system will be turned into evidence to improve health care for themselves, their families, and all Canadians. It is not an either/or choice.

TRADE-OFFS

We need to acknowledge the risks on both sides of the privacy equation. Were the protection of patient privacy given *absolute* priority—and patient data kept locked away from potential secondary use—the long-term cost to research, public health, and health systems management would be inestimable. Ultimately, these costs would be felt at the level of patient care through a failure to curb the present rate of safety failures and medical errors, improve the management of chronic conditions, better manage resources and waiting times for treatments, better deploy new technologies, and so on. Lewis argues for an open and highly diffused use of health information, and bluntly states: "Imagining that Canada can dramatically improve its health system performance without a widely accessed, first-rate health information system is a delusion."

Plainly then, the answer is not to say, in the abstract, that privacy trumps secondary usage in all cases, or vice versa. What is needed is a reasonable balancing of the privacy interests at stake against secondary uses, on a contextualized basis. As Willison, Gibson, and McGrail argue, the debate needs to shift from asking "*Should* health research be considered a permitted use of health information?" to asking "What *types* of research would qualify, and under what conditions?" At present we need to accept that there is no magic technological cure that will irrevocably guarantee the protection of personal health information in every context. If we attempt to develop hard-and-fast rules (some things are allowed, some are not), it may mean in some situations that research cannot be conducted when it ought to be. Yet in the absence of hard-and-fast rules, it appears that we must accept elevated risks to the use of personal health information. An alternative to these either/or scenarios is to accept the need for some form of decision-maker, such as a research ethics board, that exercises discretion in deciding on a case-by-case basis how best to balance privacy and the collective need for employing data in research and quality improvement.

In what follows we explore the two broad strategies, both of which figure prominently in this volume, that are generally promoted as a means of reconciling patient privacy rights with the secondary use of health information and the problems inherent in both: one is eliciting patient consent, and the other is de-identifying data. We then move to a fuller discussion of the role of Research Ethics Boards (REBs) and their potential for making the trade-offs needed on a contextual basis. First, though, it worth noting that under *existing* provincial and federal laws, secondary use of personal health information is in some cases allowed, on a discretionary basis, with no legislated requirement of consent *or* de-identification. For example, personal health information may be shared with "prescribed entities" for the purpose of processing health-care payments, or for the planning, management, and analysis of the health-care system.[20] In their chapter, Chafe, Spencer, Hudson, Milnes, and Sullivan offer us the perspective of one such prescribed entity, Cancer Care Ontario. Similarly, internationally acclaimed data centres like the Manitoba Centre for Health Policy (discussed in the contributions from, respectively, Martens and Katz) and Ontario's Institute for Clinical Evaluative Sciences (discussed by Gershon and Tu) are allowed to use de-identified personal health information data—subject to a range of robust and specific safeguards. Thus one approach is to allow "safe fortresses" to have access to personal health information for secondary use on the basis that the likelihood of disclosure, given the privacy systems and protocols in place, is substantially lessened in these environments. However, the vast majority of researchers are still not members of these data centres, a subject to which we will return. In some cases, personal health information may be shared for research purposes—without patient consent—if a REB provides approval. For example, where research requires that information from EHRs be matched with provincial administrative records, REBs may allow disclosure of identifiable information for the purposes of this cross-referencing, but stipulate that the resulting database then be de-identified.[21] Again, we discuss the role of REBs further below.

PATIENT CONSENT

As mentioned, the underlying value driving concern for patient privacy is the principle of informed consent, paramount in medical ethics. In carrying out a research project with a patient cohort over a limited time span, it may be possible to address privacy concerns by securing patient consent, and even to renew consent on an ongoing basis as new secondary uses are undertaken. For proponents of a rigorous approach to privacy rights, the burden is squarely upon those who wish to use personal health information for research and quality improvement to secure consent—no consent, no research. Although this approach may seem reasonable enough, it raises a host of problems. For example, requiring individuals to opt-in to research studies by giving specific consent can mean over time that certain types of populations, particularly vulnerable populations, are systematically excluded from research. Certainly, innovative means can be employed to enlist vulnerable populations. For example, McMurchy and colleagues describe the evolution of an Ontario HIV cohort study wherein researchers were able to track patient medical histories—notwithstanding the grave consequences of privacy breaches for this cohort (social stigmatization, denial of life insurance, job loss, and so on). The study's success was due in large part to community involvement: participants joined the cohort voluntarily, and actively participated in its oversight. It offers an inspiring picture of what can be achieved on the research front by involving patients, earning their trust, and securing their ongoing consent; however, such approaches may not always be feasible, particularly in larger population studies. With very large cohorts—say, patients in British Columbia living with cancer, or the Canadian population as a whole—it would be very difficult to rely on a consent-based model. There is much to be learned from large-scale population-based research, but the cost of gathering (and re-gathering) consent for specific secondary uses is prohibitive. There is a worry as well that consent requirements may result in selection bias if particular subpopulations are, for one reason or another, difficult to reach and to obtain informed consent from. Emerging health issues may go unnoticed if vulnerable populations or patients with particular health conditions are underrepresented in the dataset relied upon by researchers and health administrators.[22]

An option here is to ease consent requirements by settling for *presumed* consent. Tamblyn, in her contribution, describes how Alberta and Quebec have each followed the same path in developing drug repositories that track patients' prescriptions. Both provinces initially relied upon a consent-based model, with physicians asking their patients to "opt in." It quickly became evident that this would be administratively unmanageable, as doctors were spending up to 30 minutes explaining the system to individual patients.[23] Both provinces moved to a regime of presumed consent, allowing patients to "opt out" of the repository if they so desired.

Alternatively, the administrative burden of obtaining patient consent may be eased by asking patients to issue *broad* consent at the time of information collection, granting consent to a range of secondary uses. As Kosseim explains in her chapter, it is not clear that the law, as it now stands, allows broad consent as a substitute for informed consent. The ethical challenge, she goes on to explain, is to ensure that in broad consent the patient is sufficiently well-informed, which requires somehow imparting to patients a sense of the known and *unknown* risks of data sharing that exist at the time of recruitment.

Technology may be able to ameliorate but not solve some of the administrative burdens associated with a consent-based approach. Some US commentators have recommended, for example, the creation of a nationwide Health Record Trust that would collect patients' health records in one central repository, and allow patients to assign their own "privacy settings" for secondary uses. This would follow the approach taken for example with web browsers, web-based email services, and social networking.[24] No doubt there could be efficiency gains through such an approach, as doctors and researchers would no longer be burdened with having to walk patients one-by-one through a maze of consent forms for secondary uses. But one should not think of this as a "silver bullet" solution to the underlying ethical dilemmas. Patients would still face the problem of decision overload, as they would be responsible for making ongoing decisions concerning the secondary use of their health information. Many, no doubt, would simply accept the default privacy settings (as do many users online), which is to say that the consent garnered through a Health Record Trust would, in the end, be a form of implied consent. An alternate worry is that many would, for simplicity's sake, opt for maximal privacy settings, thereby compromising the dataset. The problem would be especially acute if particular segments of the population (say, people of a certain age or ethnicity) were underrepresented in datasets as a result of a general tendency toward withholding consent to secondary uses.

A social contract argument could perhaps be made for overriding the consent requirement, and mandating that all citizens submit their health information for promising secondary uses. With web-browsers and social networking websites, those who opt for strong privacy settings pay a price in terms of usability: they are denied access to some websites and applications. In the case of secondary use of personal health information for medical research, there is no analogous trade-off to guarding one's privacy to the utmost, creating a free-rider problem. *Ex ante*, all of us benefit equally from the advancements made possible by the secondary use of data in research. Arguably, it is unfair that anyone should be allowed to share in these advancements while refusing to bear his or her share of the attendant risks to privacy—provided that robust measures are taken (technological, administrative, etc.) to protect individual privacy.

In the end, as a number of contributors conclude, there is no one-size-fits-all solution to this question of how to balance a patient's privacy interests with secondary usage of personal health information. Notice, in this regard, how settling upon a consent-based approach provides only the beginnings of answer. One must further specify the *kind* of consent required (i.e., actual or presumed, specific or broad). Plainly the appropriate specifications here will turn upon the sensitivity of the health information at issue, the relative benefits of the proposed secondary usage, and the administrative costs involved in adhering to one or another standard of consent. Depending on how these variables play out, the consent-based approach may in some cases be unfeasible or inappropriate.

A conclusion that "it depends" is not particularly palatable from the perspective of promoting research and quality improvement systems. Given it is necessary to strike a balance between privacy rights and research/quality improvement goals, the critical questions become: Who makes this decision? On the basis of what principles? And how quickly?

DE-IDENTIFICATION

Privacy concerns can be addressed by de-identifying health information before putting it to secondary use. Indeed, through de-identification, researchers can and do make use of vast stores of health information that is routinely collected for administrative purposes (e.g., hospital discharge records, physician billing records). In their contributions, Katz and Lix explore, respectively, the use of administrative data to guide improvements in the delivery of health services to populations, and to ascertain chronic disease cases. The appeal of this "paper clip" solution, described by Martens, is that it makes use of information already collected for other purposes, while minimizing risks to privacy. Lix describes, for example, how researchers are able to develop algorithms to be used in ascertaining patterns of chronic disease across the population from anonymized data.

There are degrees of de-identification, which pose varying risks to privacy. If, for example, anonymized hospital discharge records are linked with anonymized physician billing records, the possibility of discerning the identity of particular individuals is greater, albeit still small. Given the great benefits to be had from secondary use, there is a need to assess the actual risk of re-identification, as opposed to purely theoretical risks. As Lowrance explains in his contribution, there are real costs to secondary usage, as datasets are stripped down and de-linked in the name of privacy:

> The redacted data tend to lack fine personal detail, and because the identifiers have been stripped away, the data cannot be readily linked to other datasets. If the de-identification is irreversible, the data sources cannot be recontacted to validate the data, obtain additional information, or invite participation in other research projects.

Again, in thinking about access to anonymized datasets (and the risk of re-identification), there does not appear to be the ease of one-size-fits-all solutions. New and improved information technologies may enable data custodians to tailor datasets for particular research projects, so as to grant access to only those data fields that are strictly required. Where Katz and Lix are optimistic about all that can, with some resourcefulness, be gleaned from existing administrative datasets, other contributors urge that new and better systems of data collection are required, and must be built from the ground up with secondary use in mind. In her examination of secondary usage of information on drug prescriptions, Tamblyn speaks of the need for a

> new generation of tools … to assess the risk of re-identification in the context of a specific study, and allow customization of the classification of personal health information variables to minimize measurement error so that the most precise and most unbiased estimates of safety and effectiveness of drugs can be provided.

Similarly, Pringle, in her contribution, argues that new and improved databases are essential to the advancement of health services research, specifically nursing service. Pringle details the many challenges involved in implementing a database for this purpose. Among other things she notes that the collection of standardized, numeric measurements—of the sort needed to ensure the comparability of hospital data—will require a kind of cultural shift among nurses on the front lines. Nurses have been resistant, for example, to recording patients' levels of pain on a scale of 1–10, as this formal quantification is thought to depersonalize the nurse-patient relationship. This is only one example, but it is telling of the subtle adjustments involved in establishing a new and improved health information database.

As mentioned earlier, large-scale repositories of health information, collected for the purposes of administering publicly funded health-care systems, do exist in some provinces, and we can learn by studying their successes and setbacks to date. In her contribution, Martens explains how a rich repository of anonymized health and demographic information is stored and used for research purposes at the Manitoba Centre for Health Policy (MCHP). The MCHP has from its inception put great emphasis on the protection of patient privacy, and it is illuminating to read Martens's account of the complex and costly measures taken to ensure secure storage of this information (which *arrives* at MCHP in de-identified form). These privacy and security measures have come at a cost to researcher access. Until 2007, only researchers working in collaboration with an MCHP scientist could access the database. Having subsequently opened the door to independently run researcher projects, the MCHP is now trying to enable remote access to the database, making it accessible to researchers geographically remote from the MCHP's data laboratory. This has been a formidable challenge, requiring the creation of a new organizational wing at the MCHP. Ontario's Institute for Clinical Evaluative Sciences (ICES) is undertaking similar reform, creating satellite hubs to expand its data fortress to locations across Ontario (e.g., a hub to Queen's University, one to downtown Toronto).

Nonetheless, although these internationally renowned data centres are making efforts to include external researchers, many researchers cannot access data from these centres or their satellite arms. Moreover, expansion is incremental at best *within* a province, thus forestalling the ability to do comparative research across provincial boundaries. And levels of security vary greatly: where some researchers will face the labyrinthine security measures implemented at the MCHP and ICES, others may be carrying around vast amounts of personal health information on their laptops with little or no security measures in place. As Willison, Gibson, and McGrail observe, "Powerful personal computers and the gradual expansion of clinical EHRs in the inpatient and outpatient settings make the development of smaller ad hoc research databases both easy and inexpensive to assemble." An enormous challenge facing policy-makers, then, is to ensure that health information is accessible to researchers, while at the same time achieving an acceptable level of security standards across the country. National leadership is needed to create or at least facilitate a coherent Canada-wide approach.

THE ROLE OF RESEARCH ETHICS BOARDS

As emphasized already in this introductory chapter, the complex trade-offs involved in the secondary use of health information cannot be balanced in the abstract. An arrangement that strikes an optimal balance in one situation may be suboptimal in others. What this implies, from a legal and policy perspective, is that discretion will have to be placed in the hands of data custodians and research ethics boards (REBs) to make decisions, on a case-by-case basis, concerning secondary usage. In a sense, therefore, the key objective for policy-makers is to ensure that these bodies have the training, technology, and independence needed to carry out this function effectively and efficiently.

There are two primary sources of REB review in Canada. The first, spelled out in the recently revised *Tri-Council Policy Statement on Ethical Conduct for Research Involving Humans 2* (*TCPS 2*),[25] applies to research supported by federal funding agencies: the Canadian Institutes of Health Research, the National Sciences and Engineering Research Council of Canada, and the Social Sciences and Humanities Research Council of Canada. All major universities and research centres in Canada have bound themselves contractually with these agencies, committing to observe the ethical guidelines set out in the *TCPS 2*. As a result, the *TCPS 2* applies virtually across the board to academic research undertaken in Canada.[26] The second source of REB review, enacted through the *Food and Drugs Act*, applies to clinical trials of pharmaceuticals and medical devices. The guidance document here, a counterpart to the *TCPS 2*, is the rather wordily titled *International Conference on Harmonization of Good Clinical Practice Guidelines* (*ICH-GCP*).[27] For simplicity's sake, the discussion that follows will focus on the *TCPS 2*.

One major concern, which a number of commentators have raised in recent years, has to do with the level of relevant expertise within REBs. Article 6.4 of the *TCPS 2* states that a REB must consist of at least five members, including both men and women, with the following qualifications:

- At least two members have expertise in relevant research disciplines, fields, and methodologies covered by the REB;
- At least one member is knowledgeable in ethics;
- At least one member is knowledgeable in the relevant law (but that member should not be the institution's legal counsel or risk manager). This is mandatory for biomedical research and is advisable, but not mandatory, for other areas of research; and
- At least one member has no affiliation with the institution.

Commentators have noted that the interpretation of membership require-ments has varied tremendously from one REB to the next.[28] There is, for example, no professional designation certifying expertise in ethics, to be incorporated by reference here, and what guidance is offered in the *TCPS 2* is open-ended: "A member knowledgeable in ethics ... needs to have sufficient knowledge to guide an REB in identifying and address-ing ethics issues. A balance of theory, practice and experience offers the most effective path to knowledge in ethics for REB membership."[29] One wonders whether it is a common occurrence for would-be recruits to REBs to decline the invitation, citing their lack of ethical reasoning skills?

It is difficult to gauge the general quality of decisions rendered by REBs because, as Knoppers notes in a recent article, "no central clearing house of decisions and supporting arguments from the letters sent by ethics review committees exists to guide future applicants, to demonstrate transparency, or to foster natural justice through a public 'jurisprudence' of decisions rendered."[30] Moreover, there is no dedicated appeal body for REB decisions to ensure that REB decisions are addressed competently and consistently, and in accordance with principles that are open to public scrutiny.[31] There is, however, a possibility that a REB could be the subject of a general judicial review challenge to a court on the basis that either its decision was unreasonable or it did not comply with procedural fairness in rendering its decision.[32]

The *TCPS 2* sets out an ethical framework to be applied by REBs that amounts to a kind of cost-benefit analysis. The *TCPS 2* instructs REBs to "attempt to achieve the most favourable balance of risks and potential benefits in a research proposal,"[33] and prescribes a "proportionate ap-proach" to research ethics review, whereby levels of scrutiny increase with levels of risk. As others have noted, assessments of risk should ideally involve a kind of actuarial work, extrapolating from statistics about previ-ous events to "turn uncertainties into probabilities."[34] The *TCPS 2* suggests that REBs should consult perspectives of the participants themselves, along with research in epidemiology, genetics, sociology, and cultural anthropology, in gauging the magnitude or seriousness of the harm.[35] In assessing the *probability* of the harm occurring, REBs are instructed to consult past experience, and to review existing publications that provide rates of harm in similar issues or "other empirical evidence."[36]

Anecdotal reports suggest that REBs are, in reality, seldom very em-pirical in their assessments of risk. Instead a kind of armchair approach is often taken, whereby REB members imagine worst-case scenarios, and impose upon researchers measures for their avoidance. The difficulty with this "probability neglect," as one critic explains, is that "with little to constrain imaginings of possible harms, researchers are being asked to mitigate a host of potentialities precisely because we do not know how likely or unlikely they might be."[37] Lewis's contribution to this volume somewhat echoes this point, as he argues that data security is not nearly so perilous as is often assumed by privacy rights advocates. "Citizens are not lurking beside dumpsters," he writes, "in the hope that a carelessly disposed paper medical record will furnish them with information to use against an individual. Very few people have any motive to learn anything about an identifiable individual's health condition." The "theoretical possibility of potentially sinister use" does not justify a closed health information culture.

Article 5.5 of *TCPS 2* addresses secondary use of identifiable information for research purposes. Such use is allowed, without individual consent, only where the REB is satisfied that the identifiable information is essential to the research; secondary use without consent is unlikely to adversely affect the welfare of the individuals; appropriate measures are taken to protect privacy and safeguard identifiable information; any known preferences previously expressed by individuals are complied with; it is impossible or impracticable to obtain the individuals' consent; and the researchers have obtained any other necessary permission for secondary use (e.g., in privacy legislation).[38] The *TCPS 2* assumes (probably erroneously) that a clear line can be drawn between identifiable and non-identifiable information, and permits secondary use of non-identifiable information without consent. Where researchers propose to link anonymized datasets in ways that might create identifiable information, they must satisfy their REB that the linkage is essential to the research and that appropriate security measures will be taken (Article 5.7).

New information technologies, and notably the implementation of EHRs, could enable secondary usage of health information on a grander scale, with bigger research payoffs but also more complicated risks. It is imperative that REBs evolve accordingly, adopting more sophisticated approaches to risk assessment. For example, it is commonly noted by strict privacy advocates that anonymized health information could, in principle, be linked back to a patient. This is one of those "theoretical possibilities" that must be evaluated probabilistically.

As things now stand, there is no formal system for monitoring the training of REB members. No orientation sessions are offered to new recruits to REBs, and there is no system of continuing education in place.[39] In fairness, there do exist training programs tailored to REBs: the Canadian Association of Research Ethics Boards (CAREB) and the National Council on Ethics in Human Research (NCEHR) both independently offer "REB 101" courses; the latter offers a REB 201 course as well—but there is no national body that presently evaluates these programs and tracks certification.

Not all critics of REBs favour increased training and accreditation as a solution. One scholar, Kevin Haggerty, worries that a move in this direction will only result in an enlarged bureaucracy, more formal and rigid in its assessment of research applications. Haggerty is most concerned about what he perceives as the creeping expansion of REB review into areas of research where the risks of harm are largely imaginary. "The more ethical roadblocks are installed for innovative and critical research," he writes, "the more we risk homogenizing inquiry and narrowing vision, as scholars start to follow what they perceive to be the path of least institutional resistance."[40]

Having said this, there are options available to streamline the ethics review process, without necessarily undermining its effectiveness. For example, where research is undertaken jointly by multiple institutions—as is becoming increasingly common—it is standard practice to have the REB of each and every participating institution review the proposal. This obviously results in needless headaches for legions of researchers across the country and often costly and unnecessarily burdensome administrative delays; moreover, different REBs might reach different conclusions regarding risks and benefits. Strictly speaking, the *TCPS 2* does not require these multiple approvals, as article 8.1 allows that "[a]n institution that has established an REB may approve alternative review models for research involving multiple REBs and/or institutions." Among these alternatives, ethics review may be delegated to an external, specialized, or multi-institutional REB.[41] Short of delegation, the REBs of multiple institutions may enter into agreements for reciprocal REB review—agreeing effectively to accept the findings of REBs from partner institutions. Yet these harmonization options, to date, are seldom pursued in practice. Perhaps this is due to a fear of legal liability or to an abundance of caution that Haggerty and others allege is endemic to the culture of research endeavour. Or perhaps it is due to a dash of hubris on the part of research ethics boards themselves.

Other countries seem to be generating solutions to the problem of multi-institutional review being required for the same piece of research. Australia's National Health and Medical Research Council is developing a system to support the *single* ethical review of a research ethics committee that is recognized by all institutions participating in a given collaborative research project. In 2007, the government of Australia allocated $5.6 million, over four years, to the Harmonization of Multi-Centre Ethical Review (HoMER) project for the development and implementation of a national approach for single ethical review. The Australian government has noted, among other things, that single ethical review, being more streamlined, is more amenable to independent verification. The HoMER project has made the ethics review process more transparent and consistent for researchers, institutions, and other stakeholders. The formalization of the ethical review process is also expected to enhance public confidence.[42]

As indicated, it is technically possible for Canadian institutions participating in collaborative research projects to harmonize their ethics review. Yet it seems that institutional REBs are reluctant to take on the liability risks associated with reviewing research that is not based in their institution.[43] In response, the *TCPS 2* might be modified to require that all funded researchers be members of institutions that have processes and policies in place to facilitate harmonization of review processes so as to allow, where possible, single ethical review. To sweeten the deal, federal and provincial funding agencies could finance the development of guidelines to inform these processes and policies and perhaps even offer specific assistance to institutions to implement harmonization policies. Given the costs and amount of planning involved in Australia's launch of HoMER, it would appear extremely optimistic to expect such coordination to arise spontaneously in Canada. It will take a concerted effort, at the national level, to effectively implement a Canadian analogue to HoMER.

CONCLUSION

This volume brings together diverse views concerning the promises and perils of the secondary use of personal health information not only for research and quality assurance purposes but also for governmental decision-making. The chapters amply display the policy tensions and challenges to be met. Yet there are inestimable benefits to Canadian patients and citizens in supporting the advancement of electronic health data collection—both for the immediate care of patients and for subsequent research and decision-making. It is simply not possible to overestimate the benefits that can flow from better management (with better research evidence) of our health-care system, currently costing $192 billion per year. As Lewis notes, "Care is not primarily driven by real-time, relevant, comprehensive information; it is driven by other forces.... In many cases we pay more for bad quality and mistakes than for excellence." Balanced against the drive for better information and better decision-making is the concern that medical information can sometimes be the most sensitive form of personal information we have. Whilst many members of the public may have few qualms about handing over personal information (as we frequently do online via Facebook and other mediums), privacy policy cannot be developed on a majority rules basis. A balance has to be struck between the potential benefits for research and the potential risks to privacy.

We conclude this introduction and overview with our take on the top ten things that need to happen for Canada to negotiate the trade-offs required between the benefits of health research and quality assurance with privacy protection:

1. Legislation, regulation, and policy should emphasize the need to *balance* privacy of personal health information with the importance of data for secondary use for the purposes of research and quality improvement.
2. No sharp distinction should be made in law, regulation, or policy between "primary" and "secondary" use; rather, it should be recognized

that there are a range of uses for personal health information that carry different levels of risks to privacy and benefits to health-care decision-making.

3. Research ethics board decision-making needs to be rationalized to eliminate duplication and to facilitate research spanning institutions and provinces, and to ensure robust ethical review and realistic appraisal of risks to privacy. Consideration should be given to modify the *TCPS 2* to require funded researchers to be situated at institutions that have such policies in place, and some funding could be provided to facilitate the development of these policies and procedures.

4. It is important in designing policy to think through the complexities of interface between human nature and both regulation and technology. For example, Tamblyn notes that if security systems are too onerous, then researchers will figure out "work arounds" that could jeopardize security. Consequently, privacy protocols for data collection should neither expect nor require superhuman effort.

5. Researchers and governments must work together (supported by national and provincial research funding agencies) so that governments can see that data used for research and quality improvement will enhance the efficiency and equity of their respective health-care systems and that research is not designed to embarrass governments into action.

6. True concerns about patient privacy need to be separated out from these other, less ethically serious concerns such as resistance by health-care professionals to change or resistance by government to better information about system performance.

7. Researchers must accept accountability for their use of personal health information and devote more time to communicating to the public the health and quality benefits flowing from secondary usage for research and quality improvement purposes, and explaining the safeguards in place to protect individual privacy.

8. Training in privacy requirements and techniques should be part of tertiary education programs in health care (public health, health services and policy, medical professional training, etc.).

9. Canada Health Infoway, in developing EHRs across the country, should work with the research community to ensure that the architecture of EHRs anticipates the need to collect data for research and quality improvement.

10. Federal and provincial agencies should support clinician researchers to use administrative and clinical data for surveillance and research purposes so that doctors, nurses, pharmacists, and so forth can see in real time the health and care benefits for patients (and for themselves) of collecting data and complying with the various privacy protocols needed to do such collection.

Effective information gathering and analysis is essential if Canadians are to receive proportional value for the hundreds of billions of dollars they invest annually in their health-care system. Our hope is that this volume will help kick-start this important conversation on how best to balance genuine privacy concerns over health information with the many gains to be had from the secondary use of data.

NOTES

1. CIA, *The CIA World Factbook 2010* (Washington, DC: Central Intelligence Agency, 2010), https://www.cia.gov/library/publications/the-world-factbook/.
2. Microsoft Corporation, *Annual Report 2010*, https://www.microsoft.com/investor/reports/ar10/10k_fh_fin.html (accessed 26 January 2011).
3. T.J. Nelson, "On the Importance of Information in Health Care" (1998), http://www.tjnelson.com/medapp.htm.
4. G.R. Baker, P.G. Norton, V. Flintoft, R. Blais, A. Brown, J. Cox, E. Etchells, W.A. Ghali, P. Herbert, S.R. Majumdar, et al., "The Canadian Adverse Events Study: The Incidence of Adverse Events among Hospital Patients in Canada," *Canadian Medical Association Journal* 170, no. 11 (2004): 1684. To account for statistical error, Baker et al. estimate a range of 9,250 to 23,750 deaths from preventable error. The figure of 16,500 is the mean of that range.
5. Quote attributed to Rutherford D. Rogers.
6. C. Schoen, R. Osborn, M.M. Doty, D. Squires, J. Peugh, and S. Applebaum, "A Survey of Primary Care Physicians in Eleven Countries, 2009: Perspectives on Care, Costs, and Experiences," *Health Affairs* 28, no. 6 (2009, Web Exclusives): w1175.
7. Organisation for Economic Co-operation and Development, *OECD Economic Surveys: Canada 2010*, 10-11.
8. An Advisory Council on Health Info-Structure was commissioned by the federal Minister of Health, under the Chretien government, back in 1997.
9. The Commonwealth Fund, *International Profiles of Health Care Systems* (New York: The Commonwealth Fund, 2010), http://www.commonwealthfund.org/~/media/Files/Publications/Fund%20Report/2010/Jun/1417_Squires_Intl_Profiles_622.pdf (accessed 26 January 2011).
10. Kaiser Permanente's first EHRs were implemented in 2004, in Hawaii. The system was "fully deployed" nationwide in March 2010. See Kaiser Permanente, "HealthConnect Electronic Health Record," http://xnet.kp.org/newscenter/aboutkp/healthconnect/timeline.html (accessed 10 November 2010).
11. C. Pagliari, D. Detmer, and P. Singleton, "Potential of Electronic Personal Health Records," *British Medical Journal* 335 (August 2007): 330-33.
12. C. Schoen, R. Osborn, P.T. Huynh, M. Doty, K. Zapert, J. Peugh, and K. Davis, "Taking the Pulse of Health Care Systems: Experiences of Patients with Health Problems in Six Countries," *Health Affairs* (2005, Web Exclusives) w5-509, http://www.commonwealthfund.org/Content/Publications/In-the-Literature/2005/Nov/Taking-the-Pulse-of-Health-Care-Systems--Experiences-of-Patients-with-Health-Problems-in-Six-Countri.aspx.

13. P. Kosseim and M. Brady, "Policy by Procrastination," *McGill Journal of Law and Health* 2 (2008): 8-9.
14. *Constitution Act, 1867* (U.K.), 30 & 31 Vict., c.3, s. 91, s. 92, reprinted in R.S.C. 1985, App.II, No. 5.
15. T. McIntosh, "Intergovernmental Relations, Social Policy and Federal Transfers after Romanow," *Canadian Public Administration* 47, no. 1 (2004): 27-51, cited in Willison, this volume.
16. Canada, Standing Senate Committee on Social Affairs, Science and Technology, *The Health of Canadians – The Federal Role,* vol. 1-6 (Ottawa: Standing Senate Committee on Social Affairs, Science and Technology, 2002), section 10.4.
17. "Whatever I see or hear in the lives of my patients, whether in connection with my professional practice or not, which ought not to be spoken of outside, I will keep secret, as considering all such things to be private." Translation by Michael North, National Library of Medicine (2002), www.nlm.nih.gov/hmd/greek/greek_oath.html (accessed 12 January 2010).
18. *McInerney v. MacDonald* [1992] 2 S.C.R. 138.
19. EKOS Research Associates, *Electronic Health Information and Privacy Survey: What Canadians Think – 2007* (Final Report submitted to Canada Health Infoway, Health Canada, and the Office of the Privacy Commissioner of Canada, August 2007).
20. K. El Emam and A. Fineberg, "An Overview of Techniques for De-identifying Personal Health Information" (14 August 2009): 5, http://ssrn.com/abstract=1456490 (accessed 26 January 2011).
21. Ibid.
22. Canada's Conservative government came under fire in the summer of 2010 when it cancelled Statistics Canada's mandatory long-form census, citing privacy concerns. The move will impoverish the dataset available to policy-makers and researchers. Some fear that the move will render the plight of vulnerable populations invisible to researchers, policy-makers, and the general public. See L. McQuaig, "Making It Easier to Ignore the Poor," *Toronto Star,* 27 June 2010.
23. N.M. Ries, "Legal Issues in Health Information and EMRs," in *The Human and Social Side of Health Information Systems,* ed. A. Kushniruk and E. Borycki (Hershey, PA: Idea Group Inc., 2008), 267.
24. D.B. Kendall, "Protecting Patient Privacy through Health Record Trusts," *Health Affairs* 28, no. 2 (2009): 444-46.
25. Canadian Institutes of Health Research, Natural Sciences and Engineering Research Council of Canada, and Social Sciences and Humanities Research Council of Canada, *Tri-Council Policy Statement on Ethics of Research Involving Humans* (December 2010), Cat. No. MR21-18/2010E-PDF, http://www.pre.ethics.gc.ca/pdf/eng/tcps2/TCPS_2_FINAL_Web.pdf (accessed 23 February 2011).
26. T. Lemmens and L. Austin, "The End of Individual Control over Health Information: Promoting Fair Information Practices and Governance of Biobank Research" (forthcoming): 34. Draft paper available at http://ssrn.com/abstract=1337695 (accessed 26 January 2011).
27. Health Canada, *Good Clinical Practice: Consolidated Guideline* (Ottawa, ON: Health Canada, 1997), http://www.hc-sc.gc.ca/dhp-mps/prodpharma/applic-demande/guide-ld/ich/efficac/e6-eng.php#fn_1.

28. H. Sampson, S. Cox, R. Saginur, and M. Owen, "Examining the Need for Canadian Research Ethics Board (REB) Member Standardized Education: Governance Views from the Field," *Health Law Review* 17, no. 2-3 (2009): 75.

29. *Tri-Council Policy Statement*, 71.

30. B.M. Knoppers, "Challenges to Ethics Review in Health Research," *Health Law Review* 17, no. 2-3 (2009): 48.

31. K.D. Haggerty, "Ethics Creep: Governing Social Science Research in the Name of Ethics," *Qualitative Sociology* 27, no. 4 (2004): 394.

32. M. Hadskis and P. Carver, "The Long Arm of Administrative Law: Applying Administrative Law Principles to Research Ethics Boards," *Health Law Review* 13 (2005): 19-32.

33. *Tri-Council Policy Statement*, 10.

34. Haggerty, "Ethics Creep," 402.

35. *Tri-Council Policy Statement*, 23.

36. Ibid.

37. Haggerty, "Ethics Creep," 403.

38. *Tri-Council Policy Statement*, 62.

39. Sampson et al., "Examining the Need for Canadian Research Ethics Board (REB) Member Standardized Education," 73.

40. Haggerty, "Ethics Creep," 412.

41. *Tri-Council Policy Statement*, 99.

42. More information on this project can be found on Australia's National Health and Medical Research Council's website, at http://www.nhmrc.gov.au/health_ethics/homer/index.htm.

43. J. Downie and F. McDonald, "Revisioning the Oversight of Research Involving Humans in Canada," *Health Law Journal* 12(2004): 164.

SETTING THE STAGE: DEFINING THE INFORMATION ACCESS AGENDA

HEALTH RESEARCH AND DATA PROTECTION: HOW CAN RESEARCHERS CONTRIBUTE TO THE POLICY DEBATE?

Patricia Kosseim

In this chapter, I briefly describe the evolution of legislative policy-making in Canada over the past decade as it relates to secondary use of personal information for health research purposes. I go on to propose three proactive ways the health research community could contribute value to the policy development process in this area. I conclude with a few guarded messages about what might happen in the absence of such proactive measures.

EVOLUTION OF LEGISLATIVE POLICY-MAKING IN THIS AREA

By virtue of its very nature, the policy dilemma that lies at the crossroads of data protection and health research is forcibly multijurisdictional. Initially, the patchwork of different data protection laws across the provinces constituted a significant hurdle for stakeholders. Indeed, for a time, it created such uncertainty that many feared it would jeopardize the vision of a Canada-wide health infostructure[1] and hamper plans for modern e-systems of health care, management, evaluation, and research.

Data Data Everywhere: Access and Accountability? ed. C.M. Flood. Montreal and Kingston: Queen's Policy Studies Series, McGill-Queen's University Press. © 2011 The School of Policy Studies, Queen's University at Kingston. All rights reserved.

Consequently, in the years immediately following the adoption of the federal *Personal Information Protection and Electronic Documents Act (PIPEDA)*[2] in 2000, the Conference of Deputy Ministers initiated a process to encourage harmonization of privacy laws across jurisdictions in order to enable the development of pan-Canadian, interoperable electronic health record (EHR) systems as a first-order priority. It tasked its then Advisory Committee on Information and Emerging Technologies to develop recommendations on how that might be achieved. While this process resulted in the publication of a helpful framework (the *Pan-Canadian Health Information Privacy and Confidentiality Framework*),[3] it was not without limitations. (Quebec did not participate in the development of the framework, and Saskatchewan withdrew near the end of the process.) Despite the political difficulties inherent in that process, jurisdictions did, over time, harmonize their laws more or less around a similar standard that allows health providers to use and disclose personal health information relatively unimpeded within a designated "circle of care." Beyond finding a common solution for immediate health-care purposes, however, jurisdictions have not shown much appetite for pursuing a concerted harmonization process with respect to other core statutory provisions, including access to personal information for health research purposes.

Rather than take the political risk of all gravitating toward a similar model, holus-bolus, jurisdictions seem to be generally more tentative, calculating, and incremental in this complex and innovative area of policy-making. Jurisdictions are patiently looking to one another's experiences to see which approaches are working out well in practice, and which are not. As a result of this incremental approach, we are seeing emerge several distinct generations of privacy laws informed by the implementation of others that preceded them. For instance, private sector privacy laws at the federal level, and in British Columbia and Alberta, are all undergoing their first legislative reviews. These jurisdictions are closely comparing their respective approaches and noting which aspects have proven to be most practical and effective in order to inform possible amendments to their own laws. Similarly, Newfoundland, New Brunswick, and Nova Scotia are drawing practical lessons from the experiences of Ontario and the Prairie provinces to help shape their policy choices and decisions as they move to introduce, adopt, or implement new health information protection regimes. The innovative model recently introduced by British Columbia's *E-Health Act*[4] and the recently adopted amendments to Alberta's *Health Information Act*[5] will no doubt be of interest to other jurisdictions as they watch to see, over time, how successful these new approaches prove to be in balancing research access with privacy concerns.

Hence, even though explicit attempts at harmonization may appear to have stalled, legislators—like most policy-makers—will naturally look to the experiences of other jurisdictions to inform the evolution of their own laws. Based on developments to date, it may be that laws across jurisdictions will eventually converge by way of incremental and practical emulation,[6] rather than by explicit and concerted harmonization per se.

In light of the policy-making phenomenon we are seeing unfold in the context of data protection laws generally, it is questionable whether continued calls to resurrect a top-down, concerted harmonization effort across jurisdictions to align existing research access provisions will bear fruit any time soon. Instead, researchers' efforts may be better spent on trying to inform how the next generation of legislative policy—whether in its formulation, interpretation, or application—can strike an effective balance between the right to privacy and access to personal data for health research. By setting their sights *ahead of the curve*, researchers can contribute to the development of a model solution which—if socially acceptable and practically feasible—may influence other jurisdictions to follow suit and eventually converge into an established norm. In the remainder of this chapter, I set out three ways by which researchers might consider doing this.

EDUCATE POLICY-MAKERS

Like any other decision-maker, policy-makers[7] have to be well informed of all the facts, hear all the relevant positions, and understand all the different perspectives in order to make well-balanced decisions. This has never been truer than it is today, particularly in light of the mind-boggling complexities brought about by rapid advances in information technologies, the revolution of genomics science, and the impact of globalization in what has essentially become a borderless world.[8]

Policy-makers need to understand technological systems and practical realities in order to enlighten their deliberations, inform their options and, ultimately, formulate their policy positions. Often, their assigned mandate or portfolio is quite expansive and they struggle to keep up with rapid advances in information technology. Some are under intense public pressure and scrutiny. They are expected to move seamlessly between files, cases, applications, complaints, emergencies, and priorities. In each instance, they must immerse themselves in the subject matter and gather required information to make effective laws, policies, choices, decisions, resource allocations, recommendations, orders and findings.

Proactive initiatives aimed at educating policy-makers are especially critical at this juncture. The health-care paradigm is undergoing a major cultural shift as significant investments in electronic health information systems raise public expectations of more transparent institutional decisions, greater accountability of health professionals, enhanced quality of health-care services, more effective health policies, more efficient management of the health system—and greater empowerment for its end-users. Scientific advances, particularly in genomics, are refining our understanding of various predictive factors affecting health, disease susceptibility, and potential reaction to therapies, ushering in whole new expectations for personalized medicine. Health providers, institutions, policy-makers, and even end-users themselves, rely on researchers to provide the evidence base needed to support and sustain these desired improvements in health care. To provide this evidence base, researchers working across jurisdictions, disciplines, and information systems require access to data for systematic investigation, evaluation, analyses, and eventual application.

Recent trends are also beginning to redefine fundamental rules and expectations within the research enterprise itself. Spurred by transformative advances in information technology and genomics science, sponsors and publishers are increasingly encouraging—if not *requiring*—researchers to share data among themselves prior to publication through controlled-access databases, and post publication through open access journals available over the Internet. Modern research initiatives recognize the value-added of large-scale research and international consortia, seek to maximize economies of scale, see greater opportunity in collaboration over competition, and focus on the need to address global health threats in the greater public interest. Expectations to share and release data reflect a new research ethos of greater transparency, stronger accountability, and fairer distribution of benefits resulting from publicly funded research.

As these trends continue to mount pressure for research access to data, we are also seeing emerge, on the converse side of the equation, a whole new wave of modern privacy risks giving rise to public fears and concerns. These concerns are not necessarily specific to the scholarly research enterprise, but arise as potential threats in neighbouring spheres of social activity that are growing increasingly interconnected despite intent efforts to keep them intellectually separate. Commercial incentives to collect and use personal information for other profit-making purposes, major data leaks resulting from technological or organizational failures, criminal uses of personal information for nefarious purposes, and government encroachment into citizens' private lives in the name of national security or law enforcement are some examples of the kinds of serious privacy risks butting up against research.

These new trends and risks on both sides of the research-privacy equation require a "re-think" of competing societal values through a whole new lens. One of the most significant and valuable contributions health researchers can make to the educative process of policy-makers wrestling with these issues is to develop real-life case studies that bring modern dilemmas to life and illustrate, in very concrete and proportionate terms, the hard risks that have to be faced and tough choices that need to be made. Case studies help ground discussions, focus attention on practical issues, and turn people's minds to the trade-offs that have to be balanced.[9] Workshops, roundtables, conferences, and summits organized around the use of practical case studies provide opportunities for researchers and policy-makers to bridge knowledge and experience, create a common platform for discussion, and begin to engage all other relevant stakeholders, so that they may together address—and eventually *resolve*—this new generation of research access and privacy challenges.

There are also many other ways researchers can contribute valuable knowledge to the policy-making process as it pertains to secondary use of personal information. Here are but a few examples:

- Legislative committees that review draft legislation, consider amendments to existing legislation, and conduct general policy reviews on the state of health care or health research will invite testimony from various experts, academics, and interest groups to explain the state of knowledge, anticipate emerging challenges, and make recommendations for improvement. The resulting reports become important reference works, are widely cited and constitute significant milestones in the policy development process. While they may be overtaken or stalled by unpredictable political events in the short term, these seminal reports can have lasting utility and influence when the same policy issue eventually gets picked up again for continued debate.

- Research funding agencies seek formal input from the broader research community on possible revisions to their ethics policies (e.g., *Tri-Council Policy Statement on Ethics of Research Involving Humans*[10]) and best practice guidelines (e.g., *CIHR Best Practices for Protecting Personal Information in Health Research*[11]). These consultation processes are vitally important to keep such policy instruments evergreen, workable, and relevant in practice.

- Research ethics boards and peer review panels are educated each time they evaluate a research protocol or grant application. Particularly effective is the iterative, two-way process that takes place when such boards or committees seek more detailed information from the principal investigator or the research team. This education process enhances members' knowledge and understanding of the field, not only for the purposes of reviewing the protocol in question, but also for informing reviews of future projects on similar questions or involving similar research methods.

- Privacy Commissioners are educated each time they conduct site reviews, perform audits, carry out investigations, and review privacy impact assessments. For example, Ontario's Commissioner will assess the personal information management practices of organizations seeking to obtain, and maintain, their status as prescribed entities under the *Personal Health Information Protection Act* (*PHIPA*), which grants them exceptional access to personal data for purposes of planning, managing, evaluating, or monitoring the health system.[12] Similarly, Alberta's Commissioner will review and approve a privacy impact assessment submitted by a health information custodian seeking to introduce new administrative practices or information systems affecting the collection, use, or disclosure of individually identifying information, or by a custodian seeking to perform data matching, including for research purposes, under the *Health Information Act* (*HIA*).[13]

All of these mechanisms, whether formal or informal, are vital to the education process. Rather than view these as slow, bureaucratic processes that impede research and add to already heavy workloads, researchers should regard these as valuable opportunities to explain the objectives of research, demonstrate why personal information is needed to fulfil such objectives, and share practical insight into various research methods. To seize such opportunities, researchers need not wait to be called, summoned, invited, or asked. They could take proactive measures to anticipate occasions, initiate contact, and offer useful information to enable better understanding of their proposed projects and programs, current challenges, and suggested solutions. Considering the potential for long-term impact, such proactive measures are well worth the time and effort expended.

STRENGTHEN ACCOUNTABILITY

De-identification and broad consent are often referred to as attractive solutions to the health research-privacy dilemma. However, before researchers throw all their weight behind these two policy options, to the exclusion of any other, they will need to address the practical limitations and broader policy implications of each alternative. We have addressed these policy options at much greater length in a recent article.[14] For present purposes, however, suffice it to say the following.

De-identification is often offered as a potential solution for de-personalizing information and exempting it from the requirements of informed consent, particularly for retrospective use of existing data.[15] However, de-identification is not, in and of itself, a panacea. In light of fast-changing information technology, de-identification has become an elusive, relative, and ever-shifting objective. Practical issues around system specification choices, inconsistent nomenclature, evolving standards, and varying thresholds of acceptable risk have made de-identification technology a moving target.[16] Moreover, increasing prevalence, interoperability, and convergence of different data sources, growing amounts of publicly released data on the web, and expanding capability to re-identify and/or draw inferences about individuals from biospecimens all add to the real challenges of achieving effective de-identification while maintaining data usefulness.[17]

Though de-identification is not a foolproof solution, de-identification technologies may provide a partial means, *among others*, to help manage the privacy risks associated with research use of personal data. The answer will be in recognizing that de-identification is not a simple black or white concept, but rather a question of degree. "How much" will depend on acceptable thresholds of risk, however ultimately defined, and any investments in de-identification technologies will have to be continually upgraded to keep the risk of re-identification well below those thresholds.

Most importantly, however, will be the assurance that appropriate accountability structures, processes, and agreements are in place to manage and oversee all the entities that play a role along the data de-identification chain. These entities include not only the individual researchers seeking access to de-identified data subject to conditions and limitations, but also those responsible for manipulating the data in the de-identification process, and those ultimately entrusted with holding the re-identification key. Effective risk management requires accountability of all custodians and potential users. Far from letting their guard down, researchers who promise de-identification as a means of recruiting and reassuring potential participants must be prepared to undergo intensified scrutiny to ensure that they actively safeguard de-identified data as per their undertaking and respect all of the attendant assumptions that participants expect as "part of the deal."

Broad consent is sometimes offered as another alternative for alleviating practical issues associated with obtaining specific informed consent, particularly in the context of prospective data collection for the purposes of creating a research platform, registry, or biobank.[18] However, it too poses significant challenges. For one, there remain fundamental legal and policy questions associated with the concept of broad consent that need to be addressed before it is too hastily adopted as a justifiable substitute for informed consent.[19] That said, even if it does evolve into a well-accepted norm, broad consent to provide personal information for inclusion in a research registry or platform that will serve future, yet unknown specific projects does not mean that individuals are prepared to cede *all* meaningful control over their personal data; it is not a blank cheque.

To preserve a meaningful degree of participant control over personal information, researchers should be prepared to inform participants of not only the knowns but also the *unknowns* at the time of recruitment, together with the risks associated with *not* being able to specify which researchers or projects will be conducted using the data collected. Although specific projects cannot be ascertained at the time of collection, researchers should be prepared to outline the general aims and parameters of the type of research that will be conducted using the data (including any commercial uses being contemplated); the general classes of researchers who will have potential access to the data (and under what conditions); and whether the data will be linked with other types and sources of data (and if so, which ones, and how linkage will occur). Researchers should describe what opportunities individuals will have for renewing, confirming, or withdrawing consent, together with an explanation of what each option entails. Researchers should also explain when and how individuals may exercise those options; what will happen to individuals' personal information should they die or lose mental capacity, or should the research platform, registry, or biobank cease to exist; whom individuals may contact to obtain further information at any time; and where they can obtain details about specific research projects as these become known.

Although we could debate at length which of the above disclosure requirements need to be included in the consent process, and at what level of detail in order to approximate as closely as possible the current "informed consent" standard at law, ultimately, the practical viability of this policy option—like de-identification—will turn on accountability. Security safeguards must be taken to protect the confidentiality of the data from potential breach. Governance structures and processes must be in place to manage the platform, registry, or biobank, oversee decisions about its development in line with the original aims and parameters described to participants, and respond to alleged breaches in protocol. Appropriate accountability must also be assured at the specific project level to conduct effective review and oversight from an ethical perspective and to make decisions about the use of individuals' personal data on their behalf. Although a discussion of the governance of research ethics boards extends beyond the scope of this chapter, its critical importance for eventually achieving the level of accountability necessary to alleviate privacy concerns, resolve outstanding public policy issues, and build public trust and support for health research cannot be overemphasized.

DEVELOP SELF-GUIDANCE

A critical step in any policy-making process is to look to existing sector-specific approaches that appear to be effective in practice and could feasibly be extended to more generalizable purposes. Policy advisers will readily point to successful grassroots initiatives that have stood the test of time, have proven to be workable, and have come to be accepted by key stakeholder groups. Such best practice models enhance the possibility of leveraging past experience, generating more widespread support, and facilitating more rapid adoption.

A prime example of this phenomenon is the legislative adoption of Canada's *CSA Model Code for the Protection of Personal Information* CAN-CSA-0830-96. This standard, developed by and for the Canadian business community, was directly incorporated into Schedule 1 of *PIPEDA* as an integral piece of federal law,[20] and has had enormous influence in shaping substantially similar legislation at the provincial level.

This ground-up approach was invoked more recently in the context of *PIPEDA* review. In its Fourth Report to Parliament on the statutory review of *PIPEDA*, the Standing Committee on Access to Information, Privacy and Ethics recommended that government consult with stakeholders to determine the extent to which elements of the *PIPEDA Awareness Raising Tools (PARTs)* document may be set out in legislative form.[21] *PARTs* is essentially a Q&A document that explains how *PIPEDA* applies to the health-care sector. It was developed by Industry Canada in consultation with the Office of the Privacy Commissioner of Canada and with major health provider associations *"within the context of their day-to-day activities in providing care and treatment to Canadians."*[22] The federal government concurred with the Standing Committee's recommendation and undertook, through Industry Canada, to work with relevant stakeholders "to discuss the possible options for according the *PARTs* document more formal status."[23]

Given the natural tendency of policy-makers to look for ready-made solutions through this type of approach where appropriate, we should not underestimate the importance of grassroots initiatives. Provided these are reasonably well balanced, have developed through open and inclusive processes, work well in practice, and are generally considered by affected stakeholders to be legitimate and acceptable, their potential to influence the policy-making process can be significant.

For example, the Office of the Information and Privacy Commissioner of Ontario had recommended that criteria similar to those developed in CIHR's *Best Practices for Protecting Personal Information in Health Research*[24] be incorporated into Ontario's *PHIPA* to clarify the concept of "impracticability to obtain consent."[25] Though in the end, the legislature elected not to include this level of detail in the final draft of the Bill, such a result would not have been inconceivable. A precedent for this already existed in the *Assisted Human Reproduction Act*,[26] in which the federal legislature incorporated CIHR's *Guidelines on Human Pluripotent Stem Cell Research*[27] right into the definition of "consent," a concept central to the operation of the Act.

Researchers can help fill policy gaps by offering solutions that are demonstrated to be tried, tested, and true through common usage in the community. The second draft of the *Tri-Council Policy Statement on Ethical Conduct of Research Involving Humans* is an ideal opportunity to evolve the relevant privacy and confidentiality provisions and provide further guidance to researchers and research ethics boards as they navigate through complex ethical considerations. The *Tri-Council Policy Statement*, as a national funding policy, has been widely accepted and adopted by other governmental departments and agencies, voluntary health organizations and charities, and independent not-for-profit organizations—both federal and provincial—as part of their own research funding conditions. As such, the *Tri-Council Policy Statement* has come to be broadly recognized as the applicable normative framework governing research involving humans in Canada and has gained significance as an instrument of "soft law."[28] To maintain its legitimacy as a socially accepted norm and its potential influence on what courts may determine to be a "reasonable standard of care," the *Tri-Council Policy Statement* must stay in keeping with well-established international principles and minimal legal standards, including well-established data protection standards. It must also strive to remain practically relevant and in common usage by evolving over time to address new privacy realities and challenges, especially in light of the rapidly changing EHR environment and revolutionary genomics era. Those, I believe, are the next two frontiers—indeed, the next two *opportunities*—for further policy guidance and development in this area.

CONCLUSION

In this chapter, I have offered a few practical observations about the policy-making process and suggested some proactive ways the research community can participate in policy debates about privacy and health research. Whether it is through these means, or others deemed to be more appropriate, my parting recommendation is this: *Don't wait too long*. If a "do-nothing" approach sets in and researchers get comfortably complacent about these outstanding policy issues, less optimal solutions will inevitably be thrust upon the research community by policy-makers having no other choice but to respond to competing pressures that could eventually overtake the opportunity for open debate.

If nothing is done until disaster strikes, this may force everyone's hand into accepting urgent and drastic reactions in order to appease immediate public concerns. A major privacy breach or, conversely, a major health pandemic, may push policy-makers to adopt quick solutions in the short term, without full regard for their impact on countervailing social values in the longer term. It could then take years to try to move the pendulum ever so slightly back toward the middle.

If researchers get complacent and do not take proactive steps to help inform and advance the policy debate, technological imperatives may move so far ahead, and interests and investments may become so heavily entrenched, that policy solutions will be driven by sheer practical necessity as opposed to well-reasoned principles and substantive policy debates. Over time, new deployments of technology have the subtle yet subversive effect of wearing down debate and forcing end results. Yet we know that technology is not value neutral. Whether its deployment is socially acceptable or not depends on its perceived benefits and potential risks, which in turn depend on the purposes for which it is intended to be deployed and how it is used to achieve those purposes. A healthy and rigorous debate must move alongside the development of technology in iterative fashion in order to address these questions early on.

If the policy debate does not advance through transparent, proactive debate, legislators might need to resort to legal gymnastics as an indirect way of adopting new policies, programs, or technologies without having to (seemingly) change the status quo. Current legal terms might be stretched in an attempt to fit new realities into existing statutory language. In the process, concepts such as "informed consent," "impracticability," and "de-identification" might get broadened and even distorted beyond recognition to accommodate needed solutions. If, in the end, the interpretation of words begins to defy logic, this approach will only aggravate the general sense of uncertainty and engender mistrust among participants. Unless complex issues are courageously tackled in open and transparent fashion, where everyone calls a spade a "spade," then the meaning and integrity of critical terms will begin to get lost on participants whose common-sense understanding no longer matches reality.

Finally, and if enough time passes, legislators may end up doing a full turn-about by reversing explicit promises of confidentiality made to people in the past. We have seen retroactive legislative amendments to the federal *Statistics Act*,[29] which now permits disclosure of census data after 92 years despite the federal government's express undertaking of confidentiality when the data were originally collected. We have also seen more recent attempts to amend Ontario's *Vital Statistics Act*,[30] which would have had the retroactive effect of allowing the Ontario government to disclose birth and adoption records despite express assurances to the contrary made to birth parents at the time the records were originally created and sealed. In the latter case, the Ontario Court of Justice found the amendments violated section 7 of the Canadian Charter of Rights and Freedoms and declared them to be unconstitutional.[31] Legislative reversal could constitute the greatest affront to public trust and confidence in the health system. It has potential to fail on constitutional grounds, leaving researchers no further ahead or, worse yet, creating a general public backlash against the research community. The antidote to such failure, I believe, is for the health research community to act proactively to encourage informed policy development in some of the ways suggested in this chapter.

NOTES

At time of writing, the author was on a two-year Executive Interchange from the Office of the Privacy Commissioner of Canada to Genome Canada. This chapter reflects the personal views of the author alone. It does not represent the official views of either the Privacy Commissioner of Canada or Genome Canada.

1.   Advisory Council on Health Infostructure, Canada Health Infoway: Paths to Better Health (Ottawa: Health Canada Publications, 1999), http://www. hc-sc.gc.ca/hcs-sss/pubs/ehealth-esante/1999-paths-voies-fin/index-eng. php.
2.   *Personal Information Protection and Electronic Documents Act*, S.C. 2000, c. 5.

3. Health Canada, *Pan-Canadian Health Information Privacy and Confidentiality Framework* (2005), http://www.hc-sc.gc.ca/hcs-sss/pubs/ehealth-esante/2005-pancanad-priv/index-eng.php.
4. *E-Health (Personal Health Information Access and Protection of Privacy) Act*, S.B.C. 2008, c. 38.
5. Alberta's Bill 52, *Health Information Amendment Act*, 2009, received Royal Assent on 4 June 2009.
6. C. Bennett, *Regulating Privacy* (New York: Cornell University, 1992). If we apply the typology offered by Colin Bennett in some of his earlier work on privacy governance, the process of convergence we are now seeing appears to be happening as a result of "emulation" rather than "harmonization" per se. Professor Bennett describes the process of emulation as a form of convergence that occurs more typically in an area of policy innovation, when no solution yet exists in the suite of policy techniques readily available at home, and the natural tendency is to look beyond one's domestic borders to draw lessons from others' experiences. According to Bennett, "Convergence (through emulation) is then the result of a pressure to conform in an insecure and tentative policy-making climate" (p. 5).
7. "Policy-maker" here encompasses the broad community of decision-makers— including political, regulatory, governmental, and non-governmental actors—whose actions and decisions directly influence the conditions under which researchers may access personal data for research purposes. Policy-makers include:
    *   legislators who make and pass data protection laws,
    *   judicial decision-makers and regulators who interpret and enforce such laws,
    *   government departments that develop and implement policies relevant to privacy and research,
    *   publicly funded research agencies that influence data access through resource allocation decisions, investment strategies, funding agreements, peer review, and moral suasion, and
    *   non-governmental bodies (such as research ethics boards or data access committees) specially designated by law or institutional policy to oversee research proposals and data access requests.
    This broad view of policy-making is supported by academic experts who have likewise adopted an expansive definition. See P. John, *Analysing Public Policy* (London: Continuum, 1998), 6.
8. As Frank Fischer has observed, "What was then an emerging concern is now a modern day imperative: government decision-makers need relevant information ... the increasing complexity of modern technological society dramatically intensifies the information requirements of modern decision-makers. Policy decisions combine sophisticated technical knowledge with intricate and often subtle social and political realities." F. Fischer, *Reframing Public Policy: Discursive Politics and Deliberative Practices* (Oxford: Oxford University Press, 2003), 2.
9. As a example, see Canadian Institutes of Health Research, *Secondary Uses of Personal Information in Health Research* (Ottawa: Public Works and Government Services Canada, 2002), http://www.cihr-irsc.gc.ca/e/1475.html.

10. Canadian Institutes of Health Research, Natural Sciences and Engineering Research Council of Canada, and Social Sciences and Humanities Research Council of Canada, *Tri-Council Policy Statement on Ethics of Research Involving Humans, 1998* (with 2000, 2002 and 2005 amendments), Cat. No. MR21-18/2005E, http://pre.ethics.gc.ca/eng/policy-politique/tcps-eptc/readtcps-lireeptc.

11. Canadian Institutes of Health Research, *CIHR Best Practices for Protecting Personal Information in Health Research* (Ottawa: Public Works and Government Services Canada, 2005), http://www.cihr-irsc.gc.ca/e/29072.html.

12. *Personal Health Information Protection Act, S.O. 2004, c. 3, section 45(4).*

13. *Health Information Act, R.S.A. 2000. C. H-5, section 72.*

14. P. Kosseim and M. Brady, "Policy by Procrastination: Secondary Uses of Electronic Health Records for Health Research Purposes," *McGill Journal of Law and Health* 2 (2008): 5-45, http://mjlh.mcgill.ca/texts/volume2/pdf/MJLH_vol2_Kosseim-Brady.pdf.

15. "De-identification," as the term is being used here, refers generally to the process of stripping personal data of all direct and indirect identifiers, coding or double-coding the data through the use of a key entrusted either to a restricted number of senior researchers on the research team or to an independent third-party on behalf of the researchers.

16. K. El Emam, S. Jabbouri, S. Sams, Y. Drouet, and M. Power, "Evaluating Common De-Identification Heuristics for Personal Health Information," *Journal of Medical Internet Research* 8, no. 4 (2006), http://www.jmir.org/2006/4/e28; K. El Emam, E. Jonker, S. Sams, E. Neri, A. Neisa, T. Gao, and S. Chowdhury, *Pan-Canadian De-Identification Guidelines for Personal Health Information* (Ottawa: Children's Hospital of Eastern Ontario Research Institute, 2007), http://www.ehealthinformation.ca/documents/OPCReportv11. (Report prepared with funding support of the Office of the Privacy Commissioner of Canada).

17. J. Couzin, "Genetic Privacy: Whole-Genome Data Not Anonymous, Challenging Assumptions," *Science* 321, no. 5894 (2008): 1278. See also W.W. Lowrance and F.S. Collins, "Identifiability in Genomic Research," Science 317, no. 5838 (2007): 600-2.

18. B.M. Knoppers, "Consent Revisited: Points to Consider," *Health Law Review* 13, no. 2&3 (2005): 33-37.

19. T. Caulfield, "Biobanks and Blanket Consent: The Proper Place of the Public Good and Public Perception Rationales," *King's Law Journal* 18, no. 2 (2007): 9.

20. *Personal Information Protection and Electronic Documents Act, S.C. 2000, c. 5, Schedule 1,* http://laws.justice.gc.ca/en/P-8.6/index.html.

21. Standing Committee on Access to Information, Privacy and Ethics, *Statutory Review of the Personal Information Protection and Electronic Documents Act (PIPEDA),* Fourth Report (May 2007), 39th Parliament, 1st Session, Http://Www2.Parl.Gc.Ca/Housepublications/Publication.Aspx?Docid=2891060&Language=E&Mode=1&Parl=39&Ses=1.

22. Industry Canada, *PIPEDA Awareness Raising Tools (PARTs) Initiative for the Health Sector,* http://www.ic.gc.ca/epic/site/ecic-ceac.nsf/en/h_gv00207e.html.

23. Government of Canada, *Government Response to the Fourth Report of the Standing Committee on Access to Information, Privacy and Ethics*, http://www.ic.gc.ca/epic/site/ic1.nsf/en/00317e.html.
24. Canadian Institutes of Health Research, *CIHR Best Practices*, see note 11.
25. A. Cavoukian, *Submission to the Standing Committee on General Government: Bill C:31 Health Information Protection Act* (Information and Privacy7 Commissioner/Ontario, 27 January 2004), http://www.ipc.on.ca/images/Resources/up-012704.pdf.
26. *Assisted Human Reproduction Act*, S.C. 2004, c. 2, http://laws.justice.gc.ca/en/A-13.4/index.html. This Act has recently come under constitutional challenge in the Quebec Court of Appeal, *Reference Concerning the Constitutional Validity of ss. 8 to 19, 40 to 53, 60, 61 and 68 of the Assisted Human Reproduction Act*, S.C. 2004, c. 2, (2008) QCCA 1167, leave to appeal to the Supreme Court of Canada allowed.
27. Canadian Institutes of Health Research, *Updated Guidelines for Human Pluripotent Stem Cell Research* (29 June 2007), http://www.cihr-irsc.gc.ca/e/34460.html.
28. For a fuller discussion of how clinical and research ethics policies may influence the development of legal standards, see A. Campbell and K. Cranley Glass, "The Legal Status of Clinical and Ethics Policies, Codes and Guidelines in Medical Practice and Research," *McGill Law Journal* 46, no. 2 (2001): 473-89; and S.V. Zimmerman, "Translating Ethics into Law: Duties of Care in Health Research Involving Humans," *Health Law Review* 13, no. 2–3 (2005): 13-18.
29. R.S.C. 1985, c. S-19, s. 18.1, as amended by *An Act to Amend the Statistics Act*, S.C. 2005, c. 31.
30. R.S.O. 1990, c. V-4.
31. *Cheskes v. Ontario (Attorney General)*, [2007] 87 O.R. (3d) 581, O.J. No. 3515 (Ontario Supreme Court).

ACCESS DECISIONS: A NEXUS
OF CONSIDERATIONS

William W. Lowrance

Around the world, there are strong pressures to increase data sharing for health research. Although policy decisions, infrastructure, intellectual property agreements, and other facilitating basics must be in place first, the final step is *access*: the actual sharing of data.

This chapter describes the general characteristics of access decisions, discusses the terms of restricted access, identifies a few issue-clusters urgently needing attention, and concludes by briefly addressing the question "What do researchers want?"[1]

WHY "NEXUS"?

Although perhaps a bit arcane, the word is not overly dramatic. When a researcher or research group requests access to information curated by others—especially information that may be personally identifiable—a whole raft of linked issues must be considered. Access cannot legitimately be granted until satisfactory answers are given, and commitments made, regarding such questions as the following:

- Does the proposed use conform to privacy and data-protection requirements? Is it consistent with the body of common law, especially that concerning medical confidentiality? Does it comply with medical, public health, genetic, and pharmaceutical research regulations, policy

Data Data Everywhere: Access and Accountability? ed. C.M. Flood. Montreal and Kingston: Queen's Policy Studies Series, McGill-Queen's University Press. © 2011 The School of Policy Studies, Queen's University at Kingston. All rights reserved.

statements, and international conventions? If there are exceptional circumstances, how will these be dealt with?

- How will human subject protections be respected? What is the status of consent? How will identifiability be handled? What are the security precautions? Are there restrictions on further transfer? What are the prospects of database linking that could increase disclosure risks?
- What is the likely payoff for the public good? What are the general public interest considerations?
- What are the funders' data-sharing requirements? What are the data custodians' self-interests? What intellectual property arrangements have been made?
- What are the plans for research ethics board review? Is other in-dependent oversight or governance in place? What are the provisions for audit, enforcement, and penalties?

These may be viewed either as hurdles—which they certainly can be—or else as assurances that, managed well, can foster trust and build goodwill all around.

Access decisions are also a *nexus* in the sense that the decisions can affect the interests of many interrelated parties:

- the individuals to whom the data may pertain (patients or other direct data-subjects, and perhaps partners or family members),
- various social or health-status population groups,
- researchers and their institutions,
- research funders,
- others (e.g., law enforcement agencies, biotechnology investors), and
- society in general.

RESPONSIBILITIES

There are responsibilities all around.

Data stewards must manage the terms of data release, respecting the obligations and commitments to the people to whom the data pertain. The stewards may well want to go beyond the basic requirements in order to nurture long-term relationships, especially in ongoing longitudinal studies or in health-care systems that glean data from electronic health records. Even as data stewards are protective of the data-subjects, though, they must consider serving the broader public interest by sharing data for research.

Data-requesting researchers must decide whether they and their teams can and will comply with the terms of access, and whether they are willing to be held accountable.

Funders, hosting research institutions, research ethics boards, and various governance bodies must exercise duties having to do with optimizing the use of data, ensuring that access is efficacious and fair, protecting data-subjects' interests, and generally watching over the health research enterprise.

THE TWO MODES OF ACCESS

Provision of access to information for health research proceeds via two basic modes: unrestricted and restricted. Often, a combination of the two is employed.

Unrestricted, Open Access

Unrestricted, open access is usually provided via public posting on a website. This can be efficacious, inexpensive, and egalitarian. Masses of useful data are made available this way. However, such open distribution tends to be limited to two types of data: (a) data that are strictly not personally identifiable, that is, data that are either thoroughly de-identified (anonymized), or else aggregated so as to be only average values, and (b) data for which consent to such public release has been granted.

Unrestricted release of data that have been de-identified is common but has several drawbacks. The redacted data tend to lack fine personal detail, and because the identifiers have been stripped away, the data cannot readily be linked to other datasets. If the de-identification is irreversible, the data sources cannot be recontacted to validate the data, obtain additional information, or invite participation in other research projects. Furthermore, de-identification itself is a demanding technical craft, trickier than most people think.

Unrestricted release of data with consent is a fairly rare circumstance for most health-related data, although it does occur for some datasets judged to be non-sensitive, and for some to which advocacy groups, such as groups promoting research on particular diseases, urge unfettered access.

Restricted Access

Restricted access is mediated by contract-like agreements with the data custodians or stewards, who may be either the original data collectors or the curators of archived or legacy data. Access can also be mediated by electronic data platforms that manage data from multiple sources.

TERMS OF RESTRICTED ACCESS

Access to data that are not in the public domain is granted via agreements specifying terms and fitting the access within the requirements of policies, laws, professional guidance, international conventions, and common decency. Similar undertakings must be made whether the application for access is made directly to a data steward or an access committee, or indirectly through an impersonal, online platform.

On the providing side, agreements may be executed by funders, data custodians (who may be senior investigators, research groups, or in some jurisdictions, corporations), supervisory committees, hosting universities or other institutions, or a combination of these parties.

On the requesting side, agreements are executed by principal investigators or other research leaders, and / or by universities or other institutions. These parties assume responsibility for ensuring that the conditions are met, including by staff and students.

Agreements take a variety of forms, from letters of understanding to website clickthroughs to complex contracts. Probably no agreement covers all of the following points, but set out here as a menu are the more common elements of data access and biospecimen transfer agreements. All of these matters must be weighed whenever policies are being developed or agreements are being negotiated, even if it is then determined that the consideration is not pertinent.

Confirmation of professional competence. Applicants may be asked to provide evidence of experience with database or genomic research, or of having published articles on the health topic of concern. Such a provision is meant to protect the reputation of the resource from incompetent analysis, avoid wasting the efforts of resource stewards, and serve some of the other concerns discussed below.

The obligation of custodians to evaluate and confirm the competence of data or sample requesters is a matter of debate. The importance (and difficulty) of such confirmation can be higher if the requesters are far away or in a different culture, or are relatively unestablished investigators or students.

Screening of scientific merit and relevance. Some custodians, either in the access agreement or by their tradition, reserve the right to screen the scientific creativity, analytic power, or relevance of proposals, and some insist on the right to vet resulting publications in draft. Others believe that such screening is simply not within the purview of the data-providing custodians. This issue, too, is a matter of debate. A widely held view is that peer-reviewed approval for research funding suffices to screen the merits of proposals.

Specification of what is to be provided. Data access agreements must specify how and when the data—and possibly also associated data codes, computer programs, and general documentation of the dataset—will be provided. Reference may be made to ancillary technical standards.

Biospecimen transfer agreements must address how and when the materials will be delivered and how they will be preserved in transit. Reference may be made to protocols on handling and storage.

Consent. Consent is a core consideration whenever personally identifiable data or biospecimens are involved. It must always be addressed in agreements. Access may hinge on some original consent, on some subsequent or special consent, or on a waiver of consent requirements such as by an ethics review board or by legislation.

Research use of electronic health records presents unprecedented challenges to conventional constructions of consent, as a fine article by Kosseim and Brady made clear.[2]

Purpose limitation. This relates to consent, and when included it most often specifies that only certain health conditions or diseases can be studied. Purpose limitation is a traditional constraint, embodied in data-protection and other laws and guidance, and it can be a concern of data-subjects or specimen sources.

One purpose-related question that occasionally must be addressed is whether data or materials can be used for case controls vis-à-vis other data. Another is whether a collection can be used to identify and contact potential subjects for clinical trials or other projects.

In many agreements the pursuit of commercial purposes—or research that is recognized as having potential to lead to profit—is disallowed unless explicitly granted and an intellectual property agreement is signed.

One can question whether narrow purpose limitation should be encouraged in this era of research on multifactorial conditions. Also, it should be noted that purpose limitation can be very difficult to audit or enforce once data or biospecimens have been transferred.

Confidentiality. Solemn reminders may be made concerning common law obligations of medical confidentiality, data-protection regulations, or other laws or professional guidance.

Aspects of anonymization or disclosure protection may be discussed; sometimes these are technically complex. If anonymization is reversible, the agreement must address how the identifiers will be held by whatever party will have authority to use the key to re-identify, and the criteria and procedures governing re-identification.

Usually agreements specify that data recipients will make no attempt to re-identify, trace, or contact the data-subjects; link to databases carrying related identifying data; or use the received data or materials in any way that could infringe upon the rights of the data-subjects or otherwise affect them adversely.

Confidentiality restrictions may also apply to information about health-care providers or institutions, other researchers, or relatives of the data-subjects.

Security. Reference may be made to physical, administrative, and informatics security standards or guidelines. Special requirements may be imposed, such as assurance that data will be held and used only in a stand-alone computer and not copied.

Research ethics approval. Usually, research ethics board or equivalent approval is a condition of access. Data providers, data accessors, or both, may have to get approval. Access agreements may specify the stage(s) in the application process at which ethics approval must be secured.

Limiting onward transfer. Almost always, the data recipients must promise not to pass the data or biospecimens on to unauthorized parties. Colleagues—even close colleagues employed in the recipient's department, university, or corporation—cannot be taken as authorized de facto. An authorized party might be, for instance, a researcher in another institution who has signed a similar agreement.

Linking. Conditions may be imposed on the linking of the provided data with other data or with biospecimens. Increasingly, agreements address the linking of health or other data to biospecimens that the applicants already hold, and vice versa.

Recontacting the data-subjects or biospecimen sources. Usually, recontacting data-subjects without intermediating representation is forbidden. Some agreements mention that contact can be facilitated by the original data collectors.

Maintaining the quality of the resource. Usually, it is required that the data-requesting researchers notify the original custodians of any errors or degradation of data, biospecimens, codes, methods, or documentation that become apparent. The agreement may state that, upon notice from the data providers, erroneous or outdated data must be destroyed.

Publication. Results must usually be published in the open scientific literature, posted on a website, or deposited in an archive. Coding formats and documentation may be specified, as may limits on delay between receiving the data and submitting manuscripts for publication.

Acknowledgements. The contributions of the resource and its curators must always be acknowledged in publications. This is usually expressed in standard acknowledgement notes at the beginning or end of articles.

Co-authoring with the data providers. Obligations to co-author with the data-providing principal investigators or research group vary with collections. A perennial issue is what co-authorship involves and whether it amounts to more than just pro forma credit. This must be considered carefully by funders and others. Although the joining of complementary skills certainly can enhance research, requiring co-authorship as a condition of access can amount to coercion.

Enriching the resource. Agreements may require returning findings to the resource, posting them in a public database, or depositing them in an archive. Methods and timing may be specified. So may who bears what costs. This kind of feeding-back enrichment is becoming customary.

Archiving. If serious, long-term, accessible archiving is expected from the start, agreements usually refer to technical specifications for submission of data and documentation, and address the attendant cost-bearing and intellectual property issues.

Assigning or waiving of intellectual property (IP) rights. IP rights may be asserted over access to data or materials in the first place, over subsequent sale of data or samples, or in relation to publications, patents, copyrights, or royalties resulting from the access.

Access agreements usually refer to separate, detailed legal IP agreements—for example, agreements to which (on the data-providing side) the funders or the database-hosting university are parties. Or the agreement may simply declare that the data providers retain no IP rights.

Sometimes, exclusivity of access to some data or biospecimens is granted, such as for periods while articles or patent applications are prepared. Or the access may be non-exclusive.

Responding if consent is withdrawn. It may be required that if a research participant or data-subject withdraws consent, or if consent is invalidated for any other reason, holders of data or biospecimens, including secondary users, must destroy the data or materials and/or sever links and certify the actions to the custodians.

Prioritization of access to limited resources. The agreement may state that access to depletable samples, analytic services, or other limited resources is subject to prioritization as determined, for example, by precedence of application, comparative scientific merit against other applications, or lottery. Mention may be made of a committee that makes or oversees priority decisions.

Access fees or royalties. Fees may be assessed to cover the costs of preparing and transferring data, biospecimens, and so on, and possibly to help offset infrastructure and staffing costs as well. For commercial users the rate may reflect the prospects of profit.

Returning or destroying biospecimens. Biospecimens may have to be returned or destroyed at the end of the project, or in the event of non-compliance with the terms of the access agreement.

Transborder enforcement. If data or materials are being provided to recipients outside of local national legal jurisdiction, then special ethics review, transborder data protection, and contract enforcement undertakings may be included, such as stipulating that the laws of the data provider's hosting nation will always apply.

Termination. A clause may state what will happen if the primary custodian responsibility has to be ceded, such as if the unit closes. Often, such a clause provides that curatorship will pass to a similar research unit or the funders.

Disclaimers. Standard legal disclaimers of responsibility for errors or inaccuracies, or for consequences of use of the provided data or materials, are invariably included.

A few concluding comments

Agreements can be drafted more tightly, and moved toward more uniformity, if they refer to established policy documents instead of rehearsing standard procedural or other requirements at length. The Canadian Institutes of Health Research (CIHR) may find it useful to develop such policies, if they are not already in place. It may also find it useful to draft access agreement templates.[3]

CIHR's 2005 *Best Practices for Protecting Privacy* carries solid guidance relevant to secondary use of data,[4] as does "Data, Data Everywhere" by Black and her colleagues.[5] *Best Practices* may now deserve to be updated; selected provisions could then be adopted more firmly into policy and embodied in, or referred to by, access templates.

A FEW ISSUE-CLUSTERS URGENTLY NEEDING ATTENTION

Management of Identifiability

Even as impressive progress has been made in recent years on the handling of identifiability, perhaps most notably with public statistics, complications have been increasing. Two significant sources of complication are genomic science and database linking.

Genomic science has been burgeoning at a breathtaking pace, and it promises to hasten progress toward truly individualized health care. But it is not unfair to say that the science is outrunning ethics and policy. There are justified identifiability and privacy concerns about the exquisitely detailed, person-specific—perhaps person-unique—information that genomics generates through

- the conducting of genome-wide analyses on large numbers of samples;
- the linking of newborn blood spots, biopsy samples, and other bio-specimens with medical records;
- the growth of research biobanks; and
- the rapid drop in the cost of genotyping, which exacerbates the scale of these concerns.[6]

An example of a knotty technical development that needs attention is the recent demonstration that the DNA from many people can be distinguished in complex mixtures.[7] Obviously such analysis does not in itself reveal names and addresses, but it can confirm that a genotype is present in a mélange. Although the technique holds clear promise to help with the investigation of crimes and the identification of disaster victims (and the identification of sample redundancies across research datasets), it presents evident challenges to civil liberties and to the protection of identities in pooled DNA research samples and even in summary statistics.[8] A number of other troublesome issues surround large-scale advanced genomic research.[9]

Database linking is another activity that increasingly needs vigilance. From the perspective of identity protection, linking does not seem to be amenable to detailed generic policy guidance (i.e., of a sort that specifies how much linking of what to what is acceptable). Rather, linking is quite case specific: some linking contributes useful substantive information without increasing identifiability, whereas other linking increases the risk of deductive or even overt identification.

Provision of Access Via Complex Multisource Data Platforms

Massive amounts of data are now distributed via large-scale research platforms that assemble, organize, and store data—and sometimes bio-specimens—often from multiple sources, and then distribute them to researchers. Examples are omnipurpose biobanks, longitudinal study databases, and genome-wide association databases. These may be linked with more conventional registries, hospital discharge records, prescription databases, or other collections.

Among the challenges are the handling of consent for secondary uses, the staging of ethics review (only before the original submission of data to the platform? again before access from the platform is granted? project-specific, or more general as to purpose?), and the locus of ultimate authority over access (the original data collector, such as a physician? the platform's managers? an independent access committee?).

Obviously, electronic health records of the sort being developed in Canada, and the consolidating databases or virtual databases that inevitably will be derived from them, will present special access issues, especially as regards consent, de-identification, and enforcement.[10]

Movement of Data and Biospecimens across Borders

Until recently, transborder transfer was handled reasonably satisfactorily by straightforward agreements between data providers and data requesters. The parties often knew each other, at least professionally, and sometimes the transfers were sanctioned by government research agencies.

Increasingly, however, access is being requested by strangers far away, often by Internet, raising new issues of vetting and enforcement (and adding a certain poignancy and geographical truth to "data data everywhere"). In response, policies may have to be revamped, and the world's governmental privacy and data-protection authorities may have to develop guidelines and regulations that are more specific to transborder transfers of data for health research than the current ones, and more uniform across jurisdictions.

WHAT DO RESEARCHERS WANT?

In answering this question, one complication is that researchers play many roles. Whereas many researchers are data requesters and users, others are data providers, and many researchers are both.

Furthermore, research scientists and their leaders and funders must speak for themselves. In this collection, for example, Pringle has clearly indicated that she wants database development in order to facilitate nursing research.

Overall, surely researchers—like everybody else, one hopes—want progress on the "complex and intertwined" challenges identified by Willison, Gibson, and McGrail in this collection:

> confusion and uncertainty regarding law and policy; absence of clarity regarding consent for research use of personal information; heterogeneity in institutional policies and procedures and in the ethics review processes; insufficient capacity for secure management of data; low comparability of data; failure to design research use into the common interoperable electronic health record infrastructure; the proliferation of electronic databases; and political hurdles.

Measures that should be welcomed by researchers might include

- continuing promotion, by public education and legislation, of a societal stance of reasonable balancing of data-subject and public-good interests, and guidance on how to assess these (not necessarily opposed) interests;
- recognition in law and regulations that a variety of health services research and other analyses are integral and essential to the provision of quality health care (but confining the data uses and further transfers appropriately);
- clearer and more specific guidance from governmental privacy and data-protection authorities on the basic issues of identifiability and consent, and on their complementary interactions;
- stronger recognition and financial support for the often underappreciated work of massaging, documenting, and providing access to data to others for secondary research;
- ethically and legally sanctioned ways for accessing data for which consent is lacking and difficult, undesirable, or impossible to obtain;
- continuing development of more effective methods for de-identifying various types of data, managing the links between reversibly de-identified substantive data and identifiers held separately, and training people to carry out these tasks;
- consideration of establishing government-operated data de-identification services;
- evaluation of the usefulness of providing access via research data centres (data enclaves to which qualified researchers come, or which they access from a distance through secure electronic connections);
- exploration of the usefulness of certifying researchers who are suitably skilled and pledged to respect confidentiality and intellectual property, with the certification then allowing robust access to a variety of sensitive databases;
- tightening the legal, cybersecurity, and other elements of the cordon around data used in health research, whether the data are strictly "health" data or not;
- pursuant to the preceding point, making sure that the barriers against third-party access to research data for non-research purposes by police, courts, insurers, and banks are as high as possible, with case-specific legal mandates required before access can be granted;[11]
- options for enforcing access commitments and sanctioning infractions committed by data-receiving researchers;
- attending to the issues of management of identifiability, provision of access via complex multisource data platforms, and movement of data and biospecimens across borders as was mentioned in the previous section;

- firmer CIHR policies on data sharing and access, and perhaps template data-access and biospecimen transfer agreements; and
- continuing to promote a *culture* of data sharing in Canada.[12]

Ideally, researchers' views should be congruent with the majority public's, and responsive to minorities' concerns. When there is such congruence, trust tends to grow. When carefully attended to, the access considerations discussed here can contribute to such trust.

NOTES

1. This chapter draws heavily, with permission, on the themes developed in the author's report to the Medical Research Council UK and the Wellcome Trust, "Access to Collections of Data and Materials for Health Research" (2006), http://www.wellcome.ac.uk/About-us/Publications/Reports/Biomedical-ethics/WTX030843.htm.
2. P. Kosseim and M. Brady, "Policy by Procrastination: Secondary Use of Electronic Health Records for Health Research Purposes," *McGill Journal of Law & Health* 2 (2008): 5-45, http://mjlh.mcgill.ca (accessed 29 September 2009).
3. An example of a template having applicability well beyond cancer research is National Cancer Research Institute (UK), "Samples and Data for Cancer Research: Template for Access Policy Development," (London, 2009), http://www.ncri.org.uk/default.asp?s=1&p=8&ss=9 (accessed 24 January 2010).
4. Canadian Institutes of Health Research, *CIHR Best Practices for Protecting Privacy in Health Research* (Ottawa: Public Works and Government Services Canada, 2005), http://www.cihr-irsc.gc.ca/e/documents/et_pbp_nov05_sept2005_e.pdf (accessed 29 September 2009).
5. C. Black, K. McGrail, C. Fooks, P. Baranek, and L. Maslove, "Data, Data Everywhere: Improving Access to Population Health and Health Services Research Data in Canada. Final Report" (Centre for Health Services and Policy Research, Vancouver, 2005), http://www.chspr.ubc.ca/node/105 (accessed 29 September 2009).
6. W.W. Lowrance and F.S. Collins, "Identifiability in Genomic Research," *Science* 317 (2007): 600-602.
7. N. Homer, S. Szelinger, M. Redman, D. Duggan, W. Tembe, J. Muehling, J.V. Pearson, D.A. Stephan, S.F. Nelson, and D.W. Craig, "Resolving Individuals Contributing Trace Amounts of DNA to Highly Complex Mixtures Using High-Density SNP Genotyping Microarrays," *PLoS Genetics* 4 (29 August 2008), http://www.plosgenetics.org/article/info:doi%2F10.1371%2Fjournal.pgen.1000167 (accessed 29 September 2009).
8. One quick response to the discovery by Homer et al. was US National Institutes of Health, "Modifications to Genome-wide Association Studies (GWAS) Data Access" (28 August 2008), http://grants.nih.gov/grants/gwas/data_sharing_policy_modifications_20080828.pdf (accessed 29 September 2009).
9. For the benefit of its own enterprise, the international genomics community should brainstorm intensively to try to anticipate possible future

technical developments, such as the one just mentioned, that could induce backlash against this promising field of health science, and prepare for the eventualities.

10. The options of consent for electronic health record data are perceptively reviewed in Kosseim and Brady, cited in note 2 above.

11. Instructive lessons may be drawn from the US Certificates of Confidentiality program; see National Institutes of Health, Certificates of Confidentiality Kiosk, http://grants2.nih.gov/grants/policy/coc (accessed 29 September 2009).

12. An excellent recent essay in the US academic context is H.A. Piwowar, M.J. Becich, H. Bilofsky, and R.S. Crowley, on behalf of the caBIG Data Sharing and Intellectual Capital Workspace, "Towards a Data Sharing Culture: Recommendations for Leadership from Academic Health Centers," *PLoS Medicine* 5, no. 9 (2008): e183, http://www.plosmedicine.org/article/info:doi/10.1371/journal.pmed.0050183 (accessed 29 September 2009).

BALANCING SAFETY, QUALITY, SECURITY, AND PRIVACY: THE CASE OF PRESCRIPTION DRUGS

ROBYN TAMBLYN

Computerization is finally making inroads into the health-care industry. Population-wide computerized administrative databases have been available for a number of decades and have fostered the development of new and exciting areas of public health, health services, and clinical research. Canada, because of its publicly funded health-care system, has provided leadership in using these data for pharmacoepidemiological studies and research on the quality and safety of health-care delivery, area variation in health-care delivery, and social determinants of health.

The increasing use of electronic health-care records is expected to bring about the next revolution in health services, population health, and clinical research. The electronic health-care record (EHR) is expected to improve the safety and quality of health services by providing timely communication and needed clinical information. The EHR is also expected to dramatically improve the ability to detect public health threats, such as emerging epidemics and adverse drug events, as well as allow clinical research into a broader portfolio of health services.

Data Data Everywhere: Access and Accountability? ed. C.M. Flood. Montreal and Kingston: Queen's Policy Studies Series, McGill-Queen's University Press. © 2011 The School of Policy Studies, Queen's University at Kingston.
All rights reserved.

Yet the EHR also brings forth a whole new family of complexities. The very advantage of the EHR in improved efficiency in retrieving and communicating essential clinical information has increased concerns about breaches in confidentiality, easier access and misuse of data by employers and insurers, and security breaches on a catastrophic scale.[1]

Legislation to protect the public against inappropriate use of personal information has been enacted in most countries. This legislation was originally intended to facilitate e-commerce, but it is also applied to health data. In Canada, the primary legislation is the *Personal Information Protection and Electronic Documents Act* (*PIPEDA*). In the United States, the primary legislation is the *Health Insurance Portability and Accountability Act* (*HIPAA*). The legislation outlines the expected requirements for organizations handling personal health information. Specifically, it stipulates provisions for how personal information is to be collected, used, and disclosed—as well as the responsibilities of organizations to protect personal information by taking appropriate security measures and using it only for the purpose for which it was collected. These new requirements for robust data protection have led to a dramatic growth in technological innovations aimed at improving the security and privacy of data.[2]

Unfortunately, these new requirements have also created a widening cultural divide. On the one side are health professionals and researchers whose primary objective is to use these new forms of information technology to improve patient care, public accountability surveillance, and research. On the other side are professionals who primarily want to improve security and privacy of information.[3] This schism jeopardizes our ability to use computerization of health information to its full potential to generate new health-care knowledge and improve patient and population outcomes.

This chapter will comment on the appropriate balance between security/privacy and patient/population benefits within the specific context of effective management of prescription drugs. This area of health-care delivery has considerable challenges with respect to the safety and quality of care that make it, arguably, a good candidate for computerization. Furthermore, Canada is fortunate to have some experience in applying different approaches to protecting the security and privacy of information that will be informative in considering policy for the use of health information. Two of the most salient issues related to secondary use of computerized drug management and electronic health record data will be reviewed: the de-identification and anonymization of data, and the issue of consent or other forms of authorization or notification.

CLINICAL BENEFITS FOR PATIENTS

Improving the Safety and Quality of Prescription Drug Management by Computerized Drug Management

Prescription drugs account for an increasing portion of health-care budgets (an estimated $34 million annually in Canada), and adverse drug events are a leading cause of mortality.[4] More than one-third of Canadians have an adverse event due to prescription drugs in a six-month period; in the United States, adverse drug events are estimated to cost over $30 billion annually.[5]

There are three preventable causes of adverse drug-related events that were expected to be resolved by computerization of drug management.[6] First, computerization was seen as a critical solution to fragmented prescription drug information. Because patients use multiple physicians and pharmacists to obtain their medications, no single provider has a complete drug profile.[7] This is particularly problematic during the transition between community and hospital care: the patient's complete current drug profile may not be known at the time of admission, 50 percent of patients' drugs are changed during hospitalization, and there is inadequate communication in the post-discharge period to the dispensing pharmacies to stop previous medication and start new medication. As a result, approximately 46 percent of preventable adverse events arise from transitions between community and hospital care.[8] Indeed, 76 percent of adverse events occurring within the first 30 days post-discharge from hospital are related to adverse drug-related events, many of which are preventable.[9] Because most pharmacies are computerized, retrieval of information on dispensed prescriptions to generate a complete drug profile was considered to be an early "win" that could substantially improve patient safety in the short term.

The second aspect of drug management that was expected to benefit from computerization was the conversion from written prescriptions to electronic prescriptions.[10] Computerized prescribing eliminates the illegible handwritten script and, as a result, reduces the risk of transcription and dispensing errors. Indeed, the advent of a legible prescription was considered to be such an early win that the US Medicare reform bill instituted a requirement for electronic prescribing by 2005.[11] Florida instituted a similar requirement as early as 2001.

Third, the opportunity to conduct an automated screen for inappropriate dosing as well as for potential drug, disease, and allergy interactions was expected to bring about early benefits.[12] Similar to computer-generated guidance and alerts for air-traffic controllers, it was anticipated that computerized decision support for drug management would act as a safety net for human error related to forgetting, fatigue, distractions, and knowledge gaps.

Strategic investments have been made in the United States, Scandanavia, the United Kingdom, Europe, New Zealand, and Australia to institute e-prescribing and drug information exchange that would realize these safety benefits.[13] Initial evaluation suggests some success in reducing transcription errors through computerized prescribing,[14] but mixed results for improving drug safety through computerized decision support.[15] Drug information exchange between providers has the greatest potential to reduce avoidable reconciliation errors that occur during transitions in care between hospital and community,[16] but unresolved privacy and security issues have created major barriers to implementation.[17]

Canadian Computerized Solutions

While slow to introduce computerization into health care, Canada is catching up, and is among the first countries to institute a national plan for an interoperable electronic record. As part of the Canadian electronic health record established by Canada Health Infoway, most provinces are in the process of instituting provincial repositories of dispensed medications. In 1996, British Columbia became the first province to create a pharmanet, a repository of all dispensed prescriptions from community pharmacies in the province. Using this leading innovation, pharmacists could view a patient's drug profile at the time a new medication was dispensed. Since that time, pharmanet systems have been introduced or are in the early implementation phases in almost every province. These systems aim to provide a complete drug profile for community-dispensed medications, and in some jurisdictions they also include hospital medications. In the future, it is expected that electronic prescriptions will also be transmitted to the repository for retrieval by community-based pharmacies, as well as stop and change orders.

Computerized Solutions and Challenges in Security and Privacy

Data repositories. The development of provincial repositories of dispensed medication has been a powerful solution to the problem of fragmented information on prescription drugs across different pharmacies. However, repositories also raise issues of consent and privacy. In the primitive paper world, access to information in another pharmacy or institution such as a hospital required written patient consent to have that information transferred to a new care provider. Needless to say, paper-based written consent requirements made it impossible to provide timely access to current drug profile information for safe clinical care decisions. Thus, one important consent issue concerns whether it is necessary for a person to consent to have his or her data placed in the repository— and, if consent is necessary, how it should be given. British Columbia, the first province to introduce a provincial pharmanet, initially included all individuals in the repository.[18] However, a review by the provincial privacy commissioner then led to the introduction of an opt-out clause allowing individuals to be excluded.

Alberta, the next province to implement a drug repository, initially legislated that residents of Alberta would need to consent ("opt in") to be included in the repository.[19] However, in pilot phases, it became evident that the burden of asking physicians to obtain consent from patients was considerable, and that physicians were not willing to engage extensively in obtaining consent even when paid extra for the service. As a result, the legislation was modified to presume implicit consent and give residents of Alberta the opportunity to opt out from having their data included within the repository.

Quebec, several years later, followed a similar pathway to Alberta, initially introducing legislation that required individuals to provide explicit consent to have their drug data included in the provincial repository. These data would then be available to all authorized users (but, oddly enough, not to the patients themselves). However, after a detailed planning exercise, it became evident that it would be difficult—if not impossible—to collect consent from all of Quebec's 8.5 million residents.[20] The Quebec legislation is currently being modified to provide an opt-out clause similar to that in Alberta and British Columbia.

Ontario used a similar approach to British Columbia and Alberta in the recent introduction of its drug profile viewer for Ontario emergency rooms. Drug profiles for all Ontario residents covered by the Ontario drug plan are made available to emergency room personnel. Individuals are given the option of opting out by submitting a written opt-out, either for any access or for access to a subset of medication.[21] In the United States, health maintenance or provider organizations use a different approach. Patients, by virtue of signing up with a provider organization, are notified (a) that their data are electronic and (b) how their information will be shared, both for primary use in delivering care and for secondary uses. Patients who do not wish to have their data made electronic can simply seek an alternate care provider organization. In Canada, such a model, by virtue of universal health insurance, could not be applied.

In essence, the creation of data repositories has addressed the problem of fragmented information on current prescription drug use. However, it has created new challenges in how to appropriately define a population authorization model that will enable patient outcomes to be optimized by providing health-care professionals with timely access to critical clinical data, while still respecting an individual's right to maintain some or all aspects of privacy over his or her health information.

Access to data. Data repositories, and electronic health records in general, that enable clinical data exchange among providers raise an important technical issue: how to ensure that only authorized individuals access a patient's electronic health information. An array of standards and security features have been established to address this requirement. Indeed, the new standard for robust identification requires the user to have three forms of proof of identity: (a) something you know, (b) something you have, and (c) something you are. Typically, passwords are used to meet the criteria of "something you know." "Something you have" includes devices such as smartcards, or RSA keys that produce random digits that need to be entered when a person logs on. "Something you are" includes voice prints, finger prints, and retinal scans.

Security features are one of the greatest barriers for health professionals to use electronic health records, not because of the procedures themselves but because of the time inefficiencies they create.[22] Typically, to reduce the likelihood of breaches in security, full level authentication is required for signing into a system, for signing into an individual application, and potentially for signing into a record for a given patient. In addition, there may be further restrictions as to where computerized files can be accessed (e.g., only in a dedicated room), and screen timeouts may be used to avoid illicit access to information when a computer is left unattended. Indeed, in some jurisdictions, regulations require that screen timeouts occur every ten minutes that a computer has not been in use.

The challenge in implementing these security systems is that users will establish work-arounds to security protocols when the requirements are excessive. For example, passwords, which are often forgotten, may be written on "stickies" and then attached to the computer for easy reference. When the log-on process is time consuming, passwords and other forms of identification are often provided to administrative assistants so that patient files can be opened in preparation for use. Indeed, this is the usual process for paper files. Ultimately, when security features of a system are sufficiently onerous, health professionals bypass or discontinue using systems because they interfere with the quality and efficiency with which they can deliver care. In these cases, neither patient privacy nor clinical benefit is achieved.

POPULATION AND RESEARCH BENEFITS

Monitoring the Safety and Effectiveness of Prescription Drugs: Optimizing Population Outcomes

There is a worldwide consensus that better methods are needed to monitor the safety and effectiveness of prescription drugs.[23] Canada is among the countries working to improve these methods. Indeed, a consortium of representatives from the Canadian Institutes of Health Research, provincial drug benefit managers, federal regulatory authorities, and Health Canada has developed a Canadian plan for post-market research that would use both administrative and, ultimately, electronic health record data to monitor the safety and effectiveness of drugs post-market.[24] This network has been recently funded by the federal government. There are several reasons why Canada critically needs to improve its post-market surveillance of drug safety and effectiveness.

Pre-market trials will not suffice: there is a consensus that the therapeutic effectiveness and adverse effects of prescription medication need to be monitored after drugs have been approved for the market. Pre-market trials that are used to assess the safety and effectiveness of drugs are typically not large enough to assess less common adverse events.[25] In addition, many drug trials measure short-term biological effects (e.g., reduction in serum lipids) rather than the long-term health outcomes for which the medications are intended (e.g., prevention of stroke or myocardial infarction). Further, several studies have indicated that drugs are often used off-label, to treat either populations or indications for which the drugs were not tested.[26]

Currently, information on adverse events is obtained through voluntary reports from health-care providers. Although it is difficult to estimate, it is thought that more than 99 percent of adverse events fail to be detected through voluntary systems of adverse event reporting.[27] Newer approaches, such as prescription event monitoring—where physicians systematically monitor new patients started on a drug—are superior to voluntary adverse event reporting in detecting potential problems. However, these methods suffer from poor response rates.[28]

These types of problems have been well recognized in public health.[29] Even when reporting of communicable diseases is mandatory, underreporting is substantial. Newer methods of surveillance have been pursued by public health researchers to provide more timely identification of emerging epidemics and disease outbreaks by using electronic administrative and health data.[30] These methods could be adapted for monitoring adverse events in relationship to prescription drugs. Indeed, Canadian researchers, using administrative databases, were among the first to pioneer the use of linked longitudinal drug exposure and outcome histories created through administrative data to identify sentinel threats to population safety.[31] The augmentation of administrative data with more detailed clinical information within electronic health records would permit timelier, more precise, and less biased estimates of the safety and effectiveness of many drugs.

Secondary Use of Electronic Health Data for Surveillance and Research

Important questions have been raised about whether it is permissible to use electronic health data for monitoring the safety and effectiveness of drugs, and for population health research, without explicit consent from patients. In general, data protection Acts that regulate the use of electronic personal information share the broad principle that individuals should be informed about the purpose of the data collection and its potential uses. The legislation varies in the extent to which consent (explicit) is required for data collection and whether explicit exemptions are made for secondary uses of data for research and quality assurance.

Regardless of the wording of national data protection Acts, the general consensus is that these Acts have had a negative impact on research in the United States, the United Kingdom, the European Union, and Canada.[32] The greater restriction in data access appears to be only partly explained by the legislation itself. The majority of problems arise because of differences in the interpretation of legislation by the various research ethics boards and privacy commissioners.[33] Further, research into the general public's opinion about acceptable conditions for secondary use of data has provided new insights and highlighted complexities in defining socially acceptable guidelines for the use of electronic health information for public health, quality monitoring, and clinical research. Indeed, the availability of electronic health records, coupled with legislation governing the use of personal health information, has called into question the acceptability of many current practices where medical records are used to conduct morbidity and mortality reviews; to monitor outcomes of health care as part of quality assurance programs; to contribute to national registries for chronic disease; and to conduct retrospective studies to assess potential risk factors, causes of disease, effects of treatment, and utility of diagnostics assessments.

In light of these new challenges, it is recognized that a framework is needed for the secondary use of electronic health information that would address issues of consent for data collection, retention and destruction after use, public trust and confidence, misuse by employers and insurers, leaks, and variability in interpretation by privacy commissioners and ethics boards.[34] While there are many sensitive issues to consider—such as the misuse of information by insurance companies and employers—the issues most central to the research enterprise are related to consent for secondary use and de-identification/anonymization of data.

A FRAMEWORK FOR SECONDARY USE: CONSENT, PERMISSION, OR NOTIFICATION

Consent for use appears to be interpreted in different ways by different jurisdictions in relation to personal information protection Acts.[35] In this respect, there are three very different interpretations of the lay term *consent*, as outlined in Table 1. These interpretations give rise to three models, and access to data depends on the model used. For both the research consent and permission/authorization models, data can be accessed only when signed consent or permission is provided. In all three

TABLE 1
Interpretations of the Lay Term *Consent*

Consent Type	Definition
Research consent	Research consent constitutes a request for participation for a specific purpose (research project/research program) for a specific time period, with the option to provide and withdraw consent at any time without affecting an individual's treatment. Further, it is expected that data will be destroyed at the completion of the project for which consent was solicited.
Permission/Authorization	Information is provided on the use of the data, including use for secondary purposes such as research and quality assurance. A one-time request for permission for secondary use is made, typically with a provision for opt-out or revocation of permission.
Notification	Information is provided on the use of the data, who accesses the data, the safeguards and the conditions for data access, the conditions under which consent would be obtained if relevant, the data to be included and excluded on a regular basis, and an opt-out provision.

models, opt-out or withdrawal of consent makes the data either partially or totally unavailable.

Blended models have been also introduced. An example would be at Partners Health Corporation, where all patients are notified about the secondary use of data, including the data that may be accessed, the conditions under which data are provided, the data to be included and excluded, and the conditions under which patient consent to access a data file would be required (e.g., for data related to psychiatric admission to a mental health facility).[36]

To date, no model for consent, permission/authorization, or notification has included a requirement that findings related to secondary use—whether that be quality assurance or research—be provided to patients, nor has any model provided for the capacity to conduct a call-back for health threats that are detected for individuals. As a result, the current research on the utility of secondary use needs to take into account both (a) the differences in the interpretations of consent, permission, and notification for secondary use, and (b) the relative absence of information on how individuals per se may benefit personally from secondary use of their information.

Recent research on secondary use reveals three major issues that will have an impact on the framework established for post-market assessment of drug safety and effectiveness, as well as for other purposes. First, studies in several countries have revealed that the general public has virtually no information about the use of health data for public health, quality assurance, or research. Indeed, only 6 percent are aware that cancer registries exist, 5 percent are aware that a birth defect registry exists, and a mere 10 percent are aware that health record data are used for quality monitoring.[37] In a recent qualitative study of health professionals and patients, health professionals admitted that they rarely—if ever—discussed the secondary uses of medical record data with their patients.[38] As a result, *the public is generally unaware of secondary uses of health data.*

The second salient issue is that public preferences on consent for secondary use are abundantly unclear. Surveys of both patients and the general public produce highly variable results depending on how the question is asked. Depending on the survey, the acceptability of secondary use of identifiable data varies from 11 percent to 84 percent; for non-identifiable data, the acceptability ranges from 11 percent to 81 percent.[39] When information is provided about why such information is needed and how it will be used, such as in the survey related to the cancer registry in the United Kingdom,[40] acceptability of secondary use without consent for both identifiable and non-identifiable data tends to be quite high. On the other hand, when the public is surveyed with respect to consent for secondary use without an understanding of the context, the acceptability of use without consent seems to be considerably lower.[41] In fact, surprisingly, up to 84 percent of the general public find it acceptable to be enrolled in intervention trials in the emergency room without consent, even at considerable risk, whereas up to 74 percent want to consent first for secondary use of their health data, where the risk is minuscule.[42] At the root of these highly variable responses is not just survey methodology but a fundamental lack of understanding on the part of the public as to how information is used and why such information is necessary for both public accountability and research. *Lack of public knowledge is one of the most critical problems that needs to be addressed for secondary use.*

The third issue is that if patients are asked to provide either permission or consent for secondary use, certain subgroups will be underrepresented. There is systematic evidence that individuals with less education and from lower income households are less likely to provide consent, producing a systematic bias in the data that will be retrieved.[43] If consent/permission was a requirement for secondary use for the purposes of monitoring adverse events related to drugs, inequities in health access and provision, appropriateness of care, wait times or other such salient topics for the general public, then an entire subpopulation of individuals would be underrepresented in these reports. The systematic underrepresentation of certain subgroups of the population by virtue of the complexities of consent, permission, or other such mechanisms of determining acceptability of secondary use will not be acceptable to the general public. *Thus, more appropriate approaches such as the possibility of notification of secondary use, with or without an opt-out, may be justified from a public accountability and responsibility perspective.*

A FRAMEWORK FOR SECONDARY USE: DE-IDENTIFICATION AND ANONYMIZATION OF DATA

A critical issue in secondary use is the extent to which individuals' privacy is protected.[44] Using modern-day anonymization methods, considerable strides have been made in reducing the risk of re-identification, particularly in complex situations that require data linkage. Approaches to the anonymization of data are currently based on limiting the amount of data collected, and on providing a "one size fits all" categorization of personal health information (age, sex, date of birth, date of death, geographic residence) that aims to minimize the likelihood that a small number of individuals would be present in any one data cell (e.g., 80-year-old women living in Whiterock, BC).[45]

There is a critical need to develop more sophisticated approaches using longitudinal studies to determine causes of diseases, prognoses of treatments, and adverse events in relation to drug therapy.[46] Indeed, there is consensus on the need for research to identify more adequate tools to reduce the risk of re-identification, particularly when using linked longitudinal data.[47] This new generation of tools must be able to assess the risk of re-identification in the context of a specific study, and allow customization of the classification of personal health information variables to minimize measurement error so that the most precise and most unbiased estimates of safety and effectiveness of drugs can be provided.[48] For example, the standard "one size fits all" approach to de-identification places all persons over 80 years of age into one group to minimize the risk of re-identification. Yet this practice not only obscures the higher risk of adverse events in the very old, but also is increasingly difficult to justify as over 25 percent of the elderly are included in this age group.

In summary, new tools are needed to anonymize longitudinal linked health data. Until these tools are available, there will continue to be capricious and variable decision making with respect to the requirements for secondary use, particularly in relation both to data granularity of personal health information and to data linkage.

SUMMARY

We live in a period of great riches, where population-wide administrative and electronic health data will become available to improve the health care that can be delivered to individual patients and the accountability of the health-care delivery system. The same environmental riches have the potential to dramatically advance the opportunities for rapid, high through-put research on key public health and clinical concerns. To master the capacity that this new generation of data will provide, there is an absolute requirement to create a robust framework for secondary use of these data for research and for quality assurance. Two central issues will require explicit definition and operationalization within this framework: first, the requirements for secondary use in relation to consent, permission, and notification; and second, adequate development of tools to ascertain the risk of re-identification and the extent of anonymization of data.

The public must be engaged in dialogue about the risks and benefits in the secondary use of health data for research. Specifically, people should be informed about both the clinical benefits for themselves as patients (e.g., identification of personal health threats) and the population and research benefits (e.g., identification of public health problems or system inefficiencies) of each and every project that uses their data. In this respect, the research community needs a method of communicating regularly with the public on funded projects that involve secondary use of data. Only this kind of systemwide approach to information translation will deliver the transparency that the general public expects for secondary uses of health data.

NOTES

1. J.G. Hodge Jr., L.O. Gostin, and P.D. Jacobson, "Legal Issues Concerning Electronic Health Information: Privacy, Quality, and Liability," *JAMA* 282, no. 15 (1999): 1466-71. See also S.A. Buckovich, H.E. Rippen, and M.J. Rozen, "Driving toward Guiding Principles: A Goal for Privacy, Confidentiality, and Security of Health Information," *Journal of American Medical Informatics Association* 6, no. 2 (1999): 122-33; A. Fraser, "Privacy and the Secondary Use of Data in Health Research in Scotland," *Journal of Health Services Research and Policy* 8, Suppl. 1 (2003): S1-S6; E.H. Kluge, "Informed Consent and the Security of the Electronic Health Record (EHR): Some Policy Considerations," *International Journal of Medical Informatics Association* 73, no. 3 (2003): 229-34; W. Lowrance, "Learning from Experience: Privacy and the Secondary Use of Data in Health Research," *Journal of Health Services Research and Policy* 8, Suppl. 1 (2003): S1-S7; E. Rynning, "Public Trust and Privacy in Shared Electronic Health Records," *European Journal of Health Law* 14, no. 2 (2007): 105-12; B. Woodward and D. Hammerschmidt, "Requiring Consent vs. Waiving Consent for Medical Records Research: A Minnesota Law vs. the U.S. (HIPAA) Privacy Rule," *Health Care Analysis* 11, no. 3 (2003): 207-18; K.D. Mandl, P. Szolovits, and I.S. Kohane, "Public Standards and Patients' Control: How to Keep Electronic Medical Records Accessible But Private," *British Medical Journal* 322, no. 7281 (2001): 283-86; D. Markwell, "Commentary: Open Approaches to Electronic Patient Records," *British Medical Journal* 322, no. 7281 (2001): 286; and R. MacDonald, "Commentary: A Patient's Viewpoint," *British Medical Journal* 322, no. 7281 (2001): 287.
2. A.J. McMurry, C.A. Gilbert, B.Y. Reis, H.C. Chueh, I.S. Kohane, and K.D. Mandl, "A Self-Scaling, Distributed Information Architecture for Public

Health, Research, and Clinical Care," *Journal of American Medical Informatics Association* 14, no. 4 (2007): 527-33. See also A.D. Boyd, C. Hosner, D.A. Hunscher, B.D. Athey, D.J. Clauw, and L.A. Green, "An 'Honest Broker' Mechanism to Maintain Privacy for Patient Care and Academic Medical Research," *International Journal of Medical Informatics Association* 76, no. 5-6 (2007): 407-11.

3.   A. Iversen, K. Liddell, N. Fear, M. Hotopf, and S. Wessely, "Consent, Confidentiality, and the Data Protection Act," *British Medical Journal* 332, no. 7534 (2006): 165-69. See also D.W. Bates, G.J. Kuperman, S. Wang, T. Gandhi, A. Kittler, L. Volk, C. Spurr, R. Khorasani, M. Tanasijevic, and B. Middleton, "Ten Commandments for Effective Clinical Decision Support: Making the Practice of Evidence-Based Medicine a Reality," *Journal of the American Medical Informatics Association* 10, no. 6 (2003): 523-30.

4.   J. Hippisley-Cox, M. Pringle, R. Cater, A. Wynn, V. Hammersley, C. Coupland, R. Hapgood, P. Horsfield, S. Teasdale, and C. Johnson, "The Electronic Patient Record in Primary Care – Regression or Progression? A Cross Sectional Study," *British Medical Journal* 326, no. 7404 (2003): 1439-43 [Erratum appears in *British Medical Journal* 327, no. 7413 (2003): 483]. See also J. Lazarou, B.H. Pomeranz, and P.N. Corey, "Incidence of Adverse Drug Reactions in Hospitalized Patients: A Meta-Analysis of Prospective Studies," *JAMA* 279 (1998): 1200-1205; Canadian Institute for Health Information, "Drug Expenditure in Canada, 1985 to 2006" (2007), http://secure.cihi.ca/cihiweb/dispPage.jsp?cw_page=PG_750_E&cw_topic=750&cw_rel=AR_80_E.

5.   Health Canada, *Public Opinion Survey on Key Issues Pertaining to Post-Market Surveillance of Marketed Health Products in Canada*, POR 298-02 (Final report, prepared by Decima Research, 2004), http://hc-sc.gc.ca/dhp-mps/medeff/research-recherche/decima_2003_final_rep-rapp_e.html. See also T.J. White, A. Arakelian, and J.P. Rho, "Counting the Costs of Drug-Related Adverse Events," *Pharmacoeconomics* 15, no. 5 (1999): 445-58.

6.   R. Koppel, J.P. Metlay, A. Cohen, B. Abaluck, A.R. Localio, S.E. Kimmel, and B.L. Strom, "Role of Computerized Physician Order Entry Systems in Facilitating Medication Errors," *JAMA* 293, no. 10 (2005): 1197-203. See also D.S. Bell, R.S. Marken, R.C. Meili, C.J. Wang, M. Rosen, and R.H. Brook, "Recommendations for Comparing Electronic Prescribing Systems: Results of an Expert Consensus Process," *Health Affairs (Millwood)*, Suppl.Web Exclusives (January 2004): W4-17.

7.   Bell, Marken, et al., "Comparing Electronic Prescribing Systems," see note 6. See also N.J. Mackinnon and C.D. Helper, "Indicators of Preventable Drug-Related Morbidity in Older Adults 2. Use within a Managed Care Organization," *Journal of Managed Care Pharmacy* 9, no. 2 (2003): 134-41; R.M. Tamblyn, P.J. McLeod, M. Abrahamowicz, and R. Laprise, "Do Too Many Cooks Spoil the Broth? Multiple Physician Involvement in Medical Management and Inappropriate Prescribing in the Elderly," *Canadian Medical Association Journal* 154, no. 8 (1996): 1177-84; and D.S. Bell, S. Cretin, R.S. Marken and A.B. Landman, "A Conceptual Framework for Evaluating Outpatient Electronic Prescribing Systems Based on Their Functional Capabilities," *Journal of the American Medical Informatics Association* 11, no. 1 (2004): 60-70.

8. D.W. Bates, "Frequency, Consequences and Prevention of Adverse Drug Events," *Journal of Quality in Clinical Practice* 19, no. 1 (1999): 13-17.
9. A.J. Forster, H.J. Murff, J.F. Peterson, T.K. Gandhi, and D.W. Bates, "The Incidence and Severity of Adverse Events Affecting Patients after Discharge from the Hospital," *Annual International Medicine* 138, no. 3 (2003): 161-67.
10. Bell, Marken, et al., "Comparing Electronic Prescribing Systems," see note 6.
11. R.J. Blendon, C.M. DesRoches, M. Brodie, J.M. Benson, A.B. Rosen, E. Schneider, D.E. Altman, K. Zapert, M.J. Herrman, and A.E. Steffenson, "Views of Practicing Physicians and the Public on Medical Errors," *New England Journal of Medicine* 347, no. 24 (2002): 1933-40.
12. Bell, Marken, et al., "Comparing Electronic Prescribing Systems," see note 6.
13. D. Protti, "IT in General Practice: A 10-Country Comparison" (Canadian Medical Association, 2005), http://www.cma.ca/index.cfm/ci_id/49047/la_id/1/print/true.htm.
14. E. Ammenwerth, P. Schnell-Inderst, C. Machan, and U. Siebert, "The Effect of Electronic Prescribing on Medication Errors and Adverse Drug Events: A Systematic Review," *Journal of the American Medical Informatics Associaton* 15, no. 5 (2008): 585-600.
15. A.X. Garg, N.K. Adhikari, H. McDonald, M.P. Rosas-Arellano, P.J. Devereaux, J. Beyene, J. Sam, and R.B. Haynes, "Effects of Computerized Clinical Decision Support Systems on Practitioner Performance and Patient Outcomes: A Systematic Review," *JAMA* 293, no. 10 (2005): 1223-38.
16. L.L. Leape, D.W. Bates, D.J. Cullen, J. Cooper, H.J. Demonaco, T. Gallivan, R. Hallisey, et al., "Systems Analysis of Adverse Drug Events: ADE Prevention Study Group," *JAMA* 274, no. 1 (1995): 35-43. See also J.R. Pippins, T.K. Gandhi, C. Hamann, C.D. Ndumele, S.A. Labonville, E.K. Diedrichsen, M.G. Carty, et al., "Classifying and Predicting Errors of Inpatient Medication Reconciliation," *Journal of General Internal Medicine* 23, no. 9 (2008): 1414-22.
17. E.G. Poon, B. Blumenfeld, C. Hamann, A. Turchin, E. Graydon-Baker, P.C. McCarthy, J. Poikonen, et al., "Design and Implementation of an Application and Associated Services to Support Interdisciplinary Medication Reconciliation Efforts at an Integrated Healthcare Delivery Network," *Journal of the American Medical Informatics Association* 13, no.6 (2006): 581-92.
18. British Columbia, Ministry of Health Services, "PharmaNet," http://www.health.gov.bc.ca/pharme/pharmanet/netindex.html.
19. Government of Alberta, "Alberta Netcare," http://www.albertanetcare.ca/210.htm.
20. Fédération des médecins omnipracticiens du Québec, "The Québec Medical Record," http://www.fmoq.org/P/English/Documentation/Detail.aspx?dId=153.
21. Ontario Ministry of Health and Long-Term Care, "Emergency Department Access to Prescription Drug History: Frequently Asked Questions," http://www.health.gov.on.ca/english/providers/project/eda_drug/eda_faq.html.
22. Bates et al., "Ten Commandments," see note 3. See also C.M. DesRoches, E.G. Campbell, S.R. Rao, K. Donelan, T.G. Ferris, A. Jha, R. Kaushal, et al., "Electronic Health Records in Ambulatory Care – A National Survey of Physicians," *New England Journal of Medicine* 359, no. 1 (2008): 50-60; D. Gans, J. Kralewski, T. Hammons, and B. Dowd, "Medical Groups' Adoption of Electronic Health Records and Information Systems," *Health Affairs (Millwood)*

24, no. 5 (2005): 1323-33; and S.R. Simon, R. Kaushal, P.D. Cleary, C.A. Jenter, L.A. Volk, E.J. Orav, E. Burdick, E.G. Poon, and D.W. Bates, "Physicians and Electronic Health Records: A Statewide Survey," *Archives of Internal Medicine* 167, no. 5 (2007): 507-12.

23. B.E. Wiholm, S. Olsson, N. Moore, and P. Waller, "Spontaneous Reporting Systems Outside the US," in *Pharmacoepidemiology*, 3rd edition, ed. B.L. Strom (Chichester: Wiley, 2000), 175-92. See also B. Carleton, A. Lesko, J. Milton, and R.L. Poole, "Active Surveillance Systems for Pediatric Adverse Drug Reactions: An Idea Whose Time Has Come," *Current Therapeutic Research* 62, no. 10 (2001): 738-42; A.P. Fletcher, "Spontaneous Adverse Drug Reaction Reporting vs Event Monitoring: A Comparison," *Journal of the Royal Society of Medicine* 84, no. 6 (1991): 341-44; and D.L. Kennedy, S.A. Goldman, and R.B. Lillie, "Spontaneous Reporting Systems in the US," in *Pharmacoepidemiology*, 3rd edition, ed. B.L. Strom, 151-74.

24. Canadian Institutes of Health Research, "Post-Market Surveillance of Prescription Drugs: Using the Evidence," http://www.cihr-irsc. gc.ca/e/36803.html.

25. Carleton et al., "Active Surveillance Systems," see note 23. See also B.H. Stricker and B.M. Psaty, "Detection, Verification, and Quantification of Adverse Drug Reactions," *British Medical Journal* 329, no. 7456 (2004): 44-47.

26. D.C. Radley, S.N. Finkelstein, and R.S. Stafford, "Off-Label Prescribing among Office-Based Physicians," *Archives of Internal Medicine* 166, no. 9 (8 May 2008): 1021-26.

27. See note 23.

28. C. Key, D. Layton, and S.A. Shakir, "Results of a Postal Survey of the Reasons for Non-response by Doctors in a Prescription Event Monitoring Study of Drug Safety," *Pharmacoepidemiol Drug Safety* 11, no. 2 (2002): 143-48. See also R.D. Mann, "Prescription-Event Monitoring," in *Pharmacoepidemiology*, 3rd edition, ed. B.L. Strom (Chichester: Wiley, 2000), 231-46.

29. L. Macdougall, S. Majowicz, K. Dore, J. Flint, K. Thomas, S. Kovacs, and P. Sockett, "Under-reporting of Infectious Gastrointestinal Illness in British Columbia, Canada: Who Is Counted in Provincial Communicable Disease Statistics?" *Epidemiology and Infection* 16 (April 2007): 1-9. See also D.J. Muscatello, T. Churches, J. Kaldor, W. Zheng, C. Chiu, P. Correll, and L. Jorm, "An Automated, Broad-Based, Near Real-Time Public Health Surveillance System Using Presentations to Hospital Emergency Departments in New South Wales, Australia," *BMC Public Health* 5 (2005): 141.

30. Muscatello et al., "Near Real-Time Public Health Surveillance System," see note 29.

31. J.M. Paterson, A. Laupacis, K. Bassett, and G.M. Anderson, "Using Pharmacoepidemiology to Inform Drug Coverage Policy: Initial Lessons from a Two-Province Collaborative," *Health Affairs (Millwood)* 25, no. 5 (2006): 1436-43.

32. W. Lowrance, "Learning from Experience," see note 1. See also Iversen et al., "Consent, Confidentiality, and the Data Protection Act," note 3; C. Metcalfe, R.M. Martin, S. Noble, J.A. Lane, F.C. Hamdy, D.E. Neal, and J.L. Donovan, "Low Risk Research Using Routinely Collected Identifiable Health Information without Informed Consent: Encounters with the Patient Information Advisory Group," *Journal of Medical Ethics* 34, no. 1 (2008): 37-40;

D. Willison, "Privacy and the Secondary Use of Data for Health Research: Experience in Canada and Suggested Directions Forward," *Journal of Health Services Research and Policy* 8, Suppl. 1 (2003): S1-23; and D.J. Willison, C. Emerson, K.V. Szala-Meneok, E. Gibson, L. Schwartz, K.M. Weisbaum, F. Fournier, K. Brazil, and M.D. Coughlin, "Access to Medical Records for Research Purposes: Varying Perceptions across Research Ethics Boards," *Journal of Medical Ethics* 34, no. 4 (2008): 308-14.

33. Iversen et al., "Consent, Confidentiality, and the Data Protection Act," see note 3; Willison, Emerson, et al., "Access to Medical Records," see note 32. See also B. Woodward and D. Hammerschmidt, "Requiring Consent vs. Waiving Consent," note 1.

34. C. Safran, M. Bloomrosen, W.E. Hammond, S. Labkoff, S. Markel-Fox, P.C. Tang, and D.E. Detmer, "Toward a National Framework for the Secondary Use of Health Data: An American Medical Informatics Association White Paper," *Journal of the American Medical Informatics Association* 14, no. 1 (2007): 1-9.

35. Iversen et al., "Consent, Confidentiality, and the Data Protection Act," see note 3. See also C. Metcalfe et al., "Low Risk Research," see note 32; and K.T. Win and J.A. Fulcher, "Consent Mechanisms for Electronic Health Record Systems: A Simple Yet Unresolved Issue," *Journal of Medical Systems* 31, no. 2 (2007): 91-96.

36. D.W. Bates, "A Proposal for Electronic Medical Records in U.S. Primary Care," *Journal of the American Medical Informatics Association* 10, no.1 (2003): 1.

37. D.J. Willison, K. Keshavjee, K. Nair, C. Goldsmith, and A.M. Holbrook, "Patients' Consent Preferences for Research Uses of Information in Electronic Medical Records: Interview and Survey Data," *British Medical Journal* 326, no. 7385 (2003): 373. See also G. Barrett, J.A. Cassell, J.L. Peacock, and M.P. Coleman, "National Survey of British Public's Views on Use of Identifiable Medical Data by the National Cancer Registry," *British Medical Journal* 332, no. 7549 (2006): 1068-72; and C. Molster, C. Bower, and P. O'Leary, "Community Attitudes to the Collection and Use of Identifiable Data for Health Research – Is It an Invasion of Privacy?" *Australian and New Zealand Journal of Public Health* 31, no. 4 (2007): 313-17.

38. M.A. Stone, S.A. Redsell, J.T. Ling, and A.D. Hay, "Sharing Patient Data: Competing Demands of Privacy, Trust and Research in Primary Care," *British Journal of General Practice* 55, no. 519 (2005): 783-89.

39. Ibid. See also D.W. Bates, "Proposal for Electronic Medical Records," note 36; B. Campbell, H. Thomson, J. Slater, C. Coward, K. Wyatt, and K. Sweeney, "Extracting Information from Hospital Records: What Patients Think about Consent," *Quality and Safety in Health Care* 16, no. 6 (2007): 404-8; L.J. Damschroder, J.L. Pritts, M.A. Neblo, R.J. Kalarickal, J.W. Creswell, and R.A. Hayward, "Patients, Privacy and Trust: Patients' Willingness to Allow Researchers to Access Their Medical Records," *Social Science Medicine* 64, no. 1 (2007): 223-35; J. Lecouturier, H. Rodgers, G.A. Ford, T. Rapley, L. Stobbart, S.J. Louw, and M.J. Murtagh, "Clinical Research without Consent in Adults in the Emergency Setting: A Review of Patient and Public Views," *BMC Medical Ethics* 9 (2008): 9; M.R. Robling, K. Hood, H. Houston, R. Pill, J. Fay, and H.M. Evans, "Public Attitudes towards the Use of Primary Care Patient Record Data in Medical Research without Consent: A Qualitative Study," *Journal of*

Medical Ethics 30, no. 1 (2004): 104-9; R. Whiddett, I. Hunter, J. Engelbrecht, and J. Handy, "Patients' Attitudes towards Sharing Their Health Information," *International Journal of Medical Informatics* 75, no. 7 (2006): 530-41; D.J. Willison, L Schwartz, J Abelson, C. Charles, M. Swinton, D. Northrup, and L. Thabane, "Alternatives to Project-Specific Consent for Access to Personal Information for Health Research: What Is the Opinion of the Canadian Public?" *Journal of American Medical Informatics Association* 14, no. 6 (2007): 706-12.

40. Barrett et al., "National Survey of British Public's Views," see note 37.
41. Willison, Keshavjee, et al., "Patients' Consent Preferences." See also R. Whiddett et al., "Patients' Attitudes," see note 37.
42. Willison, Keshavjee, et al., "Patients' Consent Preferences."
43. Iversen et al., "Consent, Confidentiality, and the Data Protection Act," see note 3. See also A.F. Klassen, S.K. Lee, M. Barer, and P. Raina, "Linking Survey Data with Administrative Health Information: Characteristics Associated with Consent from a Neonatal Intensive Care Unit Follow-up Study," *Canadian Journal of Public Health* 96, no. 2 (2005): 151-4; and N. Huang, S.F. Shih, H.Y. Chang, and Y.J. Chou, "Record Linkage Research and Informed Consent: Who Consents?" *BMC Health Services Research* 7 (2007): 18.
44. Lowrance, "Learning from Experience," see note 1. See also G.P. Sayer, K. McGeechan, A. Kemp, A. Bhasale, F. Horn, L. Hendrie, L. Swan, and S. Scahill, "The General Practice Research Network: The Capabilities of an Electronic Patient Management System for Longitudinal Patient Data," *Pharmacoepidemiology and Drug Safety* 12, no. 6 (2003): 483-89.
45. Willison, Emerson, et al., "Access to Medical Records," see note 32. See also D. Armstrong, E. Kline-Rogers, S.M. Jani, E.B. Goldman, J. Fang, D. Mukherjee, B.K. Nallamothu, and K.A. Eagle, "Potential Impact of the HIPAA Privacy Rule on Data Collection in a Registry of Patients with Acute Coronary Syndrome," *Archive of Internal Medicine* 165, no.10 (2005): 1125-29; S.L. Clause, D.M. Triller, C.P. Bornhorst, R.A. Hamilton, and L.E. Cosler, "Conforming to HIPAA Regulations and Compilation of Research Data," *American Journal of Health-System Pharmacy* 61, no. 10 (2004): 1025-31; N. Fefferman, E. O'Neil, and E. Naumova, "Confidentiality and Confidence: Is Data Aggregation a Means to Achieve Both?" *Journal of Public Health Policy* 16 (2005): 430-49; P.S. Frame, J.G. Zimmer, P.L. Werth, W.J. Hall, and S.W. Eberly, "Computer-Based vs Manual Health Maintenance Tracking: A Controlled Trial," *Archive of Family Medicine* 3, no. 7 (1994): 581-88; S.J. Jacobsen, Z. Xia, M.E. Campion, C.H. Darby, M.F. Plevak, K.D. Seltman, and L.J. Melton, "Potential Effect of Authorization Bias on Medical Record Research," *Mayo Clinic Proceedings* 74, no. 4 (1999): 330-38; K. Nelson, R.E. Garcia, J. Brown, C.M. Mangione, T.A. Louis, E. Keeler, and S. Cretin, "Do Patient Consent Procedures Affect Participation Rates in Health Services Research?" *Medical Care* 40, no. 4 (2002): 283-88; K. Purdham and M. Elliot, "A Case Study of the Impact of Statistical Disclosure Control on Data Quality in the Individual UK Samples of Anonymized Records," *Environment and Planning* 39 (2007): 1101-18; and J.V. Tu, D.J. Willison, F.L. Silver, J. Fang, J.A. Richards, A. Laupacis, and M.K. Kapral, "Impracticability of Informed Consent in the Registry of the Canadian Stroke Network," *New England Journal of Medicine* 350, no. 14 (2004): 1414-21.
46. M. Abrahamowicz, R. DuBerger, D. Krewski, R. Burnett, G. Bartlett, R.M. Tamblyn, and K. Leffondré, "Bias Due to Aggregation of Individual

Covariates in the Cox Regression Model," *American Journal of Epidemiology* 160, no. 7 (2004): 696-706.

47. K. El Emam and F. Dankar, "Protecting Privacy Using K-Anonymity," *Journal of American Medical Informatics Association* 15 (2008): 627-37. See also R. Bayardo and R. Agrawal, "Data Privacy through Optimal K-Anonymization," in *Proceedings of the 21st International Conference on Data Engineering* (Washington, DC: IEEE Computer Society, 2005); B. Hore, R. Jammalamadaka, and S. Mehrotra, "Flexible Anonymization for Privacy Preserving Data Publishing: A Systematic Search Based Approach," *SIAM International Conference on Data Mining* (Minneapolis, MN, 26-28 April 2007); K. LeFevre, "Mondrian Multidimensional K-Anonymity," in *Proceedings of the 22nd International Conference on Data Engineering* (Washington, DC: IEEE Computer Society, 2006); A. Machanavajjhala, J. Gehrke, D. Kifer, and M. Venkitasubramaniam, "L-Diversity: Privacy beyond K-Anonymity," in *Proceedings of the 22nd International Conference*; M. Nergiz and C. Clifton, "Thoughts on K-Anonymization," in *Proceedings of the 22nd International Conference*; S. Polettini, "A Note on the Individual Risk of Disclosure," Instituto nazionale di statistica (Italy, 2003); J. Xu, W. Wang, J. Pei, X. Wang, B. Shi, and A. Fu, "Utility-Based Anonymization for Privacy Preservation with Less Information Loss," *ACM SIGKDD Explorations Newsletter* 8, no. 2 (2006): 21-30; and J. Domingo-Ferrer and T. Vicenc, "Disclosure Control Methods and Information Loss for Microdata," in P. Doyle et al. (ed), *Confidentiality, Disclosure, and Data Access: Theory and Practical Applications for Statistical Agencies* (New York: Elsevier, 2001).

48. Safran et al., "Toward a National Framework," see note 34. See also E.B. Andrews, "Data Privacy, Medical Record Confidentiality, and Research in the Interest of Public Health," *Pharmacoepidemiology and Drug Safety* 8, no. 4 (1999): 247-60; C.A. Cassa, S.J. Grannis, J.M. Overhage, and K.D. Mandl, "A Context-Sensitive Approach to Anonymizing Spatial Surveillance Data: Impact on Outbreak Detection," *Journal of American Medical Informatics Associaton* 13, no. 2 (2006): 160-65; and L. Ohno-Machado, S. Vinterbo, and S. Dreiseitl, "Effects of Data Anonymization by Cell Suppression on Descriptive Statistics and Predictive Modeling Performance," *Journal of the American Medical Informatics Association* 9, no. 6 (2002): S115-19.

A KALEIDOSCOPE
OF VIEWS: PATIENTS,
PROVIDERS,
RESEARCHERS,
CITIZENS

THE EFFECT OF PRIVACY LEGISLATION ON OBSERVATIONAL RESEARCH: A COMMENTARY

ANDREA S. GERSHON AND JACK V. TU

In 2000, the Canadian government passed the *Personal Information Protection and Electronic Documents Act* (*PIPEDA*) to address, among other things, important privacy and confidentiality issues in medical research. Since then, all provinces have either adopted this legislation or passed privacy Acts of their own. When initially passed, this legislation was viewed with considerable concern by observational researchers who work with secondary personal health information such as data from disease registries, chart abstractions, or administrative databases. They were concerned that overly conservative interpretations of this type of legislation could limit the scope and quality of their research to the point that it would not be effective, accurate, or worth the investment of scarce research dollars and that consequently society would suffer from the loss

This chapter originally appeared as a commentary in the *Canadian Medical Association Journal* 178, no. 7 (25 March 2008): 871-73. © This work is protected by copyright and the making of this copy was with the permission of Access Copyright. Any alteration of its content or further copying in any form whatsoever is strictly prohibited unless otherwise permitted by law.

of an important source of medical progress. Now, a decade later, there is emerging evidence that these concerns were warranted even though the ultimate impact of *PIPEDA* and other privacy legislation in Canada remains to be determined.[1]

Privacy is important to protect, and privacy legislation in Canada and other westernized countries has been very successful at raising awareness and enforcing respect for privacy among medical researchers. As shown in Table 1, many governments have passed laws in the past decade designed to protect individual privacy based on similar privacy principles.

TABLE 1
Examples of Privacy Legislation in Different Countries

Country	Privacy Legislation	Year	Website
Canada	Personal Information Protection and Electronic Documents Act (PIPEDA)	2000	www.privcom.gc.ca
United States	Health Insurance Portability and Accountability Act (HIPAA) Privacy and Security Rules	1996	www.hhs.gov/ocr/hipaa
European Union	European Union Privacy Directive	1995	eur-lex.europa.eu
Australia	The Privacy Act	1988 (amended 2001)	www.privacy.gov.au

These laws appear to have been effective. Although the issue has not been studied formally, there have been relatively few violations of privacy in medical research brought to the public consciousness.[2] This is in contrast to privacy violations in other spheres like business and government.[3] In addition, those violations that have been revealed have been generally due to non-compliance with current privacy legislation.[4]

However, this type of legislation appears to have had a detrimental effect on some observational research, specifically the kind where a waiver of informed consent has been pursued. This is research where, for various reasons, obtaining consent from study participants is not practical (see Table 2).[5] In these cases, in order to maintain the balance of harms and benefits crucial to all research, a waiver is permitted. Of course, any risk of harm to participants must be minimal, and other means of preserving privacy must be employed.

TABLE 2
Factors Affecting the Practicability of Obtaining Informed Consent from Participants in Observational Research Studies

Size of population

Proportion of participants likely to have relocated or died since the personal information was originally collected

Risk of introducing major bias into the research, thereby affecting the validity of the results and the extent to which they can be generalized

Risk of creating additional threats to privacy by having to link otherwise de-identified data to nominal identifiers in order to contact patients or their surrogates to obtain consent

Risk of inflicting psychological, social, or other harm by contacting patients with particular conditions or families in certain circumstances

Difficulty of contacting patients or their surrogates directly when there is no existing or continuing relationship with them

Difficulty of contacting patients or their surrogates through public means, such as advertising and notices

Requirements for additional financial, material, human, organizational, and other resources in order to obtain consent, imposing an undue hardship on the research team or organization

Source: Canadian Institutes of Health Research, *CIHR Best Practices for Protecting Privacy in Health Research* (Ottawa: Public Works and Government Services Canada, 2005).

Although accepted by many as being necessary, the use of such waivers is controversial to privacy advocates because participants are denied the choice to accept or refuse the risks resulting from a privacy breach (however unlikely), and yet they are still exposed to those risks.[6] A privacy breach is the intentional or non-intentional accessing of participants' personal information by an unauthorized person, and could lead to problems such as psychological stress, embarrassment, and insurance discrimination. Therefore, to ensure that waivers are not used indiscriminately, most privacy legislation specifically addresses when and where they can be employed. A conservative interpretation of this legislation has been cited as a primary reason why many research ethics boards (REBs) and data custodians have refused to grant waivers. This has inhibited researchers' access to medical records and databases. In an increasing number of examples, such refusal has resulted in decreased participation and/or a selection bias of study populations (see Table 3), the non-completion of research, and the dismantling of disease registries.[7]

TABLE 3
Examples of Studies Where Informed Consent Resulted in Decreased Participation and/or Selection Bias

Author	Year	Country	Population	Nature of Informed Consent Requested	Participation Rate (%)	Patient Characteristics That Selection Was Biased Against
McKinnery et al.	2005	England	422 consecutive patients admitted to 7 pediatric intensive care units	Parents/guardians of children were asked for signed consent to share patient identifiable information with a clinical audit database	43	Healthier, shorter hospital stay, children ages 10–14 years of age
Tu et al.	2004	Canada	7,108 patients with acute stroke presenting to the emergency department	Written informed consent to participate in a clinical stroke registry	44	Older, less alert on admission, more likely to be alive at discharge, preferred language English or French
Angus et al.	2003	Scotland	10,000 randomly selected adults registered with a general practitioner, contacted by mail	Written informed consent to complete a questionnaire about their views on health issues (to be returned by patients in a prepaid envelope)	25	Older, female, higher socioeconomic status
Woolf et al.	2000	United States	1,106 patients from an urban family practice centre	Written informed consent to be surveyed about their general health and have the results linked to their medical records	67	Younger, male, white, better health
McCarthy et al.	1999	United States	140 patients taking an oral analgesic: 45 had suffered an adverse event, and 95 were randomly selected and contacted by mail or telephone	Written informed consent to allow their medical records to be used for a study looking at medication safety	53	Not available
Yawn et al.	1998	United States	15,997 patients visiting the outpatient clinic, emergency department, or hospital of a community health centre	Written general authorization for the use of medical records	91	Females age 41–64 years; patients seen for mental health reasons, trauma, and eye care

Sources: See endnotes 1 and 7.

Fortunately, there are not many published examples from Canada. However, we are still in relatively early days. Until the legislation is tested and precedents are set, the potential for further detrimental effects on observational research remains.

The current situation may be improved a couple of ways. The first is by recognizing that there is a potential problem and instituting standards and guidelines to clarify privacy legislation.[8] These could be developed by representatives of REBs, researchers, research organizations, ethicists, privacy advocates, and members of the public. In addition, education of REBs and data custodians would help them to understand and apply legislative rules. A second approach would be to educate REBs, data custodians, and the public about methods other than traditional "opt-in" informed consent that preserve privacy and that might be considered acceptable alternatives. Some organizations, like the Institute for Clinical Evaluative Sciences in Toronto, have been using such methods to safeguard data for many years (see Table 4).[9]

TABLE 4
Some Safeguards to Ensure Confidentiality of Personal Health Data Employed at the Institute for Clinical Evaluative Sciences (ICES)

De-identification of data or, where de-identification cannot occur, the substitution of an encrypted unique numeric identifier for personal identifiers by a designated data custodian

Designation of a Privacy Officer to implement and monitor compliance with all security and confidentiality policies and practices

Stringent physical and electronic security of data

Physical and electronic limitation to the access of data

Cultivation of an atmosphere of respect for privacy and confidentiality, confidentiality and data protection obligations in employment contracts, having employees sign confidentiality pledges yearly, and providing adequate and ongoing training in such matters

Implementation of strict policies and procedures to handle, access, use, disclose, retain, and destroy data

Established penalties for unauthorized attempts to access or disclose data, or to re-identify anonymized data

Assessment of potential privacy and confidentiality risks for every observational study

Limitations on data use to a need-to-use basis

Controls on disclosure of study results including the stipulation that only aggregate results are allowed to be reported

Regular reviews and audits, transparency to the public, firm oversight and approval by independent parties

Source: Adapted with permission from Institute for Clinical Evaluative Sciences, *Privacy Code: Protecting Personal Health Information at ICES*, Fourth Revision (Toronto: ICES, 2004).

Researchers should also be taught these methods so that data security breaches do not occur.[10] Not only are such breaches awful for the participants involved, but they also damage public trust in the research community and invariably lead to future tighter restrictions on data access. In addition, new ways of informing and gaining support from the public for observational research should be developed and evaluated. For example, some groups have adopted an informed "opt-out" policy in lieu of informed "opt-in" consent. These groups have used educational brochures, easily available in public spaces (e.g., hospital waiting rooms or nursing stations), to describe observational research projects and to publish a contact name and telephone number so that patients can call for further information or to request exclusion; otherwise, their data are included by default.[11]

In summary, there is some evidence that conservative interpretations of privacy legislation have had detrimental effects on the conduct of observational research in Canada. While the effects on published studies have been small, problems in other countries suggest that the situation could get a lot worse. Observational research has led to numerous important advances in the field of medicine, and its methodology is considered the best approach to address many types of research questions. Preserving privacy is a very important societal objective, but it can be done without sacrificing such research. We suggest that standards or guidelines that clarify privacy legislation, and alternate methods of preserving privacy and confidentiality, may improve the current situation and preserve this important source of medical progress.

NOTES

We would like to acknowledge the assistance of Pamela Slaughter, Privacy Officer, Institute for Clinical Evaluative Sciences.

Dr. Gershon is currently supported by an Ontario Ministry of Health and Long-Term Care Career Scientist Award, but at the time of writing was supported by a Canadian Institutes of Health Research, Institute of Population and Public Health, and Public Health Agency of Canada Research Fellowship. Dr. Tu is supported by a Canada Research Chair in Health Services Research and a Career Investigator Award from the Heart and Stroke Foundation of Ontario.

1.   J.V. Tu, D.J. Willison, F.L. Silver, J. Fang, J.A. Richards, A. Laupacis, and M.K. Kapral, "Impracticability of Informed Consent in the Registry of the Canadian Stroke Network," *New England Journal of Medicine* 350, no. 14 (2004): 1414-21.
2.   Information and Privacy Commissioner of Ontario, *Order HO-004* (2007), http://www.ipc.on.ca/index.asp?navid=53&fid1=7616.
3.   Office of the Privacy Commissioner of Canada, "CIBC's Privacy Practices Failed in Cases of Misdirected Faxes" (Ottawa, 2005), http://www.privcom. gc.ca/incidents/2005/050418_01_e.asp.
4.   Information and Privacy Commissioner of Ontario, *Order HO-004*, see note 2.

5. Canadian Institutes of Health Research, "Background Legal Research and Analysis in Support of CIHR's Recommendations with Respect to the *Personal Information Protection and Electronic Documents Act (PIPEDA)*" (Ottawa: CIHR, 2001), 38-39.

6. D. Manning, "Commentary: Don't Waive Consent Lightly – Involve the Public," *BMJ* 324, no. 7247 (2002): 1213.

7. Tu et al., "Impracticability," see note 1. See also P.A. McKinney, S. Jones, R. Parslow, N. Davey, M. Darowski, B. Chaudhry, C. Stack, G. Parry, and E.S. Draper, "A Feasibility Study of Signed Consent for the Collection of Patient Identifiable Information for a National Paediatric Clinical Audit Database," *BMJ* 330, no. 7496 (2005): 877-79; V.C. Angus, V.A. Entwistle, M.J. Emslie, K.A. Walker, and J.E. Andrew, "The Requirement for Prior Consent to Participate on Survey Response Rates: A Population-Based Survey in Grampian," *BMC Health Services Research* 3, no. 1 (2003): 21; S.H. Woolf, S.F. Rothemich, R.E. Johnson, and D.W. Marsland, "Selection Bias from Requiring Patients to Give Consent to Examine Data for Health Services Research," *Archive of Family Medicine* 9, no. 10 (2000): 1111-18; D.B. McCarthy, D. Shatin, C.R. Drinkard, J.H. Kleinman, and J.S. Gardner, "Medical Records and Privacy: Empirical Effects of Legislation," *Health Services Research* 34, no. 1 Pt. 2 (1999): 417-25; B.P. Yawn, R.A. Yawn, G.R. Geier, Z. Xia, and S.J. Jacobsen, "The Impact of Requiring Patient Authorization for Use of Data in Medical Records Research," *Journal of Family Practice* 47, no. 5 (1998): 361-65; C. Verity and A. Nicoll, "Consent, Confidentiality, and the Threat to Public Health Surveillance," *BMJ* 324, no. 7347 (2002): 1210-13; and J. Peto, O. Fletcher, and C. Gilham, "Data Protection, Informed Consent, and Research," *BMJ* 328, no. 7447 (2004): 1029-30.

8. Canadian Institutes of Health Research, *CIHR Best Practices for Protecting Privacy in Health Research* (Ottawa: Public Works and Government Services Canada, 2005), http://www.cihr-irsc.gc.ca/e/29072.html.

9. Institute for Clinical Evaluative Sciences, *Privacy Code: Protecting Personal Health Information at ICES*, Fourth Revision (Toronto: ICES, 2004), www.ices.on.ca.

10. Information and Privacy Commissioner of Ontario, *Order HO-004*, see note 2.

11. A.M. Clark, R. Jamieson, and I.N. Findlay, "Registries and Informed Consent," *New England Journal of Medicine* 351, no. 6 (2004): 612-14.

DATABASE DEVELOPMENT: A MAJOR NEED AND CHALLENGE TO ACCELERATE HEALTH SERVICES RESEARCH

DOROTHY PRINGLE

Research that would answer most health services–related questions relevant to the roles and effectiveness of professional and non-regulated health-care practitioners—including what influences quality health care—has not yet been done. The major constraints are the limited funds to undertake the research, and the few health services researchers relative to the size of the health-care system and health-care workforce. The amount of time, funds, and research effort to generate sufficient evidence to confidently use the information as a basis for decision-making is considerable. Most of the research to date has been limited to modest-sized samples in selected organizations. But, at best, these results provide only a snapshot of the system and a limited perspective on the question being investigated.

This insufficient information limits the ability of all sectors of the system to be responsive to changes and challenges. Policy development is impeded and solid evidence-based administrative practice curtailed. Exercises such as the major hospital reform of the 1990s are undertaken with little knowledge of the implications for patient care or for the workforces that are affected.[1]

Data Data Everywhere: Access and Accountability? ed. C.M. Flood. Montreal and Kingston: Queen's Policy Studies Series, McGill-Queen's University Press. © 2011 The School of Policy Studies, Queen's University at Kingston.
All rights reserved.

In this chapter, I will argue that we could dramatically accelerate the amount of health services research if we had more databases available with relevant clinical information that reflect whole sectors of the system. Specifically, a good place to start building these clinical databases is through the capture of patient outcomes that can be assessed during routine care. Ideally, this information could be used for research as well as for real-time clinical decision-making. The major constraint in building the databases is the current paucity of information technology infrastructure in our health-care organizations, but this is changing, and thus opportunities are developing to create databases. It is important to capitalize on these opportunities, but this will require concerted action to determine what information should be captured, in what form, and by whom. The creation of outcome-based clinical databases is not without significant challenges—and these will be discussed—but the long-term payoff has the potential to offset the initial investment.

Health Outcomes for Better Information and Care (HOBIC), an initiative funded by the Ontario Ministry of Health and Long-Term Care, will provide examples of how a clinical database housing evidence-based patient outcomes sensitive to nursing can be a useful database for health services research. This chapter will begin with a brief overview of the HOBIC initiative.

HEALTH OUTCOMES FOR BETTER INFORMATION AND CARE

In 1999, based on recommendations from a task force established to examine how to revive nursing in Ontario after the disruptions caused by the restructuring of the 1990s, the Ontario Ministry of Health and Long-Term Care established an expert panel to undertake the Nursing and Health Outcomes Project. The objective was to recommend a set of patient outcomes reflective of nursing's contribution to patient care across acute care, home care, chronic care, and long-term care that could be used to create a database for policy and planning purposes. The panel consisted of nurse researchers doing work on patient outcomes, epidemiologists, health services researchers, and database experts. After a review of the conceptual work and research of the previous two decades, five categories of potentially relevant patient outcomes were identified: functional status, symptom management, self-care ability, adverse responses to care, and patient satisfaction.

A critical appraisal of research on nursing in these five areas was commissioned and conducted by Dr Diane Doran of the University of Toronto and a team she assembled.[2] This appraisal resulted in the recommendation of eight specific clinical outcomes for which there was sufficient robust research linking them to nursing to be able to assert that nurses influenced the level of outcomes achieved. Additionally, psychometrically sound and feasible measures to assess these outcomes in the course of routine admission, care, and discharge of patients by nurses were identified and recommended. The eight outcomes address functional activities of daily living, including continence; management of four symptoms—pain, nausea, dyspnea, and fatigue; two adverse outcomes (now labelled safety outcomes)—number of pressure ulcers and number of falls; and therapeutic self-care, which may be interpreted as the adequacy of preparation of patients for discharge from acute and chronic care hospitals, and from home care. This is a 12-item measure that includes patients' knowledge of their health status, medication, treatments, community resources, and how to get assistance when needed.

The panel reviewed and accepted these recommendations and sponsored a two-year feasibility study across Ontario. Staff nurses on selected units of 16 organizations representing the four sectors of the system routinely assessed patients using the proposed measures for six months. Nurses and nurse administrators received monthly reports of the information on a unit-by-unit basis. The feasibility study was designed to determine (a) the capacity of each sector to reliably collect the information, (b) the costs (time and dollars) and issues involved in the training and the actual collection of the information, (c) the value and usefulness assigned to the information by staff nurses and nurse administrators, and (d) the feasibility of implementing the collection of this information provincewide in the four sectors. The assessment of these outcomes was completed at some sites on paper and at others by computer. Results demonstrated that a high degree of reliability could be achieved in assessing these outcomes through a short educational program, staff nurses valued the information generated, and nurse executives found the information useful in providing insight into the quality of care.[3]

The results of the feasibility study were provided to the government together with the recommendation that these eight outcomes be assessed in Ontario on admission and discharge of all patients in acute care hospitals and short-term home care programs, and on admission and quarterly for patients in residential settings and chronic home care. The recommendations were accepted, and the implementation of HOBIC began in 2006. Additionally, the HOBIC team was asked to begin planning for outcomes to be implemented in other health sectors—primary care, rehabilitation, mental health, and public health—and to involve more health professions (pharmacy, occupational therapy, and physical therapy).

A steering committee based in the Ministry of Health and Long-Term Care was established to guide the implementation of HOBIC. Based on discussion with this committee, two important decisions were made. First, HOBIC outcomes would only be assessed electronically. As a result, the information would serve two purposes: it would be immediately and continuously available to nurses to support their practice, and it would also constitute a secondary anonymized database for research and planning purposes. The second decision was to implement the collection using LHINs (Local Health Integration Networks) so that the project could be implemented in all four health sectors in a LHIN simultaneously. The research database, which was relocated to the Ontario Institute for Clinical Evaluative Sciences (ICES) in July 2008, was created to meet the standards established by the Ontario Health Informatics Standards Council so that it can be linked to other databases held at ICES such as the Management Information System and Canadian Institute for Health Information (CIHI) databases.

The implementation started in two LHINs, using early adopter sites to identify operational and technical issues and find solutions. By the fall of 2008, approximately 100 organizations were "live" or were in the process of going "live" that fiscal year across nine LHINs.

PATIENT CLINICAL OUTCOMES AS A BASIS FOR DATABASE DEVELOPMENT

It is more than 40 years since Donabedian proposed his now-classic framework of "structure-process-outcomes" as a basis for identifying the factors in health-care organizations that affect quality of patient care.[4] The use of this framework to identify and analyze these factors has not diminished over the intervening years and has fuelled an enormous research enterprise to gain an understanding of what matters.

Most of the early work based on this framework focused on hospital structures and processes, but more recent work has shifted to outcomes. The outcomes that have dominated the research emanating from this framework are cost, length of stay, patient mortality, and patient satisfaction. Provincial databases have been developed that capture these outcomes on a routine basis. The ascendance of the randomized clinical trial as the gold standard for testing new interventions has contributed to the identification of patient outcomes as the means of determining effectiveness and efficiency. Drug companies have poured billions of dollars into developing and testing new drugs in the course of which the identification of patient outcomes is an important element. Surgeons have tested new surgical techniques, physiotherapists have experimented with new exercise routines to improve mobility, and nurses have done considerable research to reduce fatigue and nausea in cancer patients, to name just a few examples of such research. The science of patient clinical outcomes reflective of the interventions of practitioners has blossomed in some disciplines such as nursing, but has not advanced very far in others such as pharmacy. Outcomes that reflect interdisciplinary practice in health-care sectors such as primary care and mental health have also developed but are at an earlier stage, with fewer outcomes identified.

That being said, even nursing-related research into the relationship between organizational attributes and clinical patient outcomes is a fairly recent phenomenon: until the mid-1990s, this topic had received little attention.[5] Rather, the emphasis was on organizational attributes and workforce outcomes, such as nursing recruitment and retention.

The determination of what patient outcomes to include on a database is not an easy task. The purpose for which the outcomes are being assessed and the type of health-care organization are the most relevant factors. Other important questions must also be addressed:

- Will the outcomes be generic in nature (relating, for example, to all patients admitted to hospital), or will they be limited to specialty areas?
- Will the outcomes be assessed by clinicians or be self-assessed by patients?
- What measures will be used to assess the outcomes?
- With what timing and frequency will outcome assessments be conducted?

Conceptual frameworks can be useful and might even be considered critical in pointing to the types of outcomes that should be included. Nursing became interested in patient outcomes as a reflection of nurses' contribution to patient care in the 1980s and since then a number of typologies, conceptual models, or frameworks have emerged.[6] The most influential, the Quality Health Outcomes Model developed by the American Academy of Nursing, was created to assist quality and outcomes research.[7] This framework proposed five outcome categories that are sensitive to nursing care: achievement of appropriate self-care, demonstration of health-promoting behaviours, health-related quality of life, perception of being well cared for, and symptom management to criterion.[8]

While this framework certainly influenced the expert panel that proposed the HOBIC outcomes, the members also used a high-level framework that they developed themselves. That framework identified the major objectives of the Ontario health-care system, the patient outcomes that would reflect quality in achieving those objectives and then, within these high-level system outcomes, those that could be expected to reflect nurses' contribution to patient care. Through an iterative process of working between these two frameworks with input from others, five categories of patient outcomes were arrived at and passed on to the critical appraisal team.

The professions that have subsequently undertaken outcome identification on behalf of HOBIC (i.e., pharmacy, and occupational and physical therapy) have not had the same conceptual thinking and frameworks to build upon. The team members from pharmacy searched but could not locate any work on a framework or model within their discipline that they could use, build on, or adapt.[9] Consequently, they drew upon research in the field of nursing by Irvine and colleagues[10] to develop their own conceptual framework for identifying pharmacist-sensitive outcomes in collaborative medication management to guide their work.

Second only to the challenge and importance of identifying appropriate outcomes is the selection of the instrument to measure them. When the outcomes are physiological, measurement is usually predetermined and well established. However, when the outcome falls into the psychosocial range (such as depression or quality of life) or is psycho-educational (such as self-care ability), then the measurement challenges are considerable. Health-care providers must be able to master the measures to a high level of reliability in a reasonable length of time. Additionally, the measures cannot require so much time that they interfere with other necessary tasks. This last feature is perhaps the most important one in getting health-care providers to buy in to the routine use of the measures.

Subsequent to the feasibility study undertaken by HOBIC in which the measures proposed by the critical appraisal team were used, the Ministry of Health and Long-Term Care developed agreements with the InterRAI group to institute the routine collection of Minimum Data Set (MDS) data in nursing homes and for the home care version to be instituted in the Community Care Access Centres, which operate the home care program. Since these are two of the sectors in which HOBIC is mandated to be implemented, and because there is significant overlap between the HOBIC outcomes and the InterRAI items, an agreement was reached that HOBIC would essentially be built in to the InterRAI assessment tools using the InterRAI versions of the measures. The unique HOBIC outcomes (nausea, fatigue, therapeutic self-care) were added into InterRAI using the HOBIC measurement. Fortunately, during the feasibility study, the research assistants had assessed patients using the InterRAI measures while the nursing staff had used the HOBIC measurement, and the results demonstrated they were highly correlated. Now, in Ontario, when a person moves to a nursing home, he or she is assessed by a nurse within 24 hours of admission on the HOBIC outcomes, and the results are transmitted to the databases. These responses are embedded in the MDS instrument, which is completed over the next 14 days by the MDS coordinator—an imperfect but nonetheless workable solution.

EDUCATION OF WORKFORCE IN USING STANDARDIZED MEASURES AND PRIVACY

Some professions are more accustomed than others to using standardized measures to assess outcomes. While occupational and physical therapists are so accustomed, nurses are less familiar with using standardized and psychometrically sound scales for assessment except to assess physiological status, for example, blood pressure and temperature. Instead of reporting patient status based on numeric scales, nurses more often use adjectives such as some, a lot, severe, slight, better, and less. In fact, a high proportion of nurses find numbers depersonalizing. The benefit of numbers, of course, is that they convey meaning that is more universally and objectively understood. For example, what one nurse understands the adjective "severe" to mean may differ from what a colleague in nursing or another discipline understands it to mean.

It has taken a cultural leap for nurses to use numeric scales to describe psychosocial or patient self-assessed conditions. For example, the introduction of the 0–10 "thermometer" scale for patients to assess their pain was a significant change at the time, even though the scale has now been embraced by nurses and most other disciplines.

This example from nursing culture shows that the need to use standardized measurement to create databases may require education not only on *how* to apply the measures but also on the *value* of standardization and the *advantages* of numeric over qualitative descriptions for database construction and for communication and reporting purposes. It needs to be stressed in this education that using numeric measures in no way precludes also capturing narratives or the unique experiences of patients, which are central to clinical care.[11]

Understanding the meaning of privacy of patient information when data reach beyond the traditional patient record—whether paper or electronic—and become housed in off-site databases must also be introduced into the education of clinicians who are doing the assessments and recording clinical information. It is important for clinicians to understand how the processes of Privacy Impact Assessments (PIA) and Threat and Risk Assessments (TRA) apply to the information they are collecting. Furthermore, clinicians must be able to answer patients' questions about how their information will be used and how their privacy will be protected.

CHALLENGES IN DATABASE DEVELOPMENT

The challenges in developing clinical databases that can be used for research purposes are not to be underestimated. Mitiku and Tu recently addressed the challenges of using data from an electronic medical record (EMR) in primary care in Ontario to measure cardiovascular-related primary care quality indicators.[12] Among the challenges they identified are

- developing the software to extract specific clinical information from the "dynamic" or live database of the EMR;
- managing the constantly evolving versions of the software across vendors so the extracted information is compatible with the software;

- de-identifying the information in the EMR so that patient confidentiality is not compromised;
- transporting the data to a central location for analysis by means that meet privacy and security standards;
- identifying specific diseases or other patient information from free text; and
- maintaining the upkeep and currency of the software over time.

Additionally, the databases that are created must meet health informatics standards such as those established by the Ontario Health Informatics Standards Council, so they can be linked to other databases that include administrative data to maximize the explanatory power of the clinical data. Stand alone databases that cannot be linked to other databases are of limited value beyond their ability to describe the phenomena they contain.

From the perspective of health services research, it would be useful if patient outcome data could be linked to workforce data held in databases established by the professional colleges (e.g., nurses, pharmacists, and physical therapists). These databases contain information about education, experience, specialty preparation, and employers that is updated on an annual basis. It would be useful to be able to examine relationships between these variables and patient outcomes on a macro basis.

However, the College of Nurses of Ontario has made it clear that its database was not established for these purposes, and that it is not within its mandate to collect information from nurses in order to link it to patient care phenomena. Furthermore, the College envisions considerable resistance from the nursing workforce should this linkage be suggested. A nurses' union pointed out that the College has the power to discipline its members; therefore, notwithstanding a commitment to de-identify the data for research purposes, members would not tolerate linkage of the College database to patient care data.

The EHR is evolving very slowly in this country. Implementation across the health-care sector is still billions of dollars and some years away.[13] As Willison, Gibson, and McGrail state in their chapter (this volume): "Certainly, the EHR is *an* answer, and in many respects a positive development, for reasons of patient care as well as the extraordinary research possibilities. However, it is not *the* answer for health services and policy research." Among the reasons for their position is that researchers have not been involved to any extent in the development of the EHR or the systems in which it is housed. On the other hand, though, researchers can be more involved in the future, because individual organizations are investing in information technology infrastructure. A minority of organizations currently have online clinical documentation, but this proportion is growing. Some organizations have clinical information systems without the clinical documentation capacity for most of the professions; these organizations are part way toward a solution. Finally, there are still some organizations that have no clinical documentation system at all. As Nagle has noted, "Notwithstanding the fact that many health care organizations are in the midst of deploying clinical information systems and the supporting technological devices for clinical use, the lack of system maturity related to clinical documentation is profound."[14] However, this is precisely the time to bring the research potential of this infrastructure development to the fore and begin to plan for research as well as clinical applications.

Given the cost and complexity, it is difficult to justify the development of clinical databases if the only purpose is to accelerate research (despite the immense value and need for such research). The databases must also support clinical decision-making and planning in order to get buy-in from the clinicians who will carry out the assessments and enter them into whatever device is selected for the purpose. An illustrative case, also from Ontario, is the entry of workload measurement data that all nurses were required to complete on every shift reflecting the activities they carried out on behalf of their patients on that shift. It was not long before nurses saw this only as an additional burden with no benefit to them and their patients. It did not impress them that the data were useful to researchers, to planners, and even to their nursing department for workforce deployment purposes and overtime. As a result, the quality of the data the nurses entered became suspect.

As organizations move toward clinical documentation in advance of the EHR, opportunities exist to capitalize on the clinical information the databases will contain to answer health services questions. However, if the databases are to be as useful as possible for research purposes, researchers must be involved in planning for the documentation. Nagle has pointed out the missed opportunity when paper documents are transferred directly to electronic versions: "Replication of the paper health record does a great disservice to clients and clinicians. The opportunity to redesign and improve upon the paper record is one that should be welcomed."[15] She acknowledges that this has resource implications for clinicians. Bringing researchers into the redesign of the clinical documentation also has resource implications.

Frankly, two enormous opportunities exist: (a) for the professions to reach consensus on standardized language, and (b) for interdisciplinary teams in sectors such as primary care to standardize how they document their assessments, ongoing interventions, and patients' responses (outcomes). These opportunities can be extended to regional authorities or to LHINs in Ontario to provide leadership in moving toward standardization that will serve clinical and research purposes. For example, all the chief nursing officers in acute care hospitals in the Central East LHIN in Ontario decided to abandon their unique paper-based nursing admission documents and worked together to develop a joint online procedure that has become a model for hospitals in other LHINs. The rethink eliminated redundancy, as well as much of the extraneous material that was being collected but then served no purpose once it got into the chart. HOBIC outcomes were built into the redesigned online format.

There are many questions that we need answers to as we build a more efficient and effective system: Do patients achieve the same status on targeted clinical outcomes when nurses work 12-hour versus 8-hour shifts, if higher proportions of nurses work full- versus part-time, if higher proportions of nursing staff are regulated versus non-regulated, or if the span of control of the nurse managers on units is under 50 direct reports versus over 100 direct reports? Does giving nurses access to best practice guidelines improve patients' clinical outcomes? What disciplinary configuration of primary care teams is associated with the best outcomes relative to the types of patients cared for? How well prepared are patients to care for themselves on discharge from hospital or home care? What is the relationship between patient self-care knowledge on discharge from hospital and subsequent visits to emergency rooms and hospital readmission, and over what time frame? Access to databases with patient clinical outcomes would help answer these and many similar questions. Rather than plan the future deployment of health-care providers on the basis of experience and the results of a few research studies, examining data from the entire system would provide much more substantial and detailed information on which to make these important decisions.

In conclusion, having research-friendly information in patient documents is only the first step in creating databases of clinical information for research and planning purposes. The creation of the databases themselves is expensive and time consuming, but the ongoing value to researchers has the potential to offset this initial commitment. Importantly, the databases will allow us to answer crucial systemwide questions for which—if we do not have the evidence to answer or the evidence is insufficient—the cost of getting the answers wrong can be even more expensive in the long run than creating the databases. Patient outcomes are a starting point that will allow us to answer many important health services questions. Ontario's HOBIC is a start that should serve nursing well. Moreover, the generic nature of the HOBIC outcomes and the fact that these outcomes are not unique to nursing should make them useful well beyond nursing.

NOTES

1. L. Aiken, J. Sochalski, and E.T. Lake, "Studying Outcomes of Organizational Change in Health Services," *Medical Care* 35, Suppl. (1997): NS6-NS18.
2. D. Doran, ed., *Nursing-Sensitive Outcomes: State of the Science* (Boston: Jones and Bartlett, 2003).
3. D. Doran, "Collecting Data on Nursing Sensitive Outcomes in Different Care Settings: Can It Be done? What Are the Benefits?" Ontario Ministry of Health

and Long-Term Care website, www.health.gov.on.ca/english/providers/ project/nursing/phase_two/phase_two.htm (accessed 5 October 2005).

4. A. Donabedian, "Evaluating the Quality of Medical Care," *Milbank Quarterly* 44, Suppl. (1966): 166-206.

5. Aiken et al., "Studying Outcomes," see note 1.

6. S.T. Hegyvary, "Issues in Outcomes Research," *Journal of Nursing Quality Assurance* 5, no. 2 (1991): 1-6; D. Irvine, S. Sidani, and L. McGillis Hall, "Linking Outcomes to Nurses' Roles in Health Care," *Nursing Economics* 16, no. 2 (1998): 58-64, 87; B.M. Jennings, N. Staggers, and L.R. Brosch, "A Classification Scheme for Outcome Indicators," *Image: Journal of Nursing Scholarship* 30 (1999): 381-88; A.M. Joseph, "The Impact of Nursing on Patient and Informational Outcomes," *Nursing Informatics* 25, no.1 (2007): 30-34; K.N. Lohr, *Impact of Medicare Prospective Payment on the Quality of Medical Care: A Research Agenda* (Santa Monica, CA: The Rand Corporation, 1985); M.T. Lush and D.L. Jones, "Developing an Outcomes Infrastructure for Nursing," in *Journal of the American Medical Informatics Association Symposium Supplement, SCAMC Proceedings* (Philadelphia: Hanley and Belfus, 1995).

7. P.H. Mitchell and N. Lang, "Framing the Problem of Measuring and Improving Healthcare Quality: Has the Quality Health Outcomes Model Been Useful?" *Medical Care* 42, no. 2 Suppl. (2004): II4-II11.

8. P.H. Mitchell, S. Ferketich, and B.M. Jennings, "Quality Health Outcomes Model," *Image: Journal of Nursing Scholarship* 30 (1998): 43-46.

9. J. Bajcar, M. Machado, G. Guzzo, S. Cornish, L. Cruz, N. Nassor, and T. Einarson, *Sensitivity of Patient Outcomes to Pharmacist Interventions* (Toronto: University of Toronto Faculty of Pharmacy, 2008).

10. Irvine, Sidani, and McGillis Hall, "Linking Outcomes to Nurses' Roles," see note 6.

11. L.M. Nagle, "Clinical Documentation Standards – Promise or Peril?" *Canadian Journal of Nursing Leadership* 20, no. 4 (2007): 33-36.

12. T.F. Mitiku and K. Tu, "ICES Report: Using Data from Electronic Medical Records: Theory Versus Practice," *Healthcare Quarterly* 11, no. 4 (2008): 23-25.

13. Canada Health Infoway, *2015: Canada's Next Generation of Healthcare at a Glance,* www.infoway-inforoute.ca/en/pdf/Vision-2015-Advancing-Canadas-next-generation-of-healthcare.pdf (accessed 5 October 2008).

14. L.M. Nagle, "Collecting Outcomes in Spite of Our Systems," *Canadian Journal of Nursing Informatics* 2, no. 3 (2007): 4-8.

15. L.M. Nagle, "What Else Does the Box Say?" *Canadian Journal of Nursing Leadership* 21, no. 3 (2008): 22-25.

PRIVACY ISSUES AND THE CANADIAN MEDICAL ASSOCIATION HEALTH INFORMATION PRIVACY CODE

Robert Ouellet

This chapter explores the current privacy environment in Canada from the physician perspective. The discussion is based on principles contained in the Canadian Medical Association Health Information Privacy Code and is intended to highlight a series of issues that the Canadian Medical Association feels must be addressed in looking at this matter.

In 1998, the Canadian Medical Association (CMA) adopted its Health Information Privacy Code to provide guidance to doctors with respect to the handling of patients' personal health information.[1] For over a decade, the Privacy Code has served physicians and patients well. During that time, however, legislative, societal, and technological changes occurred that have caused the privacy landscape in Canada and other jurisdictions to change significantly.[2]

The CMA Board of Directors decided in 2007 that the time was right for a comprehensive review of its Privacy Code to determine whether major revisions would be necessary.[3] A thorough review of the privacy landscape in Canada and elsewhere identified a number of privacy issues that either did not exist or were not well developed in 1998 and that may need to be addressed in a revised Privacy Code.

Data Data Everywhere: Access and Accountability? ed. C.M. Flood. Montreal and Kingston: Queen's Policy Studies Series, McGill-Queen's University Press. © 2011 The School of Policy Studies, Queen's University at Kingston. All rights reserved.

As part of its review, the CMA reached out broadly to stakeholders to elicit feedback on privacy issues. This chapter identifies and discusses these issues in the context of identifying additional current or potential future privacy issues such as secondary use of data by researchers that should be included and possibly addressed in a revised Privacy Code.

SECONDARY USES OF PERSONAL HEALTH INFORMATION

Secondary uses of electronically stored personal health information for diverse purposes having little or nothing to do with the *immediate* care of the patient are ethically, clinically, and socially among the most highly sensitive issues raised by large interoperable electronic health record (EHR) systems.[4]

The non-consensual use and disclosure of identifiable health information for secondary uses, including research, is a particularly contentious issue.[5] The storage of these data on large interoperable systems permits researchers and others easy access to vast stores of raw data for research and other purposes not directly related to health care. Demands for access to these personal data for secondary uses are increasing.[6]

In the context of medical research, two competing interests are at stake. On the one hand, there is the individual's human right to privacy, which is essential to human dignity and autonomy. On the other hand, there are broad societal interests in accessing personal health information to improve health-care delivery and public health, to advance scientific progress, and to exercise commercial interests in a free market.[7]

The World Medical Association's *Declaration on Ethical Considerations Regarding Health Databases* provides that "the right to privacy entitles people to exercise control over the use and disclosure of information about them as individuals.... Patients' consent is needed if the inclusion of their information on a database involves disclosure to a third party," including researchers.[8] The *Declaration* also states that wherever possible patient data for secondary purposes should be de-identified.[9]

In response to public concerns in the United Kingdom regarding the increased amount of commercial research within the National Health Service (NHS), the amount of personal information circulating freely within the NHS, and unethical non-consensual research practices at certain institutions, the Department of Health publicly stated it was no longer tenable to make "decisions about the use of confidential patient information ... out of sight of patients."[10]

Although the UK's *Data Protection Act* allows the non-consensual use of sensitive personal data for research purposes, it is generally held that express consent should be obtained from individuals to collect their information for medical research, particularly for secondary research by persons who were not part of the original clinical team.[11] This, however, is not always possible because some patients have since died and some may no longer be contactable. Some UK researchers now believe that the alternative to consent is to find a way to truly de-identify the information. To that end, the UK Medical Research Council has funded research into techniques to render anonymous any personal health information taken from a medical record.[12]

The NHS and other entities have developed guidelines for researchers wishing to use personal health information that are based on the Caldicott Principles for Data Protection.[13] With respect to consent, the guidelines state that "research should ... be designed to allow scope for consent, and normally researchers must ensure they have each person's explicit [express] consent to process personal information."[14]

In its 2002 report to the National Assembly of Quebec, the Commission d'accès à l'information du Québec noted researchers' heightened interest in personal health data:

> Government departments and agencies undeniably are the two types of holder bodies most solicited by researchers wishing to access nominative information within the context of their research. Among this nominative information, the data held in the files of the Régie de l'assurance maladie du Québec are the most coveted. In fact, health is the biggest research field by far. In the past five years, 56% of all applications [for access] processed by the Commission pertained to this field. In [the case of iniversity and hospital researchers] it is not unusual for the size of the samples constituted for research purposes to be composed of a population greater than 100,000 persons.[15]

In Canada, patients have a continuing right of control over the further uses and disclosures of personal health information that they have disclosed to their physicians.[16] In a fundamental sense this information remains the patient's to retain or disclose as he or she sees fit.[17]

Researchers point out, however, that if they were required to obtain express consent from each individual for access to his or her personal health data on an EHR, not only would it be impractical but research would grind to a halt.[18] They argue that requiring express consent—or allowing individuals an opportunity to opt out—before personal data can be gathered is neither appropriate nor feasible for certain types of databases, such as cancer registries.[19] Some researchers have argued that consent should be waived for whole classes of research, while others have argued the value of a blanket form of consent.[20]

A recent survey of Canadians shows a high level of support (84 percent of those polled) for health research using electronic health information.[21] However, this support is conditional on the removal of personal details, such as name and address, from the information prior to its access or disclosure. Support for the use of EHRs for research drops dramatically to 50 percent of those polled if personal identifiers are not removed from the record.[22]

In 2005, the Privacy Commissioner for Saskatchewan received complaints from women regarding the non-consensual collection, use, and further disclosure of sensitive personal health information by the provincial Cancer Agency,[23] which had embarked upon a provincewide program of cervical cancer surveillance. The Privacy Commissioner subsequently conducted a comprehensive investigation. He expressed concerns with certain provisions of the *Health Information Protection Act (HIPA)*,[24] particularly the extent of the no-consent provision (s. 27(2)(b)).[25]

The Commissioner noted that there are no provisions in *HIPA* requiring trustees to consider the wishes of the patient when making non-consensual collections, uses, or disclosures of personal health information. He viewed this oversight, along with the broad no-consent provision, to be a marked departure from the common law concept of patient autonomy that had applied in the province prior to the coming into force of *HIPA*, and to be likely at odds with the right to privacy guaranteed under the Charter.[26] The Commissioner recommended that *HIPA* be amended to allow women the opportunity to opt out of the Cancer Agency's screening program and have their identifiable information purged from the program's database.[27]

Do the same concerns arise with respect to the secondary non-consensual use of *de-identified* health information in research? There are two key concerns. First, is it possible to truly de-identify personal health information, or have advances in technology made re-identification too easy? Second, do individuals still retain a privacy interest in their de-identified health information such that their consent should be obtained prior to its use or disclosure?

Concerns respecting the non-consensual disclosure and use of personal health information for secondary research purposes might lessen significantly if the data could be truly de-identified or anonymized. Arguably, if data are not identifiable, then the information is not personal and thus privacy rights and professional obligations of confidentiality would not apply.[28] Data can be de-identified in a number of ways and to different degrees, either irreversibly or reversibly.[29] One research scientist has suggested that de-identification should be seen by data custodians as a risk management exercise.[30] The objective is not to minimize the re-identification risk to its lowest possible level, but rather for custodians to choose the risk they are willing to accept for a particular disclosure and manage it accordingly.[31]

However, even after stripping personal health data of direct personal identifiers, the resultant information is typically so rich that the risk of indirectly revealing the individual's identity is sufficiently high to require that the de-identified data be treated as identifiable.[32] All it takes to re-identify the majority of individuals in a particular region is their date of birth, sex, and full postal code, along with census tract information.[33]

Would individuals continue to have a privacy interest in their health information even if it has been truly de-identified or anonymized? The answer may depend on how one conceives of personal information: is it individual "property"? The Supreme Court of Canada has arguably adopted a quasi-property approach to personal health information in the pivotal case of *McInerney v. MacDonald*.[34] Justice La Forest, writing for the Court, stated that since the patient's interest is in the information, that interest continues even when the information is further disclosed. The suggestion has been made that "if the person's interest in the information flows with the information itself, one may conclude that the privacy interest runs with the de-identified information and includes subsequent uses."[35]

Although this does not necessarily mean that personal health information should be treated as property, it does mean that information placed in the hands of health-care providers is in trust for the patient's benefit alone.[36] Finding a subsisting privacy interest in de-identified health information does not mean that research must grind to a halt, nor does it mean that consent is required for every use of de-identified data.[37] Rather, it means that prior to non-consensual disclosures and uses of de-identified health data for research, a consideration of interests should occur to determine whether subsequent uses may proceed without the individual's consent.[38] For example, a balancing of interests could determine whether the social value of the research outweighs individuals' privacy interests in their de-identified health data.[39]

It is interesting to note that a very recent decision from the UK House of Lords found that, under the *Data Protection Act 1998* (*DPA* 1998) and the Scottish *Freedom of Information Act 2002*, de-identified health information is both "personal data" and "sensitive personal data" and thus subject to the conditions imposed on the data controller (trustee or information manager) by the *DPA* 1998.[40] Only if the data controller can fully anonymize the health data, such that it would be *impossible* for a recipient of the data and the data controller to identify the individual, would it no longer qualify as "personal data" and therefore fall outside the scope of the *DPA* 1998.[41]

TRANSBORDER FLOWS OF PERSONAL HEALTH INFORMATION AND DATA OUTSOURCING

Once personal information is in the custody and control of persons or entities located in another jurisdiction, the laws of Canada are not likely to apply and any confidentiality agreement made between the disclosing and receiving parties may be breached. In other words, further control over the personal information by the individual and the custodian/trustee may be minimal or non-existent once it is transferred outside Canada.

This issue has arisen as a result of some custodians sending personal information across the border to be managed by an entity in the United States and, in particular, by the BC government's plans to use a Canadian-based subsidiary of a US company to manage residents' personal health information.[42]

Special concerns arise when personal health information is transferred to the United States. Under the US *Uniting and Strengthening America by Providing Appropriate Tools Required to Intercept and Obstruct Terrorism Act of 2001 (USA Patriot Act)*, American authorities may secretly seize personal information that is in the custody and control of either an American company or a Canadian subsidiary of an American company. Despite this concern, only a couple of provinces have amended or passed legislation to restrict or limit disclosures of health information to jurisdictions outside Canada.

British Columbia's *E-Health (Personal Health Information Access and Protection of Privacy) Act* provides that disclosures of personal health information from a health information bank must be authorized by a designation order. Disclosures may be permitted depending on whether they are made inside or outside Canada. Personal health information may be disclosed outside Canada only for the purpose of assessing and addressing threats to public health (s. 5(c)).

Nova Scotia has specific legislation to govern disclosures of personal information by public bodies (including service providers) to persons or entities outside Canada.[43] Generally speaking, personal information in the custody and control of a public body must be stored and accessed only in Canada. There are, however, statutory exceptions to this general rule, such as when the head of the public body considers disclosure necessary to meet the public body's operational requirements.

It is important to note that in Alberta, Saskatchewan, Manitoba, Ontario, and Newfoundland/Labrador, the custodian/trustee is deemed to maintain (and thereby to retain legal responsibility for) any data that have been transferred to an information manager for processing. In addition, Alberta's *Health Information Act* specifically imposes a continuing responsibility on the custodian for the confidentiality of health information disclosed to, or stored or used by, a person in a jurisdiction outside Alberta.

CIRCLE OF CARE

In the "circle of care" environment, personal health information no longer remains solely within the purview of the physician: it must be freely shared among the members of the circle so that each member can deliver his or her aspect of patient care.

There are a number of concerns related to this concept. To begin with, what exactly is the circle of care? Who belongs in the circle? What are the membership criteria? Should patients be allowed to limit the disclosure of some parts of their health information to certain members of the circle, even if it might affect their care? Should medical researchers be part of the circle of care?

A document developed by Industry Canada to help health-care providers understand and comply with the *Personal Information Protection and Electronic Documents Act* of 2004 describes the circle of care as

> the individuals and activities related to the care and treatment of a patient. Thus, it covers the health-care providers who deliver care and services for the primary therapeutic benefit of the patient and it covers related activities such as laboratory work and professional or case consultation with other health-care providers.[44]

This description still leaves uncertainty as to who rightfully belongs within the circle. For example, "individuals and activities" and "related activities" could include a variety of individuals involved in different activities related to the care of a patient. Arguably, housekeepers/cleaners, dietitians, clergy, social workers, nurses, aides, and doctors all play a part in an individual's health care. But are they all therefore members of the circle of care—and thus permitted to access a patient's health information without his or her express consent?

Some provincial legislation includes definitions of the circle of care. For example, section 62 of Quebec's *Public Sector Act* permits the non-consensual disclosure of personal health information among those in the circle of care, which is more clearly defined as "every person qualified to receive personal information within a public body … where such information is necessary for the discharge of his duties."[45] In order to be qualified, the person must belong to one of the categories of persons referred to in section 76, such as health-care professionals in a health service institution.

Manitoba's *Personal Health Information Act* provides that a trustee may disclose personal health information without the individual's consent if it is to a person providing health care to the individual, but only to the extent necessary to enable that person to provide health care (s-s. 22(2)).[46] Ontario's *Personal Health Information Protection Act* allows certain health information custodians to rely on implied consent to collect, use, or disclose an individual's personal health information to another custodian for the purposes of providing health care or assisting in the provision of health care to that individual (s-s. 20(2)). Provincial legislative provisions, although clearer in their description of the circle of care, still leave room for interpretation. Thus a degree of uncertainty prevails.

The circle of care concept also relies on *implied consent.* Thus "circle of care" is used to describe health information custodians and their *authorized agents* who are permitted to rely on a patient's implied consent to collect, use, disclose, and handle personal health information in order to provide direct health care.[47]

However, the details of implied consent are far from clear. For example, consider the withdrawal of implied consent. One of the core provisions in the *Pan-Canadian Health Information Privacy and Confidentiality Framework* provides that patients have the right to withdraw their implied consent for the sharing of personal health information among members of the circle of care.[48] It has been noted, however, that this "ostensibly robust" position on patients' rights is subsequently diluted by the framework's "ancillary provisions," one of which allows non-compliance with a patient's wishes if they place an unreasonable burden on a custodian/trustee.[49] This commentator further notes that the reference to "administrative burdens" in the ancillary provision is a reflection of the challenge that occurs when patients are given too much authority to control their personal health information. It may result in patients limiting access to their health data and thus restricting the free flow of patient information among the members of the circle of care. Thus, the best advice to information custodians might be to balance "efficiency" with consent.[50]

PRESSURES FOR MANDATORY AND DISCRETIONARY REPORTING LEGISLATION RELATED TO CRIMINAL ACTS

Four provinces have implemented legislation *requiring* health-care providers or institutions to make non-consensual disclosures of specified personal health information of individuals who present with gunshot and/or stab wounds.[51] In addition, Alberta's *Health Information Act* gives custodians *discretion* to disclose certain personal health information to police if the custodian reasonably believes that the information relates to the possible commission of a federal or provincial offence and the disclosure will protect the health and safety of Albertans.[52] This reporting legislation is primarily the result of lobbying by police services in these four provinces for easy access to limited personal health information to help fight crime.

This legislation has generated criticism from some physicians and academics, and support from others.[53] Those opposed argue that it requires physicians to make an assessment as to the possible commission of a crime, something doctors are not trained to do, and that it requires them to assume responsibility for the safety of society at large, making the well-being of their patient a secondary concern.[54] A health-care provider's "proper focus is to provide appropriate treatment to the injured or ill individual—not determine if an injury may have been the result of a criminal or other illegal act."[55] Such an inquiry, critics argue, fundamentally alters the doctor-patient relationship of trust.[56]

Academics are concerned that the provinces do not have the constitutional authority to pass mandatory reporting legislation and, in any event, the legislation would most likely be found to violate the right to privacy guaranteed by the Charter.[57] Furthermore, the mandatory reporting legislation may deter persons with firearms-related injuries from seeking medical care.[58] Individuals may generally begin to view physicians as extensions of the police and could become reluctant to disclose certain personal information to their doctors, such as drug use, spousal abuse, and sexual orientation, which would negatively affect the health care they receive.[59]

Those in favour argue that mandatory and discretionary reporting provisions assist police in dealing with violent crimes involving handguns and knives. Doctors Nova Scotia supported mandatory reporting legislation because it believed the legislation could prevent further acts of violence.[60] The Ontario Chiefs of Police viewed the legislation as a positive step in protecting "medical staff, police officers, victims and the public from gun violence."[61] The Ontario Medical Association (OMA) also supported mandatory reporting legislation. Dr. Howard Owens, a member of the OMA's Executive Association of Emergency Medicine, stated that only the victim's name and the location of the health-care facility is disclosed to police. He noted that in those US states (at least 45) that have similar legislation, there have been no reports of victims not seeking the necessary medical care because of mandatory reporting laws.[62]

In the past, personal health information about an injured victim in the custody and control of a health-care provider or facility could be collected by police only if the victim consented or if the police had a judicially authorized warrant permitting them to seize private information. The requirement of a warrant acted as a check and balance on police/state powers.[63] The mandatory and discretionary reporting legislation replaces this judicial check and balance. Without it, the police are free to collect health information about individuals who present with certain injuries at hospitals and clinics, no matter how those injuries occurred—for example, whether self-inflicted or accidental—and without the consent of the individual concerned.

RESEARCH ETHICS BOARDS

Provincial legislation specific to health information typically allows the non-consensual disclosure of patients' personal health information by a custodian/trustee for purposes of medical research provided a number of conditions are met.[64] Among other things, the pre-approval of a research project by a research ethics board (REB), a data stewardship committee, or an institutional research review committee is routinely required as a necessary condition. The legislation generally lists a number of factors that a REB must consider in its review, such as whether the research should require the express consent of those individuals whose health data are required for the project.

If the REB review and approval process is to replace an individual's right to control the further uses and disclosures of his or her identifiable health data for research purposes, the individual members of the REB should be eminently qualified. They should understand and appreciate the legal and ethical significance of permitting a non-consensual disclosure of highly sensitive identifiable information. Furthermore, the REB members should be conflict-free in order to participate in these decisions.

FUTURE ISSUES

Function Creep

Function creep is the term used to describe the phenomenon whereby the uses of data that are stored and accessed electronically expand over time to encompass activities not originally foreseen, including the matching of personal health information accessible in an EHR database with other databases containing personal information, such as criminal databases.[65] Function creep is driven by human nature: the creation of comprehensive records in the form of large interoperable databanks naturally creates an interest among researchers, academics, police, national security officials, and others to obtain easy access to those records.

For some persons and organizations who are promoting the establishment of EHRs, "the computer is being viewed not as a technical device to make an essentially private record quickly available to physicians (and, in exceptional circumstances, to other parties), but instead as a device to transform that private medical record into a semipublic record used routinely for a wide range of investigations."[66] For example, a committee of the American Institute of Medicine that is promoting EHRs in the United States (in order to improve patient safety) has speculated that "the proposed national health information infrastructure will yield many other benefits in terms of new opportunities for access to care, care delivery, public health, homeland security, and clinical and health services research."[67]

Once large databanks of electronically stored identifiable health information exist, different government departments and agencies will want access, even to masked or sealed information, for purposes unrelated to health care.[68] This concern was raised in the United Kingdom by the British Medical Association after the NHS suggested that it might grant other government departments access to the EHR database.[69]

In Canada, once personal information is in the hands of a government department, individuals might reasonably expect to retain privacy of information and that it will be disclosed no further. If that is the case, the information may still be disclosed for the same or a similar purpose, but if the government discloses it for a new or different purpose, even if just to a different department within the government, the individual's reasonable expectation of privacy may arise anew, in which case the department would require a reasonable lawful authority (to disclose) in order to comply with the Charter.

Personally Controlled Health Records

The private sector has recently begun to provide online services to allow individuals in the United States to electronically store and maintain their own health records. These private sector companies include Google Health and Microsoft HealthVault, along with other Web services.[70]

HealthVault, announced by Microsoft in 2007, allows consumers to collect their health information—such as lists of medical problems, medical history, medications, allergies, immunizations, test results, insurance information, and doctor's visits—from their physician and other health-care providers, add information of their own, and store it electronically at no charge.[71] Individuals have the ability to access, augment, and share their health record with whomever they choose, such as family members.[72]

In February 2008, Google announced its health records project, Google Health. It promises consumers "complete control over your data," meaning the information will not be sold or disclosed without the consumer's express consent.[73] It allows individuals to put health-related information in one place by importing the information from participating institutions or entering it manually.[74]

Concerns, however, have been raised with respect to the privacy protection of information stored in online repositories.[75] Although Microsoft and Google have comprehensive privacy policies, and individuals can always remove their health information or cancel their accounts, it is unlikely that existing privacy laws would protect personal data on these sites.

The US *Health Insurance Portability and Accountability Act* (*HIPAA*) does not apply to online data stored outside the health-care system.[76] Thus, the data stored may not be as secure and private as consumers assume, and an individual's control could turn out to be limited.[77] Furthermore, it is not clear that physicians with EMRs will agree to allow their patients to receive this information in online standardized electronic formats and use it as they wish.[78]

If and when these services come to Canada, Patricia Kosseim, General Counsel, Office of the Privacy Commissioner of Canada, confirmed that the *Personal Information Protection and Electronic Documents Act* and its provincial counterparts will apply to health information stored in databases operated by private companies, such as Microsoft and Google.[79] As noted earlier, however, the *USA Patriot Act* should make Canadians wary of storing their health information on Internet servers based in the United States or managed by a Canadian subsidiary of an American company.

If these private sector health-record services prove to be secure and user friendly, the public may embrace them. Canadians may prefer to retain control over their own health information rather than relinquish control to government or a government agency.

A FINAL WORD

Physicians have a proven track record for managing sensitive health information—protecting the privacy of patient information is and always has been at the core of the physician-patient relationship. Polling conducted by Ipsos Reid for the Canadian Medical Association in 1999 and 2004 found that the majority of Canadians trusted physicians to keep their health information confidential, supported the release of their health information *with consent*, and preferred to have their physician act as data steward for their health information. The latest poll, in the summer of 2007, found that Canadians' perceptions of health information confidentiality have not really changed.

The 2007 Ipsos Reid poll for the CMA shows that the majority of Canadians still trust doctors to look after their information and share it appropriately with others. A majority of Canadians (85 percent) trust that physicians keep their health information confidential, up from 74 percent in 1999. This increase in confidence is significant particularly in light of increased media reports of health information being lost or stolen, most often from large institutions and government data holdings. The CMA believes the trust Canadians have in their doctors is important to bear in mind as Canada builds electronic health record systems.

A majority of Canadians (74 percent) also believe that their consent should be sought for the release of personal health information (down slightly from 77 percent in 1999), and just over half of Canadians (51 percent) remain concerned about *non-identifiable* health information being released without their consent (similar to 52 percent in 1999). Consent therefore remains a critical component for sharing health information. The CMA believes that appropriate consent mechanisms must be built into the design of health-care databases and electronic health record systems to ensure patients remain confident their information is well protected.

Where information is stored and who manages it are also key privacy considerations for the public. Almost three-quarters of Canadians (74 percent) find it acceptable if they can consent up front for their physician to provide electronic access to their health information to other medical professionals for diagnosis and treatment, for example, to specialists or hospital emergency rooms. A similar proportion (72 percent) say it is either very or somewhat acceptable if a patient's personal health record is stored and managed by his or her physician and no information is released without the patient's consent.

However, only one-third (33 percent) of Canadians find it either very or somewhat acceptable to have some (core) clinical data from a patient's record "stored and managed centrally by local regional health authorities or agencies"—making this the public's least favoured option for how personal health information should be shared outside of the physician's office. Also, three-quarters of Canadians (75 percent) either strongly or somewhat agree that there are parts of their medical record—paper or electronic—that only a limited number of health-care team members should have access to, and that should not be seen by third parties such as governments and researchers.

Concerns over who can see their information have led some Canadians to withhold it—something that could compromise their care. The percentage of Canadians who have held back information from a health-care provider because they were concerned about who it would be shared with, or what purposes it would be used for, has remained steady at 11 percent since 1999. To discourage this practice and strengthen trust in providers, the CMA believes that we must do everything we can to preserve and enhance the confidentiality (sanctity, trust) of the patient-physician relationship.

These results once again show that Canadians continue to place their trust in their physicians' commitment to patient confidentiality and prefer to see their personal health records remain in the custody of their physicians. For physicians, the ethical principle of protecting patient privacy is basic and fundamental, and the CMA has been at the forefront of ensuring that technological advances do not impinge on or endanger the privacy of that information. Careful stewardship of sensitive health information protects the privacy of patient information and preserves and even enhances the patient-physician relationship.

These are important messages for government and health stakeholders to keep in mind when making decisions on privacy legislation and local or pan-Canadian electronic health record initiatives. With respect to secondary use and research, the pursuit of information cannot infringe upon privacy. The onus remains on researchers to show that their research is being pursued for meritorious purposes, specifically to advance health-care delivery, improve health research, and advance medical science.

NOTES

This chapter relies extensively on a research paper, "Privacy Issues and the CMA Privacy Code," 22 July 2008, written by Judy Hunter (Legal Counsel) while she was on contract with the Canadian Medical Association as a Senior Policy Analyst in the Office of Ethics, Professionalism and International Affairs. The chapter is based on a speech delivered in Toronto at the CIHR "Data Data Everywhere" Summit on 20 October 2008 by Dr. Ouellet on behalf of the Canadian Medical Association.

1. The term *personal health information* is used in this chapter to describe health information about an identifiable individual.
2. The Canadian privacy landscape is made up of federal and provincial privacy laws, the common law (i.e., decisions of the courts regarding privacy rights), and codes and guidelines respecting privacy, such as the CMA Privacy Code and the Canadian Standards Association Model Code for the Protection of Personal Information.

3.   The project consisted of four phases. Phase one entailed a comprehensive review of the privacy landscape in Canada, as well as in the United Kingdom and Australia. Phase two consisted primarily of stakeholder consultation and the creation of a draft revised Privacy Code. The third phase culminated in a presentation of the draft Code and a background report to the CMA Board, along with a request for Board approval to circulate the draft Code to stakeholders. The final phase, expected in spring 2011, includes a presentation of the revised Code to the CMA Board for its consideration.

4.   D.J. Roy and F. Fournier, *Secondary Use of Personal Information Held on National Electronic Health Records Systems: Key Developments, Issues and Concerns* (Montreal: Centre for Bioethics, Clinical Research Institute of Montreal, 2007), 16. In Canada, an electronic health record (EHR) system is generally understood to be a compilation of personal health information, drawn from multiple sources (providers and locations), on large numbers of patients, and to be regional, provincial, or national in scope.

5.   Secondary research uses for health-related purposes may include academic or commercial research, as well as research regarding public health and policy-making.

6.   K. El Emam, "Heuristics for De-identifying Health Data," *IEEE Security & Privacy* (July / August 2008): 72, www.computer.org / security.

7.   World Health Organization, European Partnership on Patients' Rights and Citizens' Empowerment, *Genetic Databases: Assessing the Benefits and the Impact on Human and Patient Rights* (Geneva, 2003), cited in T. Caulfield and N.M. Reis, "Consent, Privacy and Confidentiality in Longitudinal, Population Health Research: The Canadian Legal Context," *Health Law Journal* (2004 Supplement): 9.

8.   *World Medical Association Declaration on Ethical Considerations Regarding Health Databases* (adopted by the WMA General Assembly, Washington, 2002), http:// www.wma.net / en / 30publications / 10policies / d1 / index.html. A "third party" would include anyone not directly involved in providing health care to the individual, for example, a researcher.

9.   Ibid., Article 24.

10.   Roy and Fournier, *Secondary Use of Personal Information*, 57, see note 4. Research can be conducted in the UK without patient consent but only with permission of a patient information advisory group and only in exceptional circumstances for important research and where obtaining patient consent would be impractical, for example, registers of cancer patients (see also Roy and Fournier, p. 73).

11.   D. Kalra, R. Gertz, P. Singleton, and H.M. Inskip, "Confidentiality of Personal Health Information Used for Research," *British Medical Journal* 333 (2006): 196.

12.   Ibid.

13.   NHS Trust, *Guide to Data Protection Issues for Researchers*, 7, http:// www. wwl.nhs.uk / library / igov / policies_and_procedures / ig_policy_guidetodata-protectionissuesforresearchers.pdf.

14.   Ibid., 5.

15.   Commission d'accès à l'information du Québec, *Reforming Access to Information: Choosing Transparency* (Quebec: Gouvernement du Quebec, 2002), 12, http:// www.cai.gouv.qc.ca.

16. *McInerney v. MacDonald*, [1992] 2 S.C.R. 138, 16 and 25, http://www.canlii. org.

17. *R. v. Tessling*, [2004] 3 S.C.R. 432, paras. 21-24; *R. v. Dyment*, [1988] 2 S.C.R. 417.

18. V. Steeves, "Data Protection and the Promotion of Health Research," *Healthcare Policy* 2, no. 3 (2007): 27, http://www.ncbi.nlm.nih.gov/pmc/articles/ PMC2585459/.

19. B. von Tigerstrom, M. Deschenes, B.M. Knoppers, and T.A. Caulfield, "Use of Cancer Patient Information for Surveillance Purposes: A Systematic Review of Legislation, Regulations, Policies, and Guidelines," prepared for the Canadian Coalition on Cancer Surveillance (2000), 64, http://www.phac-aspc.gc.ca/ ccdpc-cpcmc/cancer/publications/pdf/ucpisp_e.pdf.

20. D.J. Willison, "Trends in Collection, Use and Disclosure of Personal Information in Contemporary Health Research: Challenges for Research Governance," *Health Law Review* 13, no. 2 & 3 (2005): 107-13. See also L.J. Melton, "The Threat to Medical Records Research," *New England Journal of Medicine* 337 (1997): 1466.

21. EKOS Research Associates, "Electronic Health Information and Privacy Survey: What Canadians Think – 2007," report submitted to Canada Health Infoway, Health Canada, and the Office of the Privacy Commissioner of Canada (August 2007).

22. Ibid., 6.

23. Saskatchewan Office of the Information and Privacy Commissioner, *Investigation Report H-2005-002: Prevention Program for Cervical Cancer* (27 April 2005), http://www.oipc.sk.ca/Reports/H-2005-002.pdf.

24. *The Health Information Protection Act*, S.S. 1999, c. H-0.021.

25. Saskatchewan Office, *Investigation Report H-2005–002*, 8, see note 23.

26. Ibid., 8-9.

27. Ibid., 12. The Cancer Agency has since made a policy decision to allow women to opt out. See also Saskatchewan Office of the Information and Privacy Commissioner, *Re: The Vital Statistics Act, 2007* (Bill 61, 9 May 2007), 13. The Saskatchewan Privacy Commissioner noted that electronic databases of records can be used in Saskatchewan for research purposes. He stated that the use of personal health information for research purposes should occur only with the consent of the individual concerned or, at the very least, with notice and an opportunity to opt out.

28. W.W. Lowrance, "Privacy, Confidentiality, and Identifiability in Genomic Research," *Terra Incognita: Privacy Horizons: 29ᵗʰ International Conference of Data Protection and Privacy Commissioners* (Montreal, 26 September 2007), Workbook Series 7, 10.

29. Ibid., 10.

30. El Emam, "Heuristics for De-identifying Health Data," 74, see note 6.

31. Ibid.

32. Willison, "Trends in Collection," 107-8, see note 20.

33. Ibid., 108.

34. E. Gibson, "Is There a Privacy Interest in Anonymized Personal Health Information?" special issue, *Health Law Journal* (2003): 97-129. See *McInerney v. MacDonald*, [1992] 2 S.C.R. 138.

35. Gibson, "Is There a Privacy Intererst," 111.

36. Ibid., 111-12.

37. Ibid., 112.

38. Ibid.

39. Ibid.

40. *Common Services Agency v. Scottish Information Commissioner*, [2008] UKHL 47, para. 35. Note that the definition of "data controller" in the *Data Protection Act 1998* is generally synonymous with the definitions of trustee, custodian, and information custodian in Canadian provincial privacy legislation.

41. Ibid., para. 26 and 27.

42. In 2004, the BC government had plans to outsource the administration of its public health insurance program to a US-linked contractor. Concerns were raised that if US contractors based in Canada possessed sensitive personal information, they could be secretly forced to disclose it to US authorities under s. 215 of the *USA Patriot Act* of 2001. The issue became the subject of a comprehensive investigation and report by the BC Privacy Commissioner (see Information and Privacy Commissioner for British Columbia, *Privacy and the USA Patriot Act: Implications for British Columbia Public Sector Outsourcing*, October 2004). The Commissioner's final report "examined the impact of foreign law on British Columbia residents living in British Columbia, not abroad" (p. 5). In preparing the report, the Commissioner received input from the public, the BC and US governments, civil society groups, and private sector organizations in Canada, the United States, and Europe. The BC government subsequently addressed the concerns in s. 5 of BC's *E-Health (Personal Health Information Access and Protection of Privacy) Act* (3rd Reading, 29 May 2008) by limiting the disclosure of personal health information to jurisdictions outside Canada. In addition, BC's *Freedom of Information and Protection of Privacy Act* was amended to include provisions restricting disclosures of personal information by public bodies to entities outside Canada (see ss. 30.2, 33.1, and 33.2).

43. *Personal Information International Disclosure Protection Act*, 2006, c. 3, s.1.

44. Industry Canada, *PIPEDA Awareness Raising Tools (PARTs) Initiative for the Health Sector* (Ottawa: Industry Canada, n.d.), 4, http://www.ic.gc.ca/eic/site/ecic-ceac.nsf/eng/h_gv00207.html.

45. *An Act Respecting Access to Documents Held by Public Bodies and the Protection of Personal Information* ("Public Sector Act"), R.S.Q. c. A-2.1.

46. *The Personal Health Information Act*, C.C.S.M. c. P-33.5.

47. T. McQuay, president, Nymity Inc., "Interview with Dr. Ann Cavoukian" (Information and Privacy Commissioner for Ontario), *Nymity News* (December 2004), 5-6.

48. Health Canada, *Pan-Canadian Health Information Privacy and Confidentiality Framework* (27 January 2005), Provision 5, p. 7, http://www.hc-sc.gc.ca.

49. N.M. Ries, "Patient Privacy in a Wired (and Wireless) World: Approaches to Consent in the Context of Electronic Health Records," *Alberta Law Review* 43, no. 3 (2006): 681-712 (accessed electronically).

50. Ibid., 700.

51. Saskatchewan, *The Gunshot and Stab Wounds Mandatory Reporting Act*, S.S. 2007, c. F-22.01; Manitoba, *Bill 20: The Gunshot and Stab Wound Reporting Act* (2nd Reading April 2008); Nova Scotia, *Gunshot Wounds Mandatory Reporting Act*, 2007, c. 30; Ontario, *Mandatory Gunshot Wounds Reporting Act*, 2005, S.O. 2005, c. 9.

52. Alberta has a discretionary reporting provision in s. 37.3 of *The Health Information Act*, R.S.A. 2000, c. H-5.
53. See M. Rose, "A Practitioner's Response to the Final Report of the Select Special Health Information Act Review Committee," *Health Law Review* 14, no. 1 (2005): 12; B. Bokenfohr, "Police Experience with the Health Information Act: The Edmonton Police Service's Submissions to the Select Special Health Information Act Review Committee," *Health Law Review* 14, no. 1 (2005): 9; W. Renke, "The Constitutionality of Mandatory Reporting of Gunshot Wounds Legislation," *Health Law Review* 14, no. 1 (2005): 3; T.M. Bailey and S. Penney, "Healing, Not Squealing: Recent Amendments to Alberta's Health Information Act," *Health Law Review* 15, no. 2 (2006): 3; W. Kondro, "Gunshot Reporting Mandatory in Ontario," *Canadian Medical Association Journal* 173, no. 3 (2005): 242; College of Nurses of Ontario, "Reporting Gunshot Wounds – The College's Position," *Quality Practice* 3, no. 3 (2004): 1; College of Physicians and Surgeons of Ontario, "Mandatory Gunshot Wound Reporting: An Exception to Patient Privacy and Confidentiality," *Dialogue* (November–December 2005), 15-17; Ontario Hospital Association, "Respecting Bill 110: Mandatory Gunshot Reporting Act, 2004" (presentation to the Standing Committee on Justice Policy, Toronto, 3 March 2005); M.A. Pauls and J. Downie, "Shooting Ourselves in the Foot: Why Mandatory Reporting of Gunshot Wounds Is a Bad Idea," *Canadian Medical Association Journal* 170, no. 8 (2004): 1255; H. Owens, "Commentary: Why Mandatory Reporting of Gunshot Wounds Is Necessary: A Response from the OMA's Executive of the Section on Emergency Medicine," *Canadian Medical Association Journal* 170, no. 8 (2004): 1256; M.A. Pauls and J. Downie provide a rebuttal to Owens, *Canadian Medical Association Journal* 170, no. 8 (2004): 1258.
54. Rose, "A Practitioner's Response," 13, see note 53; Bailey and Penney, "Healing, Not Squealing," 5, see note 53.
55. Bailey and Penney, "Healing, Not Squealing," 5, see note 53.
56. Ibid.
57. Renke, "Constitutionality of Mandatory Reporting," 4-6, see note 53.
58. Ibid., 7.
59. Ibid.; Pauls and Downie, "Shooting Ourselves in the Foot," 1255, see note 53. The College of Nurses of Ontario held the same view and was opposed to mandatory reporting legislation; see College of Nurses, "Reporting Gunshot Wounds," 1, see note 53.
60. "Legislation Input," available on the Doctors Nova Scotia website, http://www.doctorsns.com/Content.aspx?active_mid=628&cid=1247.
61. Ontario Association of Chiefs of Police, "Police Leaders Welcome Passage of Law Making Reporting of Gunshot Wounds Mandatory," News room, 1 June 2005, http://www.oacp.ca/content/news/article.html?ID=140.
62. Owens, "Commentary," 1257, see note 53.
63. In order to obtain a warrant, the police must provide a judge with sufficient information under oath and in writing to establish reasonable grounds to believe that an offence has or will be committed, and the judge (a neutral party) must be satisfied that it is in the best interests of the administration of justice to issue a warrant. Given that the patient would likely have a reasonable expectation of privacy in the health information he or she disclosed to the health-care provider, the information or evidence relied on to obtain the

warrant must be sufficient to make the police search-and-seizure of private information reasonable. If for some reason the search is found not to be reasonable, a breach of the patient's s. 8 Charter right to privacy will likely have occurred.

64. Under BC's *E-Health (Personal Health Information Access and Protection of Privacy) Act*, individuals may make a disclosure directive, if allowed to do so by the minister. It is therefore possible, under BC's Act, for an individual to make a disclosure directive prohibiting a disclosure of personal health information from the EHR for research purposes (see ss. 8, 3(2)(d), and 5).

65. N.M. Ries, E. Robertson, and F. Moore, *Electronic Health Records and the Personal Information Protection and Electronic Documents Act* (report prepared by University of Alberta, Health Law Institute; and University of Victoria, School of Health Information Science, with partial funding from the Office of the Privacy Commissioner of Canada, April 2005), 50-51, 63.

66. B. Woodward, "The Computer-Based Patient Record and Confidentiality," *New England Journal of Medicine* 333, no. 21 (1995): 1419-22, http://content.nejm.org/current.shtml.

67. Committee on Data Standards for Patient Safety, Board on Health Care Services, and Institute of Medicine of the National Academies, *Patient Safety: Achieving a New Standard of Care* (Washington, DC: National Academies Press, 2004), 8, http://www.nap.edu/books/0309090776/html/ (accessed 26 November 2009).

68. The BMA has stated that it opposes any plans to allow other government agencies access to the NHS Care Records Service by, for example, the Home Office. It is concerned that large interoperable databases of patient health information will be used in the fight against crime or be abused by criminal access. See British Medical Association, "BMA Evidence to the House of Commons Home Affairs Select Committee Inquiry into 'A Surveillance Society'" (Memorandum of Evidence, April 2007).

69. British Medical Association, "Inquiry into the Electronic Patient Record and Its Use – Response from the British Medical Association" (BMA submission to the Health Select Committee Inquiry, March 2007), para. 13, http://www.bma.org.uk.

70. CBC Newfoundland and Labrador, "Online Health Records: Convenience vs. Privacy," *cbcnews.ca* (5 May 2008), www.cbc.ca/health/story/2008/05/05/fhealth-digitalrecords.html; R. Steinbrook, "Personally Controlled Online Health Data – The Next Big Thing in Medical Care?" *New England Journal of Medicine* 358, no. 16 (2008): 1653.

71. Steinbrook, "Personally Controlled Online Health Data," 1653, see note 70.

72. CBC Newfoundland and Labrador, "Online Health Records," see note 70; K.D. Mandl and I.S. Kohane, "Tectonic Shifts in the Health Information Economy," *New England Journal of Medicine* 358, no. 16 (2008): 1732.

73. Steinbrook, "Personally Controlled Online Health Data," 1653, see note 70.

74. CBC Newfoundland and Labrador, "Online Health Records," see note 70.

75. Mandl and Kohane, "Tectonic Shifts," 1735, see note 72.

76. Steinbrook, "Personally Controlled Online Health Data," 1655, see note 70.

77. Ibid.

78. Ibid., 1653.

79. CBC Newfoundland and Labrador, "Online Health Records," see note 70.

USING ADMINISTRATIVE DATA FOR QUALITY IMPROVEMENT: CAPACITY AND OPPORTUNITY

Alan Katz

The Canadian health-care system, like other single-payer systems, has over an extended period of time developed an increasingly sophisticated activity-based data collection system. The purposes for which these data are collected vary according to the specifics of each dataset, but it is normal practice for these data to be used in the management of the larger health-care system. They are thus often known as administrative data. These datasets include medical claims data submitted by clinicians who are paid on a fee-for-service basis, hospital discharge abstract data, pharmaceutical data, vital statistics data, and a growing number of other datasets that are linkable using non-nominal identifiers embedded in the data.

Uses of these data for system management, planning, and even quality measurement are within the mandate of system administration and as such clearly should not be regarded as secondary uses.

For many years, however, the potential of these data for *quality improvement* has also been recognized. Should quality improvement be classified as system management, making it a type of system administration—and therefore one of the original primary purposes for which these data were collected? This is no longer really an issue of debate. The answer is yes. We now function in an era of health-care administration that recognizes

Data Data Everywhere: Access and Accountability? ed. C.M. Flood. Montreal and Kingston: Queen's Policy Studies Series, McGill-Queen's University Press. © 2011 The School of Policy Studies, Queen's University at Kingston.

and actively supports the need for quality improvement. Data that are routinely collected (for "administrative purposes") are valuable tools that can improve our health-care system.

Calling the use of these data for quality improvement "secondary use" is, in my view, a misnomer. It implies, incorrectly, that the data were not primarily intended for administrative purposes. Even more problematically, it implies that this use is less important than other ("primary") uses.

Furthermore, the use of these data for *research purposes* is so important that this purpose should also be considered "primary use." It is now widely recognized that these data represent a valuable, rich source of research data, and this recognition is reason enough to enhance the data collected for this purpose alone.

So, whether aspects of quality improvement fall into the categories of system management or research, the use of administrative data for quality improvement should be recognized as an important, primary use, rather than categorized as a secondary use.

QUALITY IMPROVEMENT: RESEARCH OR SYSTEM MANAGEMENT?

Health services researchers have in recent years been encouraged, like those working in other fields, to actively translate their findings into system application. The dramatic growth in interest in knowledge translation has been supported by the Canadian Institutes of Health Research in the realm of health services research in various ways including the development, support, and subsequent refinement of grants (e.g., Partnerships for Health System Improvement) specifically designed for this purpose.

As we encourage researchers, system managers, and decision-makers to become partners in these (and other) grants, the boundaries between research and system management become blurred. Within these partnerships, all partners develop an understanding of other partners' goals, their methods of addressing those goals, and the constraints they face as a result of the paradigm in which they function. Inevitably, cultures clash as professionals with two very different approaches build collaborative relationships. However, the common goal of system improvement—combined with mutual understanding—nourishes the relationship while what is literally *a new hybrid model of data use* evolves.

Thus, quality improvement in health services today is best understood as being a matter of neither research nor system management, as these domains have been traditionally understood. As the relationship between the use of routinely collected data, the process of data collection, and the users of the data continues to evolve, the door opens to significant possibilities for refining the data available for the purpose of quality improvement.

ROUTINELY COLLECTED OR PURPOSE-SPECIFIC DATA?

The recognition that quality improvement is a fundamental requirement for all aspects of our health-care system—an important and primary use of routinely collected data—should impact *what* data we collect routinely and *how* we collect it. It is not unreasonable to suggest that the intended use of the data should influence, if not dictate, their content and structure. Although the different datasets come from a variety of sources, each of which faces its own particular challenges and realities with regard to data collection and input, in general quality improvement should be considered whenever we routinely collect data.

It may at first blush seem counterproductive to put significant energy into trying to mould the routinely collected administrative data to address the needs of quality improvement. Why not develop data collection mechanisms specifically for this purpose, thus ensuring that we collect the best possible data for this purpose? Surely purpose-specific data will address the needs of quality improvement better than adapting data already collected for other purposes.

This assumption fails to address two realities. First, currently collected datasets have huge untapped capacity to measure quality indicators (as I will describe in the next section). Second, there are significant costs associated with purpose-specific data collection.

The "cost" argument has become particularly important in Canada since the economic downturn of 2008–09. Let us not forget the larger political context within which this discussion takes place. The Canadian health-care system is often compared with that of the United States, and one of the significant differences between the two is the much higher costs of administering the US for-profit system because of the need for detailed financial and costing information. As we develop and implement new data collection processes to address specific needs as they are identified, such as quality improvement, we add significantly to the administrative costs of the Canadian system. In an environment where the continuing increase in health-care costs has placed significant pressure on provincial budgets and the sustainability of the system is continually being questioned, any changes to the system that may significantly increase administrative costs should be viewed with caution, especially where more cost-effective alternatives already exist.

Moreover, shifting to a mode of new purpose-specific data collection mechanisms would fail to exploit the emerging collaborative relationships (discussed above) between researchers, system managers, and decision-makers that will facilitate the refinement and evolution of datasets that are routinely collected. Health services researchers are increasingly advocating for and assisting with refinements to data collection and architecture to support quality improvement—and there is every reason to expect this trend to continue.

MEASURING QUALITY USING ROUTINELY COLLECTED DATA

Indicators of health-care quality are commonly divided into three key domains: [1]

1. *Process measures* refer to the actual care given, and encompass both clinical effectiveness and interpersonal effectiveness.
2. *Structure measures* refer to the organization of the system in which the care is delivered, which has a major impact upon access to care.
3. *Outcome measures* reflect the consequences of care rather than the components of care.[2]

While the indicators within each domain have limitations, together they can encompass the breadth of health-care delivery.

Indicators are single summary measures, expressed in quantitative terms, that represent a key dimension of health status, the health-care system, or related factors. They should be measurable, comparable, clearly defined, and sensitive to variations.

There is no question that many valuable indicators of quality cannot be adequately measured using routinely collected data. For example, indicators that measure satisfaction with the system, interpersonal care, and some outcomes of care require other mechanisms of data collection. However, studies have shown that a significant number of indicators that use routinely collected data are very useful for quality improvement.[3]

In Canada, many of these indicators come out of studies conducted using data from the Population Health Research Data Repository housed at the Manitoba Centre for Health Policy. The repository is a comprehensive database developed to describe and explain patterns of health care, and profiles of health and illness. It includes information routinely collected from the population's contact with the health-care system: physicians, hospitals, nursing homes, home care, and pharmacies. Numerous studies have established the reliability of the repository data when compared to other sources of data.[4]

POPULATION-BASED MEASURES OF QUALITY

Quality can be measured at different levels within the health-care system. At the most basic level, the care received by each individual patient is an important aspect of quality in the health-care system. At the other extreme, a bird's-eye view of the system—using population-based indicators—provides a broader perspective and is another important aspect of quality.

Routinely collected data present the opportunity to measure population-based quality as well as quality for segments of the population. A segment-based approach could be geographical (small area variations in care), disease-based (care provided to those diagnosed with a specific condition or group of conditions such as mental illness), site-based (specific to an institution), or provider-based (e.g., a designated surgeon or group of surgeons). Within this last option, providers could be grouped according to a variety of factors such as practice characteristics (e.g., productivity or how busy they are) or personal characteristics (e.g., gender, age, or where they received their training). Each approach helps us understand how different factors affect the quality of care, thus opening the door to specifically focused interventions.

The work of the British epidemiologist Geoffrey Rose has had a fundamental impact on our understanding of the value of population-based prevention.[5] He eloquently demonstrated that shifting the whole population curve a small amount in the desired direction has a more significant effect than shifting the small group at highest risk a large amount.

The same principle applies to the concept of quality improvement. A population-based focus that aims to improve the quality of health care for the whole population by a small amount will result in greater benefit for the system and population as a whole than an approach that focuses on quality improvement for a small group of providers based on the collection of a limited number of purpose-specific data.

RELATIONSHIP-BASED QUALITY IMPROVEMENT

Quality improvement activities are context specific. The success of any intervention or program is highly dependent on the context in which it is introduced. There are enabling factors that help ensure success, and there are barriers that contribute to failure.

While it is beyond the scope of this chapter to discuss all of these enabling factors and barriers, the *relationship* between the target group (whether providers or system managers) and the improvement intervention design and implementation group (e.g., decision-makers or regulatory bodies) is critical. The target group should understand the sources of the data used to measure quality, as well as the advantages and limitations of these data. This understanding is best achieved in the context of a trusting relationship with decision-makers who respect the values and concerns of the target group. This relationship can facilitate the acceptance and use of indicators that resonate with the target group, resulting in a sense of ownership and commitment to a positive outcome.

In most jurisdictions, routinely collected data do not generally meet the standards of relationship-based quality improvement. Data collection is usually government or institutionally mandated and often lacks face validity in the eyes of those who are not privy to the big picture. The limitations of the data are readily apparent, while the advantages are often obscure.

To collect routine data in a way that creates and maintains relationships, health services researchers and decision-makers could

- explore creative solutions to address data shortcomings with the potential target group in a respectful, open dialogue;
- consult the target group regarding changes to what data are routinely collected or how they are collected; and
- take seriously the target group's feedback and recommendations.

These collaborative approaches could alleviate the significant barriers to achieving the full potential of routinely collected data for quality improvement.

QUALITY INDICATORS BASED ON ROUTINELY COLLECTED DATA

There are many examples of quality indicators based on routinely collected datasets from multiple jurisdictions in Canada. I will highlight a few that have been developed at the Manitoba Centre for Health Policy over the past five years. In many cases, researchers at the Manitoba Centre for Health Policy developed these indicators in partnership with the target audience. Using the indicators has improved the quality of health-care delivery in Manitoba despite the lack of organized quality improvement programs supporting these changes.

One study by Patricia Martens and colleagues helped change the way mental health services are delivered in Manitoba.[6] This study developed a series of population-based indicators that reflected access to mental health services. These indicators, which fell within the structural domain, were unlikely to be measured when using purpose-specific quality indicators because their usefulness would not have been intuitively known—but the mere act of measuring has profoundly influenced service organization and delivery.

Unlike most of the work using routinely collected datasets, which has focused on population-based indicators or institutional care, a study by Katz et al. developed quality indicators reflecting the ambulatory care that Manitoba residents received from their family physicians.[7] The indicators are all measurable using data from the Repository, and their development included extensive provider consultation to ensure both face validity and provider acceptance. These indicators were included in the Pan-Canadian Primary Health Care indicator list developed by the Canadian Institute for Health Information[8] and represent the majority of the indicators on that list that are currently measurable. The indicators reflect processes of care that are known to lead to improved patient outcomes and that are supported by published evidence. These indicators provide the basis for a pay-for-performance primary care reform initiative in Manitoba.

Bruce et al. developed institution-based safety indicators using data available in the Population Health Research Data Repository.[9] These indicators include procedure-specific outcome data as well as broader indicators of morbidity and mortality. While scorecards are commonly used in the United States to compare providers and institutions,[10] the readily available data in Canada have not previously been used in this way. Bruce et al.'s *Patient Safety Indicators* report precipitated both data validation studies and changes in care delivery.

In a final example, Doupe et al. used the repository data to develop quality indicators for personal care homes.[11] For many of these indicators, it is not possible to determine a "correct rate." There are, however, clear patterns that indicate problems in the quality of care received in some regions or institutions that are consistently outliers across multiple indicators.

CONCLUSION

There is significant potential for quality improvement using data that are currently routinely collected. The advantages of using these data include availability and cost. These data can provide population-based quality measures, thus avoiding the tendency to focus on participants in quality improvement programs rather than on the population as a whole. There are challenges to the routine use of these data for quality improvement, but rather than focus on shortcomings, we should improve the data that are available and use this information for the benefit of all.

NOTES

1. A. Donabedian, *Explorations in Quality Assessment and Monitoring*, vol. 1, *The Definition of Quality and Approaches to Its Assessment*, ed. J.R. Griffith et al. (Ann Arbor, MI: Health Administration Press, 1980).

2. S.M. Campbell, M.O. Roland, and S.A. Buetow, "Defining Quality of Care," *Social Science & Medicine* 51, no. 11 (2000): 1611-25.

3. P. Martens, R. Fransoo, N. McKeen, The Need to Know Team, E. Burland, L. Jebamani, C. Burchill, et al., *Patterns of Regional Mental Illness Disorder Diagnoses and Services Use in Manitoba: A Population-Based Study* (Winnipeg: Manitoba Centre for Health Policy, 2004); A. Katz, C. De Coster, B. Bogdanovic, R. Soodeen, and D. Chateau, *Using Administrative Data to Develop Indicators of Quality in Family Practice* (Winnipeg: Manitoba Centre for Health Policy, 2004); S. Bruce, H. Prior, A. Katz, M. Taylor, S. Latosinsky, R. Martens, C. De Coster, M. Brownell, E.O. Sorensen, and C. Steinbach, *Application of Patient Safety Indicators in Manitoba: A First Look* (Winnipeg: Manitoba Centre for Health Policy, 2006); M. Doupe, M. Brownell, A. Kozyrskyj, N. Dik,

C. Burchill, M. Dahl, D. Chateau, C. De Coster, A. Hinds, and J. Bodnarchuk, *Using Administrative Data to Develop Indicators of Quality Care in Personal Care Homes* (Winnipeg: Manitoba Centre for Health Policy, 2006).

4.   J.E. Hux, V. Flintoft, F. Ivis, and A. Bica, "Diabetes in Ontario: Determination of Prevalence and Incidence Using a Validated Administrative Data Algorithm," *Diabetes Care* 25, no. 3 (2002): 512-16; L.L. Roos, Jr., N.P. Roos, S.M. Cageorge, and J.P. Nicol, "How Good Are the Data? Reliability of One Health Care Data Bank," *Medical Care* 20, no. 3 (1982): 266-76.; L.L. Roos, C.A. Mustard, J.P. Nicol, D.F. McLerran, D.J. Malenka, T.K. Young, and M.M. Cohen, "Registries and Administrative Data: Organization and Accuracy," *Medical Care* 31, no. 3 (1993): 201-12.; L.L. Roos and J.P. Nicol, "A Research Registry: Uses, Development, and Accuracy," *Journal of Clinical Epidemiology* 52, no. 1 (1999): 39-47.

5.   G. Rose, *The Strategy of Preventive Medicine* (Oxford: Oxford University Press, 1992).

6.   Martens et al., *Patterns of Regional Mental Illness*, see note 3.

7.   Katz et al., *Using Administrative Data*, see note 3.

8.   Canadian Institute for Health Information, *Pan-Canadian Primary Health Care Indicators*, Report 1, vol. 1, 1-1-2006 (Ottawa, 2006).

9.   Bruce et al., *Application of Patient Safety Indicators in Manitoba*, see note 3.

10. D.L. Robinowitz and R.A. Dudley, "Public Reporting of Provider Performance: Can Its Impact Be Made Greater?" *Annual Review of Public Health* 27 (2006): 517-36.

11. Doupe et al., *Using Administrative Data*, see note 3.

GETTING LOST IN DOING GOOD: A SOCIETAL REALITY CHECK

Wendy Armstrong

Increasingly, value judgments that can profoundly affect someone's life are made by public and private bodies based on surreptitiously collected information that may or may not be accurate or even relevant. Today, sellers choose their customers and governments scrutinize their citizens. It should be the other way around in a healthy market economy and a healthy democracy.

—Consumers' Association of Canada (Alberta), 1997

THE SOCIETAL LANDSCAPE

Over the past two decades, new technologies have led to dramatic growth in the collection of information in electronic databases about the circumstances and activities of individual Canadians, and equally dramatic growth in the uses of this information. Most Canadians are unaware of the extent to which this occurs.

The social and political landscape has also changed—and been changed by—these technologies and activities. Canadians have become more reliant on fewer, more distant, and larger sellers of goods and services. Former public services have been turned over in whole or in part to corporate interests through delegation, deregulation, and outsourcing. Regulations have been loosened and public protections eliminated to encourage foreign investment and trade. New public-private partnerships

Data Data Everywhere: Access and Accountability? ed. C.M. Flood. Montreal and Kingston: Queen's Policy Studies Series, McGill-Queen's University Press. © 2011 The School of Policy Studies, Queen's University at Kingston. All rights reserved.

abound. Responsibilities for policing the marketplace have shifted from public to private hands. Hard won social security programs designed to help families weather the economic storms of unemployment, child-rearing, disease, disability, and old age have eroded, leaving Canadians more dependent on private markets and charity. While public debt has dropped, family debt has skyrocketed.[1] Many historical checks and balances have disappeared—including strong consumer, human rights, and public interest voices.

Despite the growth in information surveillance of individual Canadians, there has not been a commensurate increase in availability of information about the activities of governments, public agencies, and corporations. In fact, government secrecy and commercial confidentiality (not privacy protections) have become more widespread because of the nature of many of the above changes.

THE CHANGING HEALTH-CARE LANDSCAPE

There have also been changes in the nature, funding, and focus of health care, public health, and health research in Canada. During the 1990s, encouraging foreign investment to grow domestic health-care companies and expand the research industry trumped the safety and security of Canadians as the primary driver of federal and provincial health policy.[2] As a consequence, the "life sciences" industry (a term adopted by Industry Canada to get around growing public resistance to the practices of biotechnology and pharmaceutical companies) and the health research, health-care services, and public health sectors have become far more entwined.

Once discouraged partnerships between universities and industry have become a major plank in Canada's industrial policy, which focuses primarily on the commercialization of new products and services protected by intellectual property regimes. Janet Atkinson-Grosjean uses the term "merchant scientists" to describe a new breed of researchers in Canada who "move confidently" between academia and business.[3]

Public agencies, health ministries, government bureaucracies, regional health authorities and even disease advocacy groups have been drawn into the web of industry partnerships, money, and influence.[4] While these new partnerships do not necessarily buy support for industry objectives, they almost always buy silence when it comes to public criticisms or challenges of industry practices.

A shift in focus from care of individual patients and health promotion to "population health" in the early 1990s has also led to an upsurge in poorly understood and communicated epidemiological research on risk factors affecting health and illness in populations,[5] and the marketing of screening tests and pharmaceuticals to "manage risk." In the face of widespread professional and public confusion around correlation and cause, and relative versus actual risk, individual Canadians are increasingly cast as authors of their own medical misfortunes for failing to manage these risk factors in their lives. Social stigma is now attached to an expanding number of diseases and traits.

We must keep this background in mind when we see many of the authors in this book argue that any barriers to the creation of widely accessible electronic health records and linkages of databases for research purposes are an impediment to informed decision-making in the health system and improved health for Canadians. The experiences of the Canadian public, the websites of provincial and federal privacy commissioners, and volumes of social sciences research suggest otherwise. In their enthusiasm, these authors are failing to take into account the current social and political context, the limitations of electronic databases and controls, and what Kim Vicente calls "the human factor."[6]

Therefore, the purpose of this chapter is to provide some "real world" examples of how expanding information surveillance and applications of database technologies are negatively influencing relationships in our society and important social determinants of health such as meaningful work, income, and a sense of self-worth. There are many lessons to be learned from these examples, including how the tools we use shape *what* we do and the danger of "getting lost in doing good."

Market Research by Stealth and Stealth Marketing

> Corporations have moved swiftly and definitively to exploit the advantages of new information technologies and consolidated their power as never before.
>
> —Bricker and Greenspan, *Searching for Certainty*, 2005

One of the most significant developments over the past two decades has been the widespread commercial adoption of *stealth marketing* based on new market research techniques that use "unobtrusive" information surveillance and data mining. This has been facilitated by the decreasing cost of data storage, the increasing use of "virtual" money (credit and debit cards, preauthorized payment, and online banking), and the commercialization of the Internet in 1993.

According to a former marketing executive, the word *stealth* is used to describe these strategies because "consumers are usually unaware that their personal information is being collected, used, or sold for market research and marketing purposes," and because "there is a great deal of fakery and trickery in the industry."[7]

Companies gather personal information from myriad sources, including the digital footprint we leave every time we make a purchase with credit or debit or Air Miles cards or visit a website. Collected information reveals (and infers) much about our activities, our beliefs, our health, and our vulnerabilities. This information is then used and/or sold to interested and willing purchasers, including companies in market research, data management, and public relations, which are now often one and the same.

"Fat" databases can include credit and rental history; family make-up; assets; employment history; education; history of home, auto, and health insurance claims; visited websites; magazine subscriptions; and driving record. Below are examples of lists for sale that are tied to an individual's name and address:[8]

- types of books purchased
- subscriptions to particular magazines
- registrations on and visits to websites
- responders to direct mail/TV/radio/Internet solicitations
- holders of particular credit/reward cards, purchases using those cards
- ailments and medications
- diets and nutritional concerns
- causes (associations) to which we donate

With remarkable ease, new generation software can take even anonymized data, match it with other lists, and effectively re-identify many individuals.[9] Psychologists working for market research companies then manipulate and analyze the collected information to develop sophisticated campaigns—including the use of news outlets and "thought leaders"[10]—for clients to sell products, services, and ideas. With today's strategies, few people are even aware they have been marketed to.[11]

No industry has been as effective in using these strategies as the pharmaceutical industry in its efforts to influence government regulators, medical knowledge structures, and the public. For example, in the space of little more than a year Paxil's manufacturer GSK took a little-known and once-considered rare psychiatric condition and helped transform it into a major epidemic called "social anxiety disorder"—claimed at one point to affect one out of eight.[12]

Everyone likes to think they are not influenced by these strategies, but the evidence says otherwise. Governments also hire these market research companies to create the spin necessary to convince citizens of the merits of specific policies and actions. Regardless of actual research findings or intent, money and messaging drown out the facts.

Electronic Databases and Market Segmentation

> Technology switches the opportunities for subversion from individuals to organizations.
>
> —Mark Lisac, *Edmonton Journal*, 1995

Electronic databases have also allowed corporations—particularly dominant telecommunication, banking, and energy companies—to segment their large customer base into high value customers and low value customers. High value customers obtain high quality service, special pricing benefits, and regular contact. Low value customers are shifted to voice messaging systems and call centre staff who have no authority to act.

Michael Janigan, general counsel and executive director of the Public Interest Advocacy Centre in Ottawa, describes how, now that governments have retreated from the traditional role of protecting small consumers in these inherently non-competitive sectors, a consumer "caste" system is emerging in Canada:

> We've segmented the market to the extent that you now have different castes of consumers. There are the upper castes of consumers in industries such as telecommunication and energy where big business and high volume purchasers are able to construct whatever deal they can with suppliers of goods and services. These discounts are largely paid for by the rung of customers in the lower or middle caste who effectively don't get any discounts and have little means of affecting any kind of change. Finally, there is a lower caste of "untouchables" and their business is not really welcomed by any suppliers, as evidenced by what has happened in banking over the past decade.[13]

In the early 1990s, as the financial services sector was being deregulated, banks reduced their hours and closed hundreds of branches. They shifted to electronic banking and also got out of the small loans business. High end customers were shifted to high interest credit cards. Low end customers were shifted to new (and even higher cost) cheque cashing and "payday" loan companies, which rushed in to fill the gap. According to a 2007 Manitoba study, when converted to annual percentage rates, the combined interest and fees for payday loans averages 778 percent.[14] Comparatively, someone obtaining a line of credit at a bank could expect to pay between 8 and 14 percent. Traditional banking services are commonly required to rent an apartment, hook up utilities, or obtain employment. Barriers to access to these services in this era of automatic deposits and preauthorized withdrawals are an important social determinant of health.

Janigan goes on to illustrate the appropriateness of the metaphor of the caste system as it relates to the lack of contact between castes, resulting in the development of completely different perceptions of the price and quality of service within the population because of this market segmentation. This is in sharp contrast to situations where a product or service is marketed in a similar fashion to all customers, such as when "everyone pulls up to the pump for gasoline." In these circumstances, it is far more likely that there will be an outcry over price or quality because everyone is affected.

And what about claims of greater efficiency? Although the major argument put forward by the big banks for mergers is to take advantage of efficiency gains arising from shared databases, studies on bank mergers have shown that, over a certain size, economies of scale are absent or unimportant.[15] There is no evidence that any efficiency gains from shared electronic databases are routinely passed on or fairly distributed to customers. And technology is expensive to service.

Function Creep and New Employment Screening Companies

> Computer matching turns the traditional presumption of innocence into a presumption of guilt: in matching, even when there is no indication of wrong-doing, individuals are subject to high technology search and seizure.
>
> —Bruce Phillips, Privacy Commissioner, 1995

Information housed in multiple public and private databases is now beginning to influence many other relationships in our lives, a phenomenon called "function creep." It is now commonplace for potential and current employers or agencies to obtain or require access to detailed personal information as a condition of establishing a relationship.

Verification Inc. is a US-based company that offers Canadian employers both background checks and ongoing monitoring of employees. The purpose of these services, according to promotional materials, is to enable employers to "manage risk."

In 2007, an Edmonton woman in her forties was contacted by a former employer, a large North American investment firm with thousands of Canadian employees, and encouraged to apply for a new position. She applied and was hired on the spot. She was then asked to sign a form authorizing Verification Inc. and all its agents to conduct a background check—now a required practice for all the firm's employees. This check could include *but was not limited to*

> information from personnel files, educational institutions, government agencies, companies, corporations, credit reporting agencies, law enforcement agencies ... academic, residential, achievement, job performance, attendance, litigation, personal history, credit reports, driving records, and criminal history records for which an absolute discharge or full pardon has not been granted.[16]

She also had to undergo a criminal check and be fingerprinted. Uncomfortable, the woman contacted Verification Inc.: "I wanted to know just who were the contracted agents, why there was no time frame for destruction of the record, and what did the phrase 'not limited to' really mean, particularly about my health information," she told a consumer advocacy organization in 2007.[17] She also went searching to find out what she could about the company, its owners, and track record.

The company advised her that an example of a company agent would be the RCMP and that, yes, there was no specified period for record retention. The company would also continue to monitor her personal records while she remained with her current employer. She could find no information on the company's owners or track record. She did, however, find out that Verification Inc. also offered tenant screening, drug testing, and occupational medical screening. No one could give her a clear answer about her medical records.

She told her new boss she did not want to sign. He urged her to sign, saying, "After all, there is so much information floating around out there already and you can't do anything. Why not sign it?" *When she refused, she was summarily fired.*

The woman said her biggest concern was the potential for identity theft and resulting financial losses with so much information stored in one database and the information being transferred across international borders (the example the company gave her was India; personal interview by author, 16 April 2007). Other observers have raised additional concerns about the growth of such screening:

- How might it influence the job opportunities of someone with a past cannabis charge, a different sexual orientation, or membership in the wrong political party or religious group?
- What about someone treated in the past for medical conditions such as breast cancer or depression that can increase the premiums for a company's benefit plan?
- Will the cult of efficiency ensure many do not make the first cut—*or even apply?*
- Will this create a new caste of "unemployables"?

Having to expose such detailed personal information (and explain any discrepancies) to strangers and individuals with whom we hope to establish relationships plays into human fears of being labelled in ways that can lead to embarrassment, strained relations, lost opportunities, and social exclusion. Although such fears are often dismissed, they have a legitimate basis. The files of human rights and civil liberties organizations, privacy commissioners, and public interest groups are filled with cases.

Social exclusion is now a well-recognized social determinant of health and well-being. Chronic social stress can lead to continuous output of cortisol in the body, which in turn negatively influences disease processes.[18] Social exclusion also exerts a powerful influence on someone's sense of self-worth and response to others.[19]

Medical labelling is particularly problematic—and often wrong. A 2004 compilation of essays edited by psychologists Paula J. Caplan and Lisa Cosgrove, *Bias in Psychiatric Diagnosis,* provides many examples of how a simple visit to a therapist for counselling, or documentation of a highly subjective diagnostic label in a medical chart, can have consequences ranging from loss of child custody, to denial of health insurance and employment, to removal of one's right to make decisions regarding legal affairs.[20]

In addition, a 1993 survey by the Canadian Medical Association found 7 percent of Canadians had not sought out diagnosis or treatment because of worries about how it might affect other aspects of their lives such as insurability or employment.[21] By 2007, 11 percent reported holding back information from a health provider because they were concerned about who it would be shared with or what purposes it would be used for.[22] Will this number rise as Canadians become aware of how many more people with no established relationship now have access to their health information? What are the implications of people choosing not to disclose relevant information? How will it affect the accuracy of diagnosis, the safety of treatment, the spread of contagious diseases, and the reliability of research data?

Gary Marx, a sociology professor at the Massachusetts Institute of Technology, has shown that public resistance to information surveillance occurs in many invisible ways, including individuals obscuring their identities and providing false or incomplete information.[23] Nevertheless, the function creep of electronic databases is difficult to control or monitor.

The Segmentation of Citizens and Loss of Data

> A culture of inequality may be more significant than material inequality.
>
> —Richard Eckersley, "Is Modern Western Culture a Health Hazard?"
> *International Journal of Epidemiology*, 2005

Over the past two decades, provincial and federal governments in Canada have adopted many of the practices of corporate interests, including the use of electronic databases to more efficiently monitor and segment citizens. This has led to decreased social cohesiveness, increased individualism, and a less egalitarian society.

The increasingly restrictive nature of social benefits has led to greater intrusion into the financial and family life of many Canadians.[24] On top of an applicant's financial or health worries is added the pain of having his or her family life judged (both morally and financially) by strangers. In order to avoid this discomfort, some people eligible for benefits do not apply.[25] Avoiding moral and financial scrutiny is also often cited in private by supporters of private health-care options and online commercial medical record repositories such as Google Health.

Gaps in basic data arising from the loss of universality of public programs and the shift to private spending have already created problematic bias in research results and public discourse. There are even greater barriers to obtaining reliable information in the commercial realm.

The Catch 22

> The Catch 22 of having [the right to control access] over one's own medical records or information is that other parties can request authorization for access as a condition for being considered for a service or product or employment. Denying access is interpreted as having something to hide.
>
> —Office of the Information and Privacy Commissioner of Ontario,
> *Interim Order PO-1881-I*

In many of the previous examples, broad authorizations for vaguely described sharing and uses of personal information are buried in application forms or conditions of service that few people give a second thought to signing.[26] Below is an excerpt from a typical medical authorization form in the Canadian health and life insurance industry that applicants are required to sign.

> I/We authorize any health care professional, as well as any health or social service establishment, any insurance company, the Medical Information Bureau, financial institution, personal information agents or security agencies, my/our employer or any former employer and any public body holding personal information concerning me/us, particularly medical information, to supply this information to [the life insurance company] and its reinsurers for the risk assessment or the investigation necessary for the study of any claim…

Lack of awareness of *which* particular establishments might be contacted and *what* information is contained in each establishment's file can create problems.

When a young woman starting her own business in Ontario applied for a disability insurance policy, she was surprised to be turned down because the company said her medical records showed that she had a history of repeat physician visits for "psychological counselling." It turned out her physician—someone her family had gone to for years because the physician never rushed them and always encouraged them to talk about other things in their lives when they went in for routine problems—had been billing all the appointments as psychological counselling. When confronted by the woman, the physician said, "Well, how else am I going to get paid for the real amount of time I spend to provide you with good care?" Ironically, even this visit was billed as "psychological counselling." No disability insurer will touch this young woman because all such information is shared with other health and life insurers through an industry-run North American database. Nor does she feel she can destroy her parents' relationship with the doctor by filing a complaint.[27]

Lack of Redress and Remedies for Harm Done

Sloppy data entry, coding errors, confusion with common names, software problems, bias or prejudice, internal and external breaches, unauthorized uses, and fraud all contribute to remarkably inaccurate information in databases.

Fraud and identity theft. The existence of electronic databases and the ease of access to so much personal information in these databases have been major drivers in the success of an international fraud industry dominated by organized crime. Identity theft, an emotionally and financially debilitating experience, is the fastest-growing crime in Canada. Once false information has been spread far and wide, it is impossible to track down and correct.

Inappropriate responses. The response of merchants and public agencies to date has been to collect and store *even more* personal information in electronic databases in order to authenticate someone's identity. Ironically, this creates an even greater risk if data breaches occur, which they do with remarkable regularity, including many involving sensitive medical records. Worse yet, many of the same companies whose information practices are contributing to fraud are now marketing "identity theft insurance" and "protection services" to the public.

Multiple uses of databases. Problems with data integrity, interpretation, and user-friendliness arise when databases are used for more than one purpose. This last issue came into focus in 2001 when an Ontario farmer spent over $40,000 attempting to correct his acknowledged incorrect OHIP records due to fraudulent billing by his physician. The province initially refused because the record was also used for accounting purposes.[28] In Alberta, a proposal to merge detailed electronic *medical* records in physicians' offices with provincial electronic *health* records has many physicians worried that the interface will be less useful for clinical care and will compromise their code of ethics and obligations to patients.

Three important conclusions follow:

- While good decisions can, in theory, be made with good information, bad decisions (that result in harm) can be made with bad information.
- Most of the financial, social, and emotional harm from inaccurate or biased information in electronic files is borne by individuals and their families.
- The more users and uses (authorized and unauthorized) and the greater the amount of data collected, the greater the likelihood that data will be corrupted. Designing a database for many purposes often limits the usefulness of the database for some of the purposes.

The Holy Grail of Automation

> Professionals need to think more about the interaction between technology
> and moral values, particularly in today's world where there are so many
> pressures to put economic concerns ahead of everything else.
>
> —Kim Vicente, *The Human Factor*, 2004

Opportunities to influence physician behaviours through built-in prompts,
performance measures, and "evidence-based" treatment algorithms are
frequently cited benefits of electronic patient records and databases. But
are there downsides?

A 2008 article by Sarah Bowen and Sara Kreindler looking at Manitoba's
experience with indicators suggests a need for caution.[29] So do anecdotal
reports from patients. As the wife of a man with diabetes wrote in an
email to a family support group,

> We definitely are trusting less and less. Our physicians (a husband/wife
> team) try to follow all the best practice guidelines. She still wants Lloyd
> [a Type 1 diabetic] to be on the altace, which lowers blood pressure even
> though his pressure is normal for a 20-year-old and he turns 60 this year!!
> He discontinued after one dose when he had a hypotensive episode while
> operating a power saw nearly two years ago and had to have his finger
> reattached. Also he had an appointment after his fasting blood work. The
> lab had switched over to a new computer system and he was in a lineup
> for 2 1/2 hours waiting. His blood pressure at the appointment was 78/50
> and she still wanted him to take the altace!! Just following the guidelines
> makes no common sense.

While automation and standardization have benefits, there are also
pitfalls, particularly when users become too reliant or trusting of the applications. And when something goes wrong, it affects far more people.
How quickly can embedded algorithms in electronic records be changed
given the "here today, gone tomorrow" nature of medical wisdom? Who
designs these algorithms? Who is responsible for harm done? Given all we
know about the variations in human biological and emotional responses,
just how standardized and automated can we afford to be?

Broken Promises

The province of Alberta now has the most comprehensive electronic health
record system in the country and a trail of broken promises regarding
citizen safeguards. The Alberta *Health Information Act* (*HIA*), passed in
1999, required prior one-time patient consent for uploading patient information in the custody of health-care providers (e.g., hospitals, doctors,
pharmacists) to a central provincial government-controlled electronic

health record system. The legislation restricted its scope to wholly or partly publicly funded services and providers, with some notable exceptions such as pharmacies and pharmacists.

A 2003 survey by the Privacy Commissioner of Alberta found that although many Albertans expressed support for (undefined) electronic health records, *"exercise of individual consent over who can obtain access to an Electronic Record was considered extremely important to 89% of Albertans"* (emphasis added).[30] In 2003, the Alberta government quietly eliminated Section 59—the requirement for patient consent prior to uploading records in Wellnet (now Netcare)—and gave patients the right to request that their health service provider withhold certain information from Netcare, although providers were not obligated to comply. The reason given for these changes was that providing information to patients about how their information might be used prior to obtaining authorization was administratively burdensome. In short, it cost time and money. The government news release read, *"Health Information Amendment Act* Protects Patient Confidentiality While Providing Needed Access."[31]

Later revisions to the Act in 2006 allowed disclosure of certain health information by health services providers to *police* and other authorities as well as *third party payers* (insurers) without a patient's prior knowledge or consent.[32]

In 2007, there were 24,000 registered users eligible to access Alberta Netcare based on an honour system and the "need to know," including retail pharmacists, managers, administrators, evaluators, and educators. The same year, a health-care worker was caught and charged for improperly surfing a patient's record and fined $10,000. She was checking up on her boyfriend's ex-wife.[33]

In 2008, the Privacy Commissioner of Alberta released a report.[34] It revealed that a 2003 amendment to *HIA* that allowed masking of specific fields of health information by patients had not been communicated to the public, and that there were no administrative tools to support it. It also provided the first real insight into just what information was being housed in Netcare. Also in 2008, the Alberta Auditor General reported that information technology (IT) security within the government of Alberta was woefully inadequate.[35]

In 2009, proposed amendments (Bill 52) to *HIA* included expanding the Act to cover privately funded services and removing the requirement of health service providers to at least consider a patient's wishes with regard to uploading information to Netcare. Amendments would also allow for the creation of undefined "health information repositories" for research purposes with no identified governance model. Other amendments would effectively limit auditing of the trail of sites accessing someone's records as well as oversight of new applications of health information by the Privacy Commissioner. The icing on cake was a provision making it an offense (with massive fines) for doctors and other service providers to refuse to upload their in-house medical records to Netcare upon the Minister's request, including such things as notes about private conversations.

For the first time in the history of the legislation, the Alberta Medical Association and the Alberta Privacy Commissioner raised a public alarm. Albertans began to stir. The Standing Policy Committee on Health heard from more organizations and individual Albertans than they had in the history of the legislation.[36] While some significant accommodations were made, others were not, and the regulations that will reveal the nuances in these amendments are not yet complete.

The problem with all these broken promises is that history has shown repeatedly that if people are not dealt with in good faith, they in turn will not deal in good faith. This creates a definite lose-lose proposition for just about everyone in society.

CONCLUSION

Sometimes the measurable drives out the important.

—Howard Brody, Director, Institute for the Medical Humanities

In the Canadian health research community, there is a widely held pro-electronic health record and database linkage agenda that makes four key assumptions.

1. The creation and linkage of broadly defined health and administrative databases will provide more accurate and meaningful information.
2. Any harm done to the public or society by the creation and uses of electronic records for health research will be more than offset by the benefits.
3. Research results will be unbiased and available to all.
4. This information will be used only in ways that will improve the health system and the health of Canadians.

These four assumptions are optimistic and naive. They are not borne out by the experiences of Canadians. Nor do they take into account the social and political landscape, the nature of the technology itself, and human nature.

In his best seller, *The Human Factor*, engineer Kim Vicente points out how technological innovation is progressing so quickly that we have fallen behind in our ability to manage it, and it now poses significant threats to our quality of life.

Therefore, extreme caution is urged in continuing to promote the creation of ever more databases and linkages—including the many different faces of electronic health records—without more protections for individuals. Because there is such a high risk of unintended harm in this area, health researchers must be vigilant to avoid "getting lost in doing good." What if the failure of health researchers to respect and protect the interests of individuals in this information age turns out to be the cause of many of our current health and social problems—and not the cure?

NOTES

1. Vanier Institute of the Family, The Current State of Canadian Family Finances Series (Annual Reports, 1999–2007), www.vifamily.ca (accessed 26 November 2009).
2. C. Fuller, *Caring for Profit: How Corporations Are Taking Over Canada's Health Care System* (Vancouver: CCPA and New Star Books, 1998). In the mid-1980s, areas of health care with the potential to attract foreign investment included home care, long-term care, and health information systems.
3. A. Silversides, "Merchant Scientists: How Commercialization Is Changing Research in Canada," *The Walrus*, May 2008, http://www.walrusmagazine. com/articles/2008.05-science-and-commercialization-ann-silversides/ (accessed 21 October 2009).
4. S. Batt, *Marching to Different Drummers: Health Advocacy Groups in Canada and Funding from the Pharmaceutical Industry* (Toronto: Women and Health Protection, 2005), http://www.whp-apsf.ca/pdf/corpFunding.pdf (accessed 21 October 2009).
5. N. Krieger, "Questioning Epidemiology: Objectivity, Advocacy and Socially Responsible Science," Editorial, *American Journal of Public Health* 89, no. 8 (1999): 1151-53.
6. K. Vicente, *The Human Factor: Revolutionizing the Way We Live with Technology* (Toronto: Vintage Canada, 2004).
7. T. Young (President of Drug Safety Canada), interview with author, 4 June 2005.
8. P. Lawson, Canadian Internet Privacy and Public Interest Centre, "Consumer Health Information as a Commodity" (presentation to Electronic Health Information and Privacy Conference, Ottawa, 13 November 2006), http://www.idtrail.org/files/lawson_ehealth-nov2006.pdf (accessed 21 October 2009).
9. K. El Emam, E. Jonker, S. Sams, E. Neri, A. Neisa, T. Gao, and S. Chowdhury, *Pan-Canadian De-identification Guidelines for Personal Health Information* (report prepared for the Office of the Privacy Commissioner of Canada, 2007), http://www.ehealthinformation.ca/documents/OPCReportv12.pdf (accessed 21 October 2009).
10. A. Ries and L. Ries, *The Fall of Advertising and the Rise of Public Relations* (Toronto: HarperCollins Publishers Inc., 2002).
11. A. Cassels and R. Moynihan, *Selling Sickness: How the World's Biggest Pharmaceutical Companies Are Turning Us All into Patients* (New York: Nation Books, 2005).
12. Ibid.
13. M. Janigan, interview by author for an unpublished paper, "The Changing Face of Consumer Protection in Alberta; What's Below the Waterline?" March 2005.
14. J. Buckland, T. Carter, W. Simpson, A. Friesen, and J. Osborne, "Serving or Exploiting People Facing a Short-Term Credit Crunch? A Study of Consumer

Aspects of Payday Lending in Manitoba" (Manitoba Public Interest Law Centre, 15 September 2007), http://publicinterestlawcentre.ca/files/payday_lending_report.pdf (accessed 21 October 2009).

15. R. Kerton, "Consumers Assess Mergers among Big Banks" (presentation by the Consumers' Association of Canada to the Honourable Ralph Goodale, 31 December 2003), http://www.consumer.ca/pdfs/bank_mergers.pdf (accessed 21 October 2009).

16. "Verification Inc. Pre-Employment Form" (2006), in the Consumers' Association of Canada (Alberta) "Submission to the Standing Policy Committee on Health, Alberta Legislature, Re: Bill 52, Amendments to the Alberta Health Information Act," Appendix 4 (4 February 2009), http://www.assembly.ab.ca/committees/health/submissions/HE-B52-008B.pdf (accessed 3 March 2010).

17. Caller to Consumers' Association of Canada (Alberta) in Edmonton; and interview by author, 16 April 2007.

18. CBC Ideas, "Sick People or Sick Society," Part 1, produced by Jill Eisen (Podcast, 3 March 2008), http://podcast.cbc.ca/mp3/ideas_20080303_4892.mp3 (accessed 21 October 2009).

19. Jane Elliott's famous Blue Eyes–Brown Eyes Exercise demonstrates this response.

20. P.J. Caplan and L. Cosgrove, *Bias in Psychiatric Diagnosis* (Lanham, MD: Jason Aronson, 2004).

21. Survey of Canadians by Canadian Medical Association (1993, personal files).

22. R. Ouelett, President of the Canadian Medical Association, "Physician-Patient Relationship: Trust" (presentation to the CIHR Health Information Summit, Toronto, 20–21 October 2008), http://www.f2fe.com/cihrsummit/Robert%20Ouellet.pdf (accessed 3 March 2010).

23. To explore the research and writing of Prof. Gary Marx, see his home page at http://web.mit.edu/gtmarx/www/garyhome.html#Online (accessed 21 October 2009).

24. For example, while over 300,000 manufacturing jobs have been lost in Canada, less than 40 percent of these unemployed workers qualify for Employment Insurance benefits.

25. W. Armstrong and R. Deber, "Missing Pieces of the Shift to Home and Community Care: A Case Study of the Conversion of an Alberta Nursing Home to Designated Assisted Living" (M-THAC working paper, 2006), http://www.teamgrant.ca/M-THAC%20Greatest%20Hits/M-THAC%20Projects/All%20info/Hinton/Publications/p401090.pdf (accessed 3 March 2010).

26. Canadian Internet Policy and Public Interest Clinic, "On the Data Trail: How Detailed Information about You Gets into the Hands of Organizations with Whom You Have No Relationship" (Ottawa, 2006), http://www.cippic.ca/documents/May1-06/DatabrokerReport.pdf (accessed 21 October 2009).

27. Personal interview by author, by phone, 2003.

28. Information and Privacy Commissioner of Ontario, *Interim Order PO-1881-I*, http://www.ipc.on.ca/.

29. S. Bowen and S.A. Kreindler, "Indicator Madness: A Cautionary Reflection on the Use of Indicators in Healthcare," *Healthcare Policy* 3, no. 4 (2008): 41-48.

30. Office of the Information and Privacy Commissioner of Alberta, "OIPC Stakeholder Survey" (GPC Research, March 2003). Of those Albertans polled, 89 percent also felt their consent should be required before disclosure of identifiable health information to someone doing health research, and about one-third would not agree to having their de-identified health information disclosed to researchers without consent.

31. Government of Alberta, *"Health Information Amendment Act* Protects Patient Confidentiality While Providing Needed Access" (News release, 25 February 2003). Although Albertans' support for the concept of electronic health records has increased over the years, complaints to advocacy groups suggest that most Albertans incorrectly assume information cannot be accessed without an individual's expressed consent.

32. See Part 5: Disclosure of Health Information, *Health Information Act* (Alberta), for a full list of allowed disclosures (not including 2009 amendments), http://www.qp.alberta.ca/574.cfm?page=H05.cfm&leg_type=Acts&isbncln=9780779746682 (accessed 21 October 2009).

33. R. Lombardi, "Alberta Health Care Cases Highlight Future Privacy Issues," *IT World Canada* (6 June 2008), http://www.itworldcanada.com/news/alberta-health-care-cases-highlight-future-privacy-issues/00036 (accessed 3 March 2010).

34. Office of the Information and Privacy Commissioner of Alberta, "Investigation Report Concerning the Disclosure of Health Information Using Alberta Netcare," Report H2008-IR-001 (15 May 2008), http://www.oipc.ab.ca/ims/client/upload/H2008-IR-001%20FINAL%20FOR%20RELEASE_20080515_.pdf (accessed 1 October 2009). See details of Netcare in the appendix of the report.

35. Government of Alberta, *Report of the Auditor General of Alberta* (Edmonton, April 2008), http://www.oag.ab.ca/files/oag/April_2008_Annual_Report.pdf (accessed 3 March 2010). Also see more details in the October 2008 *Report of the Auditor General of Alberta* at http://www.oag.ab.ca/files/oag/Oct_2008_Report.pdf (accessed 3 March 2010).

36. Bill 52 and presentations by groups to the Standing Committee on Health, Alberta Legislature (2009), http://www.assembly.ab.ca/committees/health/ (accessed 11 October 2009).

UNIQUELY CANADIAN APPROACHES TO DATA LINKAGE

HOW AND WHY DOES IT "WORK" AT THE MANITOBA CENTRE FOR HEALTH POLICY? A MODEL OF DATA LINKAGE, INTERDISCIPLINARY RESEARCH, AND SCIENTIST/USER INTERACTIONS

Patricia Martens

MANITOBA CENTRE FOR HEALTH POLICY: VISION AND MISSION

A Brief Overview

The Manitoba Centre for Health Policy (MCHP), a unit of the Department of Community Health Sciences of the Faculty of Medicine at the University of Manitoba, has been in existence since 1991. The founding directors, Noralou Roos and Les Roos, have worked on administrative database research since the mid-1970s. A world-renowned research centre in health services, population, and public health research, MCHP's activities span both health and social services uses of secondary data.

Data Data Everywhere: Access and Accountability? ed. C.M. Flood. Montreal and Kingston: Queen's Policy Studies Series, McGill-Queen's University Press. © 2011 The School of Policy Studies, Queen's University at Kingston. All rights reserved.

Strategic Plan

MCHP's Strategic Plan outlines its vision and mission, as well as the three pillars of activity around which it formulates goals and objectives (see Figure 1).

Vision: "The Manitoba Centre for Health Policy sets the international standard for using population-based secondary data to create new knowledge that informs health policy, social policy and service delivery." [1]

Mission: "The Manitoba Centre for Health Policy (MCHP) is a research centre of excellence that conducts world class population-based research on health services, population and public health, and the social determinants of health. MCHP develops and maintains the comprehensive population-based data repository on behalf of the Province of Manitoba for use by the local, national and international research community. MCHP promotes a collaborative environment to create, disseminate and apply its research. The work of MCHP supports the development of policy, programs and services that maintain and improve the health of Manitobans." [2]

FIGURE 1
How MCHP Carries Out Its Mission

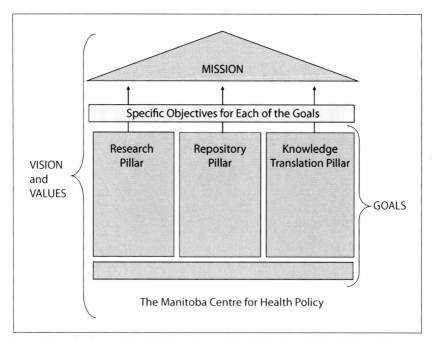

Source: Manitoba Centre for Health Policy, "Strategic Plan" (Winnipeg, 31 May 2007), p. 2, Figure 1.

Since its creation in 1991, MCHP has had a long-standing grant relationship with Manitoba Health, through five-year renewable grants. The most recent grant is from 2010 to 2015. This funding is to support the following three activities (MCHP's three pillars): research, repository, and knowledge translation.

Research – five research projects a year (referred to as "deliverables")
These projects are determined by the Minister and Deputy Minister of Manitoba Health in negotiation with the director of MCHP, and through consultation with the assistant deputy ministers, MCHP scientists, and regional health authorities (RHAs) where appropriate. Each of these projects is an independent research study that requires approvals from the Research Ethics Board of the Faculty of Medicine, as well as from the Health Information Privacy Committee of government. Databases beyond the "health" realm also require separate approvals from the relevant stakeholders (for example, the Minister of Family Services and Housing, in the case of social assistance data). Each deliverable takes approximately two years to complete. The terms of the MCHP/Manitoba Health agreement allow for independence of research scientists in accordance with academic freedom within the university. This includes publication rights, and a clause that allows for distribution of the research findings in a timely manner, presently defined as two months after Manitoba Health receives the first draft. This time frame has proven to be very reasonable, since the processes of peer review, checking data, formatting the publication, writing a "lay" summary (called the "four-pager") and media releases, and briefing the relevant stakeholders (including the Minister of Health) take at least two months, and often longer, to complete.

Repository – maintain, upgrade, and continually expand the Population Health Research Data Repository housed at MCHP
As of March 2010, the repository held 90 data files representing more than 60 different databases in the health services, population and public health, and social program areas, all linkable at the person level but anonymized prior to receipt by MCHP. Data are accessed through highly secure settings and procedures. Files are linked only temporarily for the duration of the research project, and for research purposes defined in approved proposals. The "key" to linkage is the Population Health Registry file, which contains an encrypted version of the personal health information number as well as demographic information (age, sex, geographic residence, etc.). All files contain "crosswalks" to this registry file, to allow for temporary linkage during an approved research study. This is discussed further below.

*Knowledge Translation – facilitate knowledge translation of
research findings*

MCHP produces reports on various health-related topics, with all reports available in hard copy and web-based formats. To communicate results, MCHP uses four-page lay summaries, news releases, peer-reviewed journal publications, and conference presentations and posters.

MCHP supports extensive knowledge translation activities through three annual workshop days (currently, one for non-Winnipeg Regional Health Authorities, one for the Winnipeg RHA, and one for Manitoba Health). These highly interactive workshops are designed to help decision-makers understand the data and to help research scientists understand the context from the decision-makers' lens. Participants come from various backgrounds and include the CEOs and vice presidents of RHAs, chairs and board members of RHA boards of directors, high-level planners (e.g., from the Community Health Assessment, Quality Improvement, and Planning and Evaluation sectors), medical officers of health, and front-line care providers. The workshop for RHAs outside of Winnipeg, the Rural and Northern Health Care Day, often attracts up to 200 people to discuss current MCHP reports. MCHP research scientists have also travelled to RHAs throughout the province to do similar roundtable workshops in regional settings. People from all across Canada—from Saskatchewan, Nova Scotia, and Quebec, to name a few places—and from the offices of the Canadian Institute for Health Information (CIHI), have attended these workshops as observers to learn about this unique model of researcher/user interaction. As well, the Western Regional Training Centre students (from the University of British Columbia and the University of Manitoba) often participate in these workshops to see knowledge translation in action.

Beyond the annual workshops, MCHP scientists have an ongoing and intensive research collaboration with all 11 Regional Health Authorities in the province, and with top-level planners from Manitoba Health, through *The Need To Know* Team funded by the Canadian Institutes of Health Research (Director: Patricia Martens; Co-Director: Randy Fransoo). This team meets three times a year, for two days at a time, to (a) co-create new knowledge of critical interest to planners and policy-makers, (b) engage in three-way capacity building among the three groups involved, and (c) encourage dissemination and application of the research. Considered a model of integrated knowledge translation, the team received the 2005 CIHR Knowledge Translation Award for Regional Impact. As of fall 2008, this team had produced five major research reports (an *RHA Indicators Atlas* in 2003,[3] the *Mental Illness* report in 2004,[4] the *Sex Differences* report in 2006,[5] the *What Works* report in 2008,[6] and the *RHA Indicators Atlas* update in 2009[7]). The evaluation component of the team has been described in various publications.[8]

HOW MCHP ENSURES OPTIMAL USE OF THE REPOSITORY WHILE MAINTAINING DATA SECURITY AND PRIVACY

The Manitoba Centre for Health Policy seeks to attain the highest level of data security and privacy for the repository housed on site. Funding through the Canadian Foundation for Innovation (CFI) in 1999 enabled MCHP to build the first CFI-funded "data laboratory." More recently, CFI funding granted in 2009 will expand the data holdings and extend access through secured remote-access sites. Besides routine security measures to control access to the laboratory itself (card swipes, sign-in procedures for all visitors, security cameras, limited access outside work hours), MCHP maintains its de-identified (anonymized) repository as if it contained named data.

MCHP ensures data security and privacy through the following mechanisms and processes:

- No named data are ever stored within the repository housed at MCHP.
- Crosswalk files are created in such a way that no agency has access to the complete information (see Figure 2), yet data are linkable at the person level. Databases are stored non-linked prior to project approvals, and linked only temporarily for the duration of the project.
- An encrypted number that is specific to MCHP alone is created for cross-linkage across files.
- Two-step authentication mechanisms are used by all data analysts to log on to the repository (this refers to the use of regular passwords, as well as a random number-generator device in the possession of data analysts).
- Researcher agreements are signed by each scientist prior to accessing any data, outlining the roles and responsibilities of researchers accessing the repository.
- Before any analyses are performed, all projects must have an ethics review by the Research Ethics Board of the Faculty of Medicine, and a Health Information Privacy Review by the Government of Manitoba, as well as any stakeholder reviews for non-health department databases.
- There is continual monitoring of data users, including updates as to progress or ethical approvals, and vetting by MCHP and by the Health Information Privacy Committee of all publications arising from repository use.
- MCHP's *Pledge of Privacy* brochure, available on the centre's website, outlines the ways in which data are secured.[9]
- Procedures are audited regularly, and MCHP has helped develop auditing tools.

- MCHP's Directorship has an ongoing relationship with the Ombudsman's Office in Manitoba, with meetings held at least once a year for mutual updates.
- With CIHR funding, MCHP and ICES (Institute of Clinical Evaluative Sciences, in Ontario) organized workshops and produced a toolkit on cross-Canada provincial legislation for using administrative data for research purposes without individual consent. This toolkit is available on MCHP's website.[10]
- All analyses are vetted to ensure suppression of data if the rate is based on one to five "events" in the population (it is considered legitimate to report a rate of zero), similar to Statistics Canada data rules.
- MCHP is working toward an annual accreditation process for all researchers (new and experienced), to ensure awareness of all updated procedures, protocols, and privacy considerations.

FIGURE 2
De-identification Process for Databases in the MCHP Repository

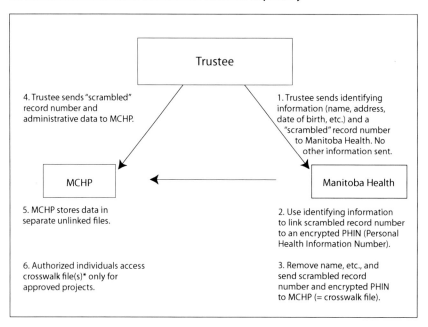

Note: *Crosswalk file accessed only by authorized individuals at MCHP to link Trustee data to other approved data in the Population Health Research Data Repository.

Source: Author's compilation.

ISSUES OF ADMINISTRATIVE DATABASES FOR RESEARCH: IDENTIFYING AND OVERCOMING BARRIERS

There are many barriers to using administrative databases within provinces and across provinces. These include jurisdiction, comparability of data, access to data (including analysis of complex data as well as expectations of data access), and relationships with data stakeholders.

Jurisdiction

Jurisdictional issues can be a problem even within one province. For example, some databases are considered "regional" databases, and identifying who is the stakeholder or custodian of the data is sometimes confusing. The provincial health department and RHAs sometimes have differing opinions on who is the ultimate stakeholder. As well, clinical databases that are held by physicians have a whole layer of uncertainty about them—are they collected for purposes of administering health care (similar to the regular billing claims or shadow billing data collection within physicians' offices), or are they research databases? If the data are considered outside the realm of administrative health-care databases, questions concerning informed consent might be raised. Researcher access to Statistics Canada databases linkable to the repository at MCHP is an ongoing issue—at present there is a legal barrier to these linkages unless the research is being done by provincial decision-makers. Thus, MCHP researchers requiring linkage between a repository database and a Statistics Canada survey (such as the Canadian Community Health Survey) are able to access the linkage for purposes of a "deliverable" only, since these reports are for government planning purposes and are funded through Manitoba Health. In contrast, scientists working on individual projects cannot use CCHS/repository linked databases.

Comparability of Data

Data are not necessarily consistently collected across Canada (and often not even across regions within one province), although national efforts are advancing the comparability of different databases (e.g., the Emergency Department Information Systems [EDIS] for emergency department data). Moreover, some provinces have more extensive data collection systems within certain database areas because of the administration of unique funded programs. One example is pharmaceutical data. Because Manitoba has had comprehensive pharmaceutical coverage for its entire population since the mid-1990s, the repository contains information on community-dispensed drugs for all residents, no matter their age or income. This is not necessarily the case in other provinces, where coverage may be limited to seniors or to those on social assistance. Standard database collection systems for key critical health information are essential if we are to do cross-Canada comparisons, and CIHR is working toward greater comparability of collected data.

Access to Data

One of the seldom-mentioned challenges to broader access and use of repository data is the complexity of these data. I have often referred to the databases as "paper clip" data—the paper clip was not originally designed for purposes other than clipping together paper, yet it makes an extremely handy tool for many other uses, including resetting a watch, becoming a zipper pull, and even replacing surgical tools to alleviate pressure underneath a damaged fingernail! However, sometimes the user of the reinvented paper clip tool needs to be satisfied with something less than perfect. So, too, administrative claims data or even clinical datasets are rarely ever collected as research data, and yet can be used for research as long as scientists know the limitations of the data collected.

Administrative databases are *not* survey data, with a survey's standard coding systems, easy-to-understand fields, and well-documented data dictionaries over time. There are also billions of administrative records, necessitating a great deal of human resources spent in understanding the nuances, the ways in which data collection has changed over time, the meanings of fields, and the creation of research concepts from these fields. Supposedly simple concepts, like "continuity of care," "grade 12 graduation," and "receiving social assistance" require extensive work to be derived from administrative databases. Here is a rather funny but enlightening scenario. During the validation of an educational database, one field appeared to be the number of days a student was absent in a given school year. Because of the importance of this predictor on long-term school outcomes, the researchers were delighted that this field existed (despite the fact that they had been originally told that absenteeism data were not collected). When the scientists looked at the distribution of the data field, they noted very distinct values—such as 10, 28, and 50—with many in-between values missing. Someone from the department finally discovered that the people inputting the data were aware that absenteeism records were not being collected. But they needed a place in which to enter bus numbers of travelling students, so they used the absenteeism field!

MCHP scientists have made major strides in documenting how databases are structured and how concepts are derived. Through the efforts of Les Roos since the mid-1990s, information on concepts derived from administrative databases has been made public through the MCHP website's Glossary[11] and Concept Dictionary.[12] This shared understanding has fostered a collaborative team approach within the organization, and continuity from research project to research project. However, there may be future barriers to this collaborative approach, as scientists not associated with MCHP sometimes bring a more proprietary mindset to their research using the repository data. Is this sense of "proprietary-ness" good for future health services and population health research? Is it good for the health of Canadians?

For several years, MCHP wrestled with the idea of making data accessible to scientists beyond the "core" MCHP research group. Until January 2007, provincial legislation did not allow repository access unless a scientist collaborated with an MCHP scientist. However, changes in the data-sharing agreement in 2007 made it possible for scientists to use the repository without having a core MCHP collaborator.

In contrast to MCHP, some provincial database centres actually create datasets on CDs for researchers to use in their own environments. Recently, heightened awareness of privacy issues has made this model problematic, and MCHP will not adopt this approach due to the potential of a breach in the use of repository data. In response to the challenges of ensuring privacy, MCHP requires researchers or data analysts to use data within the centre's secure environment, to ensure that all uses of the data are audited and that these data will not be used by people beyond the original proposed research. For this reason, geographical location has been a barrier for some researchers who are not located near the MCHP data laboratory.

To overcome this geographical barrier, MCHP has been working since 2008 to develop a "virtual organization" model that supports remote access sites (RAS). Two of the many challenges are how to maintain the high levels of security and collaboration made possible by the secured physical environment at the centre. The first pilot site opened in 2009. Implementing this new model took extensive effort, including creating a new organizational "wing" to oversee RAS models, reformatting all the databases within the repository to restrict users to certain fields or databases, and reviewing all protocols and security measures both within MCHP and for distant access arm sites. MCHP was determined to find a cost-effective model of remote access, since cost can be a huge barrier to researchers using small grants. Costing out such access is a difficult process, since MCHP must remain viable through a cost-recovery approach. So how does one estimate the costs to MCHP for RAS use? How do these costs differ from a researcher hiring a programmer/data analyst to work on site at the MCHP data laboratory? How do we ensure affordable access to students? The chief administrative officer of MCHP (Paulette Collins) and the associate director of the Population Health Research Data Repository (Mark Smith) are working on creating an algorithm to help estimate access costs.

Relationships with Data Stakeholders

Maintaining and updating a data laboratory and an extensive resource such as the repository is essential to keeping MCHP operational and leading edge. The Canadian Foundation for Innovation (CFI) has been critical to the establishment of MCHP's state-of-the-art laboratory through the 1999 and 2009 grants. The MCHP/Manitoba Health grant supports the five research projects, the ongoing maintenance costs of the repository, and the knowledge translation strategy. However, applications to CFI are essential when costly infrastructure innovations are envisioned, such as RAS pilots or acquisition of complex, expensive databases. MCHP's first CFI grant in 1999 allowed acquisition of the education and the social assistance data, which required immense human resource support. Not only does MCHP require staff to undergird such endeavours, but the supporting agency (the Department of Family Services and Housing) provided a secondment of a senior person to help MCHP understand and document the data from a research perspective.

KEYS TO SUCCESS, BARRIERS TO SUCCESS (AND OVERCOMING THESE)

A key to the past, present, and future of MCHP is its vast "information-rich" environment of linkable databases across both health and social programs. Models of working collaboratively with the many research scientists who could benefit from such data constantly require updating, as discussed above. The repository of data continues to expand, and in the past few years it appears that MCHP has turned a corner. Formerly, most of the database acquisitions resulted from MCHP scientists reaching out to the stakeholders of these data (such as the education and the social assistance data). More recently, however, it has become evident that MCHP has taken on somewhat of a "magnet centre" position, with many people approaching MCHP with ideas about housing new clinical, health, or social databases within the repository. In 2008 alone, we acquired several clinical databases—intensive care unit data, pediatric diabetes types 1 and 2 data, and clinical fetal alcohol spectrum disorder data, to name a few. This is a "good news, bad news" category of success: although the wealth of information to link to the repository seems to expand daily, the barrier to bringing in these data is financial.

It costs money to acquire a database, since administrative data are rarely compiled with research as the goal. Documenting and understanding data elements is a complex process that requires stakeholder and researcher interaction. Acquiring new databases involves six extremely intensive steps, all requiring the time of highly trained personnel: (a) relationship building and negotiating data-sharing agreements, (b) understanding and cataloguing the data ("annotating"), (c) transferring the data to

MCHP in a de-identified form, (d) validating the data, (e) measuring (i.e., figuring out new algorithms or concepts, and ways to measure these), and (f) documenting and sharing information about the database in the MCHP Glossary and in the Concept Dictionary. Only then can these data be used for further research projects (with proper permissions). Thus any discussion concerning acquisition of new databases by the repository must also involve discussions about funding, and granting agencies are sometimes hesitant to fund this sort of endeavour.

Not only is there the problem of financially supporting database acquisition, but there is also the problem of supporting a new cadre of interdisciplinary researchers and data analysts who may not have previous experience with using large administrative databases. Due to the small group of core MCHP researchers, and their own limited areas of expertise, it takes creative models to ensure that researchers investigating new areas of health research are supported. MCHP is piloting an annual accreditation process (for both new and experienced researchers and data analysts) in 2010 to guarantee that all users of the repository have the requisite knowledge about how to use the data, the regulations and requirements to use the data, and the ongoing reporting mechanisms during use, publication, and dissemination of results.

INTERACTIONS BETWEEN RESEARCH SCIENTISTS AND STAKEHOLDERS OR FUNDERS

The Manitoba Centre for Health Policy is a unit of the Department of Community Health Sciences within a university. As such, it is important for MCHP scientists and collaborators to maintain academic freedom in their research involving the repository data. MCHP scientists also have a long-standing funding relationship with government, so how do scientists exercise their academic freedom yet avoid "blindsiding" government or other data stakeholders with their findings?

The funding agreement between MCHP and the Manitoba government guarantees academic freedom, but requires that all research publications and reports using the repository be sent to government stakeholders 60 days prior to public release. MCHP scientists maintain an active knowledge-translation strategy with all stakeholders of reports, briefing all who are likely to be affected by the report within that 60-day time period. Government stakeholders acknowledge that the reports will remain true to the data, but the briefings make them aware of what will be made public (and hence, allow them to prepare for media interviews, etc.). This relationship has proven successful over the many years of operation since 1991. Although there are times when research findings are not what the government would call "good news," at least officials are given time to prepare for the questions that inevitably will come their way.

With increasing numbers of databases in the repository, there are increasing numbers of data stakeholders, and each group is given the opportunity to specify in the data-sharing agreement how it wishes to be informed or involved when someone wants to use that database for research purposes. MCHP also has processes for vetting all research proposals for alignment with its mission, and for cost based on estimated resource implications to analyze the data. MCHP has a separate vetting process for any research funded through private companies. These "Guidelines for Private Sector Sponsorship" are available under the Research Resources section ("Data Access") of the MCHP website. The basic intent of this extra review is to ensure the academic freedom of the researcher who is receiving the private sector funding, and to limit the private sponsor's involvement in the actual research analyses and publications.

MCHP'S VISION

With so much national support for electronic health records, there is an unofficial mandate to ensure that health information is collected in a useable, confidential, and accessible form for use by health-care providers. Given that agenda, however, the needs of planners and researchers often come second to those of clinicians. People in the driver's seat of many of these initiatives believe that "if you build it right for clinicians, others will come." But the basic needs of clinicians do not always match the basic needs of planners or researchers. To avoid many of these pitfalls, Manitoba's E-Health, under the guidance of Roger Girard, has approached provincial e-health initiatives from a more holistic view, integrating all three "users"—clinicians, planners, and researchers—in discussions from the start. Manitoba E-Health realizes that simply focusing on the clinical uses of electronic records does not guarantee that these data will meet the needs of planners or researchers. Various integrated committees have been set up to ensure that all voices are heard along the decision-making pathway.

People are realizing the incredible potential of administrative database research to produce population-based rates or prevalence, and to follow large cohorts over many years to detect long-term health or social outcomes. Administrative claims data have often been faulted for being "bad surveys," as if survey data were the gold standard. Let's remove this dichotomous thinking, just as we discarded the dichotomies of qualitative and quantitative research in the past decade, and adopt multi-method approaches and greater appreciation of the strengths (and weaknesses) of both paradigms. Survey research is able to measure domains often not captured in administrative data, and vice versa. The power of mixing the two through linkages is even more exciting, where survey data from one point in time can be linked to longitudinal datasets for a much more complete picture. The other dichotomy that still exists is in the hierarchy of what is considered "gold standard research design"—the randomized controlled trial (RCT). Although we all acknowledge the incredible strength of the RCT in demonstrating causation (i.e., having good internal validity), we have also seen the downsides of RCTs in recent years, including short follow-up times, restrictive inclusion criteria that might not generalize to the population using the intervention, and potential surveillance biases when people know they are being studied.

MCHP seeks to encourage RCT studies to take advantage of the repository of data housed at the centre, so that researchers can do more extensive follow-up and better understand the potential biases of their study group compared with the overall population. MCHP will continue to stretch the methodologies of quasi-experimental intervention/comparison group study designs, adapting administrative database research to address "what works" at the population level in terms of large-scale policy or program interventions. These types of quasi-experimental designs are relatively high in causal inference, and extremely high in terms of generalizeability (i.e., high external validity). MCHP's vision is to stretch the methodology needed to use administrative databases to address research questions about population health intervention (knowing the limitations of non-randomized trials), and to ensure that this information is shared with users so they, in turn, can make evidence-informed decisions.

There are unlimited potential uses of the databases found in the Population Health Research Data Repository. The scope is exciting, the questions that can be researched are seemingly endless, and so the future of administrative claims-based research is boundless. This is a good scenario when we need to address questions like "how do we keep up with demand," "how can we find funds to incorporate new databases to fill gaps in information," and "how do we work cross-provincially and nationally to share methods and findings without breaching privacy and confidentiality legislation?" MCHP scientists have seen two decades of progress, forging through new territory as research expands and requirements change. The question is not necessarily "where are the data?" but "what are we going to do with this natural resource?" How can we ensure that this resource is used for the benefit of Manitobans and Canadians?

NOTES

Patricia Martens would like to acknowledge the grant support of the Canadian Institutes of Health Research and the Public Health Agency of Canada through the CIHR/PHAC Applied Public Health Chair award (2007–2012).

This chapter approaches the issues of administrative database research from a provincial perspective, based on the author's knowledge as director of the Manitoba Centre for Health Policy.

1. The vision and mission statement of MCHP is available on the University of Manitoba website at http://umanitoba.ca/faculties/medicine/units/mchp/4241.htm.
2. Ibid.
3. P.J. Martens, R. Fransoo, The Need to Know Team, E. Burland, L. Jebamani, C. Burchill, C. Black, et al., *The Manitoba RHA Indicators Atlas: Population-Based Comparisons of Health and Health Care Use* (Winnipeg: Manitoba Centre for Health Policy, 2003).
4. P. Martens, R. Fransoo, and N. McKeen, *The Need to Know* Team, E. Burland, L. Jebamani, C. Burchill, et al., *Patterns of Regional Mental Illness Disorder Diagnoses and Service Use in Manitoba: A Population-Based Study* (Winnipeg: Manitoba Centre for Health Policy, 2004).
5. R. Fransoo, P. Martens, *The Need to Know* Team, E. Burland, H. Prior, C. Burchill, D. Chateau, and R. Walld, *Sex Differences in Health Status, Health Care Use, and Quality of Care: A Population-Based Analysis for Manitoba's Regional Health Authorities* (Winnipeg: Manitoba Centre for Health Policy, 2005).
6. P. Martens, R. Fransoo, *The Need to Know* Team, E. Burland, H. Prior, C. Burchill, L. Romphf, D. Chateau, A. Bailly, and C. Ouelette, *What Works? A First Look at Evaluating Manitoba's Regional Health Programs and Policies at the Population Level* (Winnipeg: Manitoba Centre for Health Policy, 2008).
7. R. Fransoo, P. Martens, E. Burland, *The Need to Know* Team, H. Prior, and C. Burchill, *Manitoba RHA Indicators Atlas 2009* (Winnipeg: Manitoba Centre for Health Policy, 2009).
8. S. Bowen, T. Erickson, and P. Martens, "More Than 'Using Research': The Real Challenges in Promoting Evidence-Informed Decision-Making," *Healthcare Policy* 4, no. 3 (2009): 69-84; S. Bowen and P.J. Martens, "A Model for Collaborative Evaluation of University-Community Partnerships," *Journal of Epidemiology and Community Health* 60 (2006): 902-7; S. Bowen and P.J. Martens, *The Need to Know* Team, "Demystifying 'Knowledge Translation': Learning from the Community," *Journal of Health Services Research & Policy* 10, no. 4 (2005): 203-11; P.J. Martens and N.P. Roos, "When Health Services Researchers and Policy-Makers Interact: Tales from the Tectonic Plates," *Healthcare Policy* 1, no. 1 (2005): 72-84, summarized in the Canadian Health Services Research Foundation's digest, *Insight and Action* 34 (April 2008), http://www.chsrf.ca/other_documents/insight_action/index_e.php (accessed 29 October 2009).
9. Manitoba Centre for Health Policy, *Pledge of Privacy*, http://umanitoba.ca/faculties/medicine/units/mchp/privacy.html.
10. P.M. Slaughter, P.K. Collins, N. Roos, K.M. Weisbaum, M. Hirtle, J.L. Williams, P.J. Martens, and A. Laupacis, *Privacy Best Practices for Secondary Data Use (SDU). Harmonizing Research & Privacy: Standards for a Collaborative Future* (2006), http://umanitoba.ca/faculties/medicine/units/mchp/privacyToolkit.html (accessed 29 October 2009).
11. Manitoba Centre for Health Policy, "Research Tools: Glossary," Research Resources section, http://umanitoba.ca/faculties/medicine/units/mchp/resources/glossary.html.
12. Manitoba Centre for Health Policy, "Research Tools: Concept Dictionary," Research Resources section, http://umanitoba.ca/faculties/medicine/units/mchp/resources/concept_dictionary.html.

EXPLOITING THE SECONDARY USE OF HEALTH DATA FOR EFFECTIVE CANCER CONTROL: OPPORTUNITIES AND RISKS

ROGER CHAFE, PAMELA SPENCER, MELISSA HUDSON, KAMINI MILNES, AND TERRENCE SULLIVAN

Based on 2008 Canadian risk estimates, 39 percent of women and 45 percent of men will develop cancer within their lifetimes.[1] Because so many people will experience the disease, the skillful use and protection of personal health information related to cancer truly is a societal concern. This information is also deeply personal. Cancer is often life-threatening, and the very mention of the disease has powerful connotations.[2] Because of the influence genetic factors have on developing certain types of cancer, information about individuals can have considerable implications for their family members.[3] Information about a person's risk and familial history of cancer may have financial implications, for example, affecting whether a person is able to purchase private medical insurance.[4] Furthermore, inappropriate use of patients' personal health information can jeopardize the crucial trust between patients and their care teams. All of these considerations place significant responsibilities on organizations holding the personal health information of cancer patients to use this information respectfully and to protect patients from any harm that

Data Data Everywhere: Access and Accountability? ed. C.M. Flood. Montreal and Kingston: Queen's Policy Studies Series, McGill-Queen's University Press. © 2011 The School of Policy Studies, Queen's University at Kingston. All rights reserved.

may arise from its use. Many of the proposed secondary uses of these data may not directly benefit the patient, but rather aim to improve the outcomes for cancer patients more generally or even for those who do not have cancer yet.[5] While the collection and secondary use of personal health information clearly raise privacy issues, these concerns need to be balanced against the rich promise that reasonable disclosures of cancer data have for improving the prevention, detection, treatment, and palliation of the disease.

The secondary use of personal health information already plays a central role in the fight against cancer. As e-health initiatives become more widely adopted, and with them expanded opportunities for timely data collection, we can expect even greater secondary usage of cancer data.[6] Beyond use in the direct provision of care, health information collected about patients is used to determine cancer incidence rates and patients' utilization of health-care services. This information supports cancer surveillance, system planning, program management, budgeting, and quality improvement efforts. The secondary use of personal health information also plays a key role in researching the preventable and non-preventable causes and consequences of the disease, including making survival and mortality estimates. Through health services research studies, we establish the data platform to improve the quality, efficiency, and appropriateness of care. In short, access to personal health information has numerous benefits for both current and future patients as well as the general public. The use of personal health information does, however, need to be balanced against legitimate privacy concerns raised by the array of goals this information is being employed to achieve.

Ontario's experience can serve as an example of what can be achieved by using cancer data effectively while providing protections for personal privacy. The province has a long history of collecting cancer registry and patient encounter data. Its growing repositories of biological and annotated tumour data help researchers examine the genetic factors influencing cancer. Its active research community has made major contributions to the academic literature and has helped to advance patient care. The provincial government has also passed legislation, the *Personal Health Information Protection Act, 2004 (PHIPA)*, which lays a framework describing what health information can be held, by whom, and for what purposes.[7] In this chapter, drawing on Ontario's experience, we review some real-world benefits of the secondary use of cancer data and examine some current issues regarding data access. The hope is that this examination of the challenges and opportunities related to the actual use of personal health information in cancer care in Ontario will offer useful insights to those struggling with similar issues in other areas.

CANCER DATA ACCESS IN ONTARIO

Each cancer agency in Canada plays a uniquely configured role within the cancer care system in its province. In Ontario, Cancer Care Ontario (CCO) is the main advisor to the government of Ontario regarding cancer services. In addition, CCO supports improvement initiatives across all aspects of the cancer control system through its partnerships with front-line providers, hospitals, regional cancer programs, Local Health Integration Networks (LHINS), public health agencies, researchers, patients, and the general public.[8] In order to fulfill its mandate, CCO needs access to a comprehensive range of high-quality data about all aspects of the cancer system and the population's risk for developing the disease. Much of this information comes from patient encounter data provided by hospitals and regional cancer programs across the province. CCO is also often asked to provide cancer data to other organizations and stakeholders (including researchers)—for example, statistics about new cases of cancer and data relating to system performance. CCO is thus on both sides of the data access relationship: in some instances requiring access to data from its partners, in other cases being asked to disclose data to other parties.

In Ontario, the collection, use, and disclosure of personal health information are governed by provincial legislation. Originally, permissive legislative authority to collect and use cancer patient data was granted in 1990 under Ontario's *Cancer Act*. This Act enabled CCO to engage in "compiling statistics or carrying out medical or epidemiological research" and provided a limited form of indemnity for physicians and hospitals that provided cancer data to CCO.[9] Currently, however, use of personal health information in Ontario, including information relating to cancer, is governed by the *Personal Health Information Protection Act, 2004 (PHIPA)*. The purpose of *PHIPA* is "to establish rules for the collection, use and disclosure of personal health information about individuals that protect the confidentiality of that information and the privacy of individuals with respect to that information, while facilitating the effective provision of health care."[10] In other words, the legislation seeks to strike a balance: to protect the health information of individuals held by data custodians, while allowing its necessary and appropriate use within the health-care system.

Under *PHIPA*, CCO is designated as a "prescribed entity," which authorizes it to collect personal health information, without consent, for the planning and management of cancer care. CCO is also designated under *PHIPA* as a "prescribed registry," which authorizes it to collect personal health information, again without consent, to operate the colorectal cancer screening registry in support of its ColonCancerCheck program.[11] Both designations are subject to formal oversight by Ontario's Office of the Privacy Commissioner, which conducts triennial reviews of CCO's information practices and procedures.

The introduction of *PHIPA* in 2004 has provided opportunities as well as challenges for the collection and disclosure of cancer information. One advantage is that the legislation provides a clearer statutory framework for the collection and sharing of personal health information between CCO and its data-sharing partners. For example, prior to the introduction of *PHIPA*, some hospitals resisted disclosing their pathology data in electronic format to CCO's Cancer Registry. Eventually, the Minister of Health and Long-Term Care had to intervene and exercise his authority under the *Public Hospitals Act*, mandating the hospitals to provide these data to CCO.[12] Even with this ministerial directive, though, CCO still had to negotiate individual data-sharing agreements with some of the participating hospitals largely because the privacy regimen in Ontario at the time was too vague. Since 2004, *PHIPA's* clear rules for the disclosure of personal health information have facilitated the collection of pathology data from participating hospitals and have assisted many of CCO's other data collection projects. *PHIPA* is still, however, relatively new legislation; a number of issues still need to be worked through at a practical level, including the disclosure of personal health information to researchers conducting observational research studies and cross-jurisdictional studies in Canada.[13]

CCO's Privacy Program

To fulfill its obligations under *PHIPA* and to the people whose health data it is entrusted to hold, CCO has established an organization-wide privacy program.[14] Key components of this program include the establishment of privacy policies and procedures, a privacy network within CCO, an employee privacy training and awareness program, a privacy audit and compliance program, and privacy impact assessments on existing and proposed CCO data holdings. CCO's Data Use and Disclosure Policy sets out the rules governing access to personal health information by CCO employees, consultants, and others, as well as the rules governing the disclosure of these data to third parties.[15] The fundamental principles of this policy are that access to data is provided on a "need-to-know" basis and in the least sensitive form practicable (see Table 1). To ensure that these principles are applied whenever CCO discloses data to third parties, CCO has recently introduced a set of de-identification guidelines. These guidelines provide a method for determining the relative risk of re-identification within a de-identified dataset.

TABLE 1
Levels of Data Sensitivity

Level of Sensitivity	Description
Identifiable record-level data	Data that include elements that directly identify an individual. By definition, identifiable record-level data contain personal health information (PHI).
De-identified record-level data	Data that include elements that may constitute identifying information because there may be reasonably foreseeable circumstances in which the data could be utilized, alone or with other information, to identify an individual (e.g., if linked with publicly available data). De-identified record-level data may contain PHI.
Aggregate data	Summed and/or categorized data that are analyzed and placed in a format that precludes further analysis (for example, in tables or graphs) to prevent the chance of revealing an individual's identity (individual records cannot be reconstructed). While PHI may be used to create aggregate data, once created, aggregate data do not include PHI.
Previously published data	Previously published data are not considered to include PHI.

Cancer Care Ontario's Data Holdings

Although there have been challenges to expanding the base coverage of encounter data,[16] Ontario has been steadily building valuable stores of high-quality cancer data and datamarts. For example, the province's hospitals and regional cancer programs hold significant amounts of information about individual patient encounters. The Ontario Cancer Registry—the largest jurisdiction-wide, patient-specific cancer registry in Canada—has 45 years of high-quality, person-specific cancer data relating to 1.6 million incident cases of cancer. This registry now has largely automated pathology capture on all new cancer diagnoses in the province, except non-melanoma skin cancer. The registry is an essential resource in tracking trends in the incidence of different types of cancers across the province. In addition to the Ontario Cancer Registry, a non-exhaustive sample of other significant data holdings maintained by CCO is listed in Table 2.

THE USES AND BENEFITS OF ONTARIO'S CANCER DATA

We have so far outlined a number of the measures taken by the cancer system in Ontario to ensure the appropriate use of cancer data, and we have identified some of CCO's main data holdings. In order to understand

TABLE 2
Some Examples of Cancer Care Ontario's Data Holdings

Data Holding	Description	Coverage
Activity Level Reporting (ALR)/Cancer Activity Datamart	The ALR provides an integrated set of data elements from Regional Cancer Centres (RCCs).	Complete population coverage for radiation therapy. Approximately 65% coverage for systemic therapy, and increasing as data collection expands beyond RCCs.
Patient Information Management System (PIMS)/Pathology Datamart	This database is composed of patient and tumour information for cancer and cancer-related pathology reports (tissue, cytology), submitted from public hospital (and some community) laboratories.	93% of pathology reports are included in PIMS.
New Drug Funding Program (NDFP)	The NDFP database stores patient and treatment information about systemic therapy drug utilization at RCCs and other Ontario hospitals, for which reimbursement is being sought through the NDFP according to strict eligibility criteria.	Complete coverage of all funded treatments of new drugs.
Ontario Breast Screening Program (OBSP)	The Integrated Client Management System database provides an integrated set of data for each client screened in the OBSP for the purposes of program administration, management, and evaluation.	Approximately 54% coverage for screening mammography.
Colorectal Screening Data – Colonoscopy Interim Reporting Tool (CIRT)	The data collected through CIRT are used to understand current colonoscopy activities conducted within participating hospitals from both volume and quality perspectives.	Approximately 67% coverage for Ontario colonoscopies, including 90% of hospital-based colonoscopies.
Ontario Cervical Screening Program	Cytobase consists of cervical cytology data ("Pap test" results) collected from participating community laboratories.	Approximately 85% coverage for Pap tests.
Brachytherapy Funding Program	This program stores patient and treatment information about prostate cancer patients at RCC hospitals, for which reimbursement is being sought.	Complete population coverage.
Ontario Cancer Symptom Management Collaborative (OCSMC) Data Collection Database	The data collected through the OCSMC are used to evaluate the provision of symptom management to cancer patients in Ontario.	Approximately 40% of lung cancer patients treated in RCCs, or 10% of all patients treated in RCCs.
Interim Annotated Tumour Project (ATP) Database	The Interim ATP database provides an integrated set of data, combining tumour information from the Ontario Institute for Cancer Research's Tumour Bank with CCO's Cancer Registry.	Small percentage of samples.
Wait Time Information System (WTIS)	WTIS is the first information system in Ontario to collect accurate and timely wait time data.	Currently capturing 1.6 million diagnostic procedures and surgeries annually.

Source: Adapted from Cancer Care Ontario, "Cancer Care Ontario Data Holdings" (2009), CCO Toolbox section, http://www.cancercare.on.ca/common/pages/UserFile.aspx?fileId=51047.

the importance of personal health information for the fight against cancer, it will be useful now to look at specific, concrete examples of how this information is used and the benefits that come from it.

Population Surveillance

One of the most fundamental uses of cancer data is in tracking trends in the incidence, mortality, and survival rates of different cancers across different populations over time. This population-level review of the disease is crucial for designing an effective and efficient plan for cancer control, designing a system of care with sufficient treatment capacity, and identifying areas where further research and resources are needed. Population surveillance data also help inform the public debate about cancer and educate the public about the real risks of the disease.

The Ontario Cancer Registry, together with other provincial cancer registries, provides information for the *Canadian Cancer Statistics* reports, produced by the Canadian Cancer Society, the National Cancer Institute of Canada, the Public Health Agency of Canada, and Statistics Canada.[17] Valuable resources for examining the changing distribution of cancer, these reports provide "detailed information regarding incidence and mortality of the most common types of cancer by age, sex, time period and province/territory."[18] The trends outlined in these reports show the areas where Canada has made progress in the fight against cancer, such as dramatic improvements in mortality for childhood cancers, and the control and service challenges that still lie ahead, such as the need to reduce incidence rates and improve survival for lung and aerodigestive cancers.

The Ontario Cancer Registry is undeniably a foundational resource for identifying changes in cancer incidence and for researching causes of the disease within the province. Information contained within the Registry has, for example, identified a significant rise in the number of new cases of thyroid cancer in females in Ontario over the last 20 years (see Figure 1). We have also identified a rise in the rates of testicular cancer (see Figure 2). These trends raise questions about possible changes in the detection of these conditions and about environmental changes that may increase the incidence rates of these diseases. Identifying these trends is the first step in developing ways to understand the etiology and take steps to reduce the disease burden, where there are modifiable risks.

To improve cancer care, it often helps to focus on subpopulations in order to get a more accurate picture of the unique challenges they face. For example, cancer incidence and mortality rates among First Nations people differ from the averages for the non-First Nations population in Ontario.[19] Although the overall rate of new cancer cases for First Nations people is still lower than the provincial average, of concern is the fact that the incidence rate of First Nations people has nearly doubled between 1968 and 2001. In part because of these different disease burdens,

FIGURE 1
New Cases of Thyroid Cancer in Females in Ontario, 1981–2004

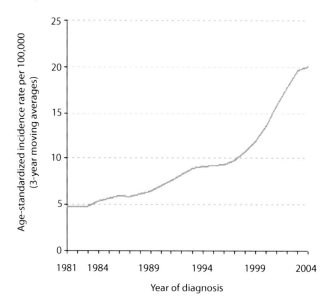

Source: Reprinted by permission from Cancer Care Ontario.

FIGURE 2
New Cases of Testicular Cancer in Ontario, 1981–2004

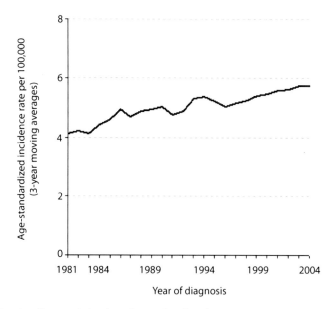

Source: Reprinted by permission from Cancer Care Ontario.

one of CCO's key priorities is to enact, in partnership with First Nation communities, a specific Aboriginal Cancer Strategy.[20] This strategy aims to be inclusive of local traditions, while clearly responding to trends in the cancer incidence rates within these communities. The importance of community for First Nations people and the long history of their being the subject of research raise particular challenges and sensitivities in collecting data.[21] Our current strategy and partnerships will hopefully allow us to negotiate these barriers and better serve these communities, while respecting the principles of ownership, control, access, and possession of data for Aboriginal communities.[22]

In 2006, Cancer Care Ontario, the Public Health Agency of Canada, and the Canadian Cancer Society completed the most comprehensive study ever undertaken on the burden of cancer in young Canadian adults, an age group often overlooked in discussions of cancer.[23] The study found that over 10,000 people between the ages of 20 and 44 are diagnosed in Canada every year, and that cancer is the leading cause of death among women in this age group. This study illustrates the impact that changes in lifestyle and environmental exposures may be having on people's likelihood of getting certain types of cancer and how these changes might affect future cancer rates. As Sir Richard Doll pointed out almost 20 years ago, trends in this age group are particularly revealing of the causes of cancer, as they reflect recent exposures to carcinogenic events. In addition, as exposures in young adults will vary according to birth cohorts, consequent changes in disease risk will be first observed in the young.[24] This type of surveillance is possible only through the collection and analysis of personal health information.

System Planning and Budgeting

One of the most important tasks for the management of the cancer system is to plan for future demand. Based on incidence rates determined through patient data and expected trends, CCO identifies the likely number of new cancers, across each of the different regions in the province, over the next ten years (see Figure 3). This level of long-term forecasting is crucial for ensuring that sufficient resources, including human resources and regional cancer infrastructure, are available to meet the growing demand for cancer services in the coming years.

Long-term forecasting of cancer rates based on current incident data also plays a role in the long-term service and financial planning of the cancer system. For example, in 2006/07, CCO funded more than 27,000 intravenous chemotherapy treatments through its New Drug Funding Program, at an annual cost of $176 million (Figure 4). Using utilization data for the program and trends in cancer incidence, it is estimated that by 2010/11 the program will reimburse more than 33,000 treatments at an annual cost of over $220 million. This rise in estimated expenditures constitutes a significant increase in the cost of the program, which the

FIGURE 3
Projected Number of Newly Diagnosed Cancers in Ontario by Region

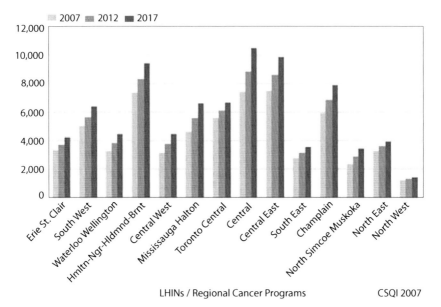

LHINs / Regional Cancer Programs   CSQI 2007

Notes: LHIN = Local Health Integration Network. CSQI = Cancer Service Quality Index. The data show all cancers combined.
Source: Reprinted by permission from Cancer Care Ontario.

FIGURE 4
New Drug Funding Program Expenditures

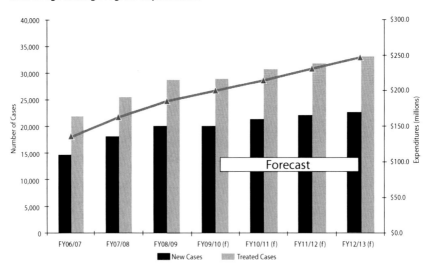

Source: Reprinted by permission from Cancer Care Ontario.

province and CCO will need to account for in their long-term budget plans. While such innocuous secondary usage of data should be clearly acceptable, governments need to ensure that the measures they enact to protect personal health information do not unduly limit our ability to plan our future cancer system.

The use of personal health information does more than just support budget forecasting and service planning: patient outcome data are also used to help better direct investments within the cancer system. For example, the Ontario Cancer-PET Registry tracks the outcomes of cancer patients who have received a Positron Emission Tomography (PET) scan in the province for the detection and staging of cancer as part of a study evaluating the effectiveness of PET technology.[25] The provincial government wants to see evidence that PET technology improves patient outcomes before committing substantial resources for its expanded use. Given the novelty of delaying the purchase of a new health technology until sufficient data are available, the Toronto Health Policy Citizens' Council recently took up the issue of whether this approach was acceptable to the public. While there have been problems in the length of time it has taken to complete the research trials, the majority of Citizens' Council members concluded that the initial "decision to base the funding of PET scans upon evidence generated by clinical studies funded by the MOHLTC was appropriate."[26] Given the high cost of many new technologies, and the apparent reasonableness of this approach to the public, more funding decisions may be directed by these types of effectiveness studies based on actual patient outcome data.

Performance and Quality Improvements

Personal health information can also be used to improve wait times—one of the public's biggest concerns about our health-care system. In order to know whether wait times are improving, health-care managers have to measure the waits patients are experiencing. The Wait Time Information System is a new information system implemented in 82 Ontario hospitals to collect accurate wait time data, including wait times for cancer surgery.[27] An important aspect of this program is that these wait time data are publicly reported. Wait time initiatives also measure other aspects of cancer care. For example, Figure 5 shows the actual waits for radiation treatment after diagnosis. This information allows patients and the public to anticipate their likely waits for services and to better hold the system to account for improving wait time performance. These important initiatives, which citizens are asking for, require the use of patient data.

CCO has been posting radiation wait times for several years, and we now post radiation, system, screen-related, and surgical waits. Ontario's collection and use of wait time information to drive improvements was honoured with the top Canadian award for Information and Productivity in 2007.[28]

FIGURE 5
Wait Times for Radiation Treatment in Ontario, 2003–2006

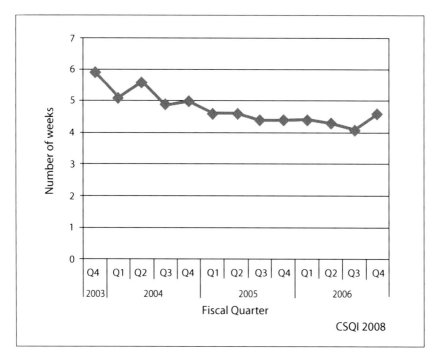

CSQI 2008

Notes: CSQI = Cancer Service Quality Index. The graph shows median waits from the time of referral to the start of radiation treatment, excluding all time intervals greater than 20 weeks and wait times for those receiving chemotherapy prior to radiation therapy. Princess Margaret Hospital is included as of March 2004 and Carlo Fidani Peel Regional Cancer Centre as of 2005. Source: Reprinted by permission from Cancer Care Ontario.

Another important area for cancer control is cancer screening. We need data about the number of people who have been screened in order to determine whether population screening targets are being met. For example, CCO's breast cancer screening program targets screening 70 percent of the female population between the ages of 50 and 69 in Ontario. Using data from a number of sources, CCO can determine how well different regions of the province are doing in meeting this important program goal and then report to the public on their success (Figure 6). Similar initiatives are underway in Ontario's cervical and colorectal cancer screening programs.

Specific quality and performance improvements also come from the analysis of outcome data. Thoracic cancer surgery is a good example. Based on a systematic review of the published research evidence, input from an expert panel, and reviews of patient data, CCO concluded that there was a relationship between high volume thoracic and esophageal

FIGURE 6
Rates for Breast Cancer Screening in Ontario, 2005/06

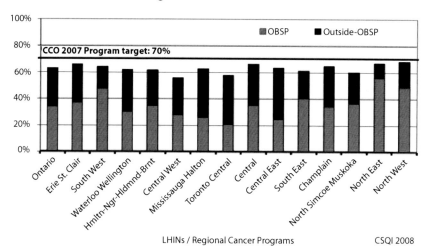

LHINs / Regional Cancer Programs   CSQI 2008

Notes: OBSP = Ontario Breast Screening Program. LHIN = Local Health Integration Network. CSQI = Cancer Service Quality Index. The bar graph shows the percentage of eligible women (ages 50–69) who received a mammogram within two years of the index year, by type of screening (OBSP vs. outside OBSP). Women were screened only once (i.e., excludes re-screens).

Source: Reprinted by permission from Cancer Care Ontario. Data were compiled from the Ontario Health Insurance Plan database; Cancer Care Ontario, Ontario Breast Screening Program; and the Registered Persons Database of the Ontario Ministry of Health and Long-Term Care. Data analysis was conducted by scientists in the Cancer Program at the Institute for Clinical Evaluative Sciences, Toronto.

cancer surgery and successful patient outcomes. The successful outcomes were also linked to surgical training, as well as a range of hospital infrastructure resources and skilled staffing.[29] In response to these findings, CCO's Program in Evidence-Based Care developed guidelines for thoracic surgery outlining the training requirements for surgeons, the number of allied and support staff required, and other expectations for sites performing thoracic surgery.[30] It also established annual volume levels that must be met by a centre performing thoracic cancer surgery. As a consequence of adopting these guidelines, the vast majority of procedures are now coordinated in just over a dozen regionally designated thoracic surgery hospitals in Ontario, down from 45 hospitals just a few years ago. All of these actions are expected to increase the survival rate of those who undergo thoracic and esophageal cancer surgery within the province.

The benefits of a greater focus on patient data do not just come from better analyzing the data we have; they also come from improving the data we collect. One example of this improved data collection is in the area of pathology reporting, where clear quality standards for clinical documentation have been established, and a concerted effort is being made to meet these standards. The use of the College of American Pathology standardized data elements led to 90 percent of cancer pathology reports meeting the new standard in 2006, a 15 percent increase from the previous year (see Figure 7).[31] Better documentation and standardization of pathology test reports help to identify unambiguous outcomes for patients.

FIGURE 7
Percentage of Pathology Reports Meeting Provincial Standards by LHIN, 2005 vs. 2006

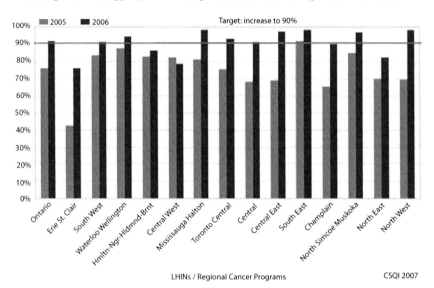

LHINs / Regional Cancer Programs   CSQI 2007

Notes: LHIN = Local Health Integration Network. CSQI = Cancer Service Quality Index. Pathology lab reports include breast cancer surgeries, colorectal and lung cancer resections, hysterectomies, and radical prostatectomies. For breast cancer only, the number of cases is reported, not the number of reports, as breast cancer commonly involves more than one surgery.

Source: Reprinted by permission from Cancer Care Ontario, "Completeness of Pathology Reporting," 2, http://www.cancercare.on.ca/search/default.aspx?q=Completeness%20of%20 Pathology%20Reporting&type=0,6-76,6-40484|-1,1377-78.

Research

CCO began as a treatment and research foundation, and it continues to support high-quality cancer research. Under *PHIPA*, CCO is subject to the same rules as "health information custodians" with respect to disclosure of personal health information without consent for research purposes. All research protocols must be approved by a research ethics board that meets the composition requirements set out in *PHIPA*, and the disclosure must be supported by a confidentiality agreement entered into by the researcher with CCO. Between 2006 and 2009, CCO received 101 completed research requests for data disclosure and approved all but three. The three requests yet to be approved involve issues relating to patient recruitment, which is an issue discussed in more detail below.

The Ontario Cancer Registry is one of CCO's data holdings of key interest to researchers. Since 1990, over 340 research articles have been published using data from the registry. Some of the many topics studied using registry data include trends in childhood cancer,[32] the influence of age and co-morbidity on mortality after radical prostatectomy,[33] the economic impact of lung cancer treatment,[34] the risk of cancer for workers in particular industries,[35] the utilization of services for breast cancer patients,[36] hospital characteristics associated with better survival for cancer surgery,[37] and genome-wide association for colorectal cancer.[38] The Ontario Cancer Registry and CCO's other data holdings continue to be a rich resource for researchers studying most types of cancer and represent a key route for making further progress in our fight against the disease.

Challenges to Data Access at CCO

While we have highlighted some of the many benefits, the secondary use of personal health information does not come without challenges. Some of the issues that we have experienced at CCO relate to cost, interprovincial data sharing, the developing field of genetics, and access to data for certain types of research studies.

Cost. Maintaining the privacy and security of large data holdings has become a standard operating cost in both the public and private sectors. We estimate that during the five years following the introduction of *PHIPA* in 2004, CCO has incurred annual privacy and data security costs of approximately $3 million, covering staffing, systems security, and the use of external consulting resources to conduct privacy impact assessments. These costs reflect CCO's need to make a substantial investment in its privacy and security infrastructure post-*PHIPA*, including conducting comprehensive privacy impact assessments on all its existing and new data holdings, and developing the privacy infrastructure for its new systems and programs that utilize personal health information, such as the Wait Time Information System and the Colorectal Cancer Screening Registry. These costs also reflect the constant need to keep pace with new security standards and new privacy-enhancing technologies, as well as with standards set by regulatory bodies such as the Office of the Information and Privacy Commissioner (Ontario).

Interprovincial data sharing. The ability to responsibly share data interprovincially would better allow for performance comparisons across provinces. It also would allow for greater opportunities to learn from other parts of the country. Data sharing in Canada, however, is hampered by the lack of consistent health privacy legislation across jurisdictions. Moreover, privacy legislation in key provinces, including Ontario, explicitly prohibits, with certain exceptions, disclosing personal health information out-of-province. In response to this issue, CCO is working closely with key stakeholders, including the Canadian Partnership Against Cancer, to facilitate and promote greater data sharing across the country.

The restriction on interprovincial transfers also impacts CCO's ability to disclose personal health information to other provinces and territories whose residents receive care in Ontario. Such disclosures facilitate cancer planning and management in the care recipient's home province or territory and are particularly critical for territories that heavily rely on Ontario for providing cancer services to their populations. For example, CCO has information on more than 50 percent of the cancer cases for Nunavut residents. As even these types of disclosures do not appear to be permitted under *PHIPA*, CCO has sought a regulatory amendment to the legislation to permit the sharing of data for defined purposes.

Disclosure and genetic information. Genetic information is playing an increasingly important role in cancer research and treatment. Yet the expanded use of genetic information raises a number of important issues for disclosure, which organizations like CCO are presently working through. First, there currently is no established definition of what constitutes genetic information, which increases the difficulty of establishing clear guidance. Because information about an individual's genetic makeup has implications for family members, rules for disclosure need to be developed regarding circumstances under which family members are informed of the results of genetic tests.[39] Finally, there need to be greater protections in Canada to ensure that people are not adversely penalized through the disclosure of the results of genetic tests, for example, in their ability to get private insurance coverage.[40]

Patient contact and research. While researchers certainly derive benefits from the protection given to their study subjects under privacy legislation, privacy protection often increases the cost and duration of studies, and decreases participation rates.[41] One specific research disclosure issue that CCO has faced since the introduction of *PHIPA* relates to patient contact for the purposes of study recruitment. The problem arises because *PHIPA* requires CCO, as custodian of the data, to obtain the individual's consent to be contacted for the purpose of participating in research.[42] This means that the researcher has to arrange to have CCO contact all study participants to get their consent to allow the researcher contact them about the study. The researcher would still need to get participants' consent to join the study. This complicated process places significant barriers on researchers who are conducting research that requires direct patient contact, as is the case for certain types of case control studies or for studies that require the patient to provide biological samples. The CCO privacy program is developing a mechanism for patient contact, informed by best practices in cancer registries elsewhere,[43] that will satisfy the Office of the Information and Privacy Commissioner while allowing studies requiring direct patient contact to continue.

CONCLUSION

Accessing and using personal health information, including cancer data, is an important investment in our future health. Appropriate and ethical access to data can improve cancer services and prevent future cases of the disease. In this chapter, we have reviewed some specific benefits. As we continue to make reforms in the protection of personal health information, we must effectively balance concerns about protecting privacy with uses of these data for purposes that will benefit both individuals and society as a whole. The Canadian constitution sets the tone for this discussion by granting individual rights but allowing for reasonable limits on these rights when there is a pressing social benefit. The key is that there needs to be proportionality between the potential harm of limiting individual rights, including the right to control one's personal health information, and the social benefit of wider secondary use of these data without re-quiring patients' consent.

There has been, to date, little empirical evidence regarding the views of the general public on what types of personal health information they would not oppose being used or for which secondary purposes. Some of the work that has been done indicates that the majority of citizens do not have concerns about many secondary uses of their health data.[44] Given that value issues are involved here, more work is needed to accurately gauge the public's views on these issues.

This chapter has reviewed some of the challenges we have faced at Cancer Care Ontario relating to the use of personal health information and has highlighted several measures that should be taken in order to increase the accessibility of our data holdings to the various actors in the cancer care system. There should be improved cooperation among entities that collect cancer data in order to allow for better comparisons both within and across provinces. The new Canadian Partnership Against Cancer could play a role here to promote greater sharing and use of comparative cancer data between provinces. We also need to prepare to address future issues that will likely arise relating to access to personal health information in the area of genetics and predictive genetic testing. The implications of having and using these new types of patient information may ultimately require further guidance from the public and from provincial legislatures.

NOTES

1. Canadian Cancer Society/National Cancer Institute of Canada, *Canadian Cancer Statistics 2008* (Toronto: Canadian Cancer Society, 2008).
2. S. Sontag, *Illness as Metaphor and AIDS and Its Metaphors* (New York: Doubleday, 1990).
3. B. Godard, T. Hurlimann, M. Letendre, N. Egalite, and INHERIT BRCAs, "Guidelines for Disclosing Genetic Information to Family Members: From Development to Use," *Familial Cancer* 5 (2006): 103-16.
4. K. Hudson, M.K. Holohan, and F.C. Collins, "Keeping Pace with the Times – The Genetic Information Nondiscrimination Act 2008," *New England Journal of Medicine* 358, no. 25 (2008): 2661-63.
5. M.P. Coleman, B.G. Evans, and G. Barrett, "Confidentiality and the Public Interest in Medical Research – Will We Ever Get It Right?" *Clinical Medicine* 3 (2003): 219-28.
6. D. Willison, L. Schwartz, J. Abelson, C. Charles, M. Swinton, D. Northrup, and L. Thabane, "Alternatives to Project-Specific Consent for Access to Personal Information for Health Research: What Is the Opinion of the Canadian Public?" *Journal of the American Medical Informatics Association* 14 (2007): 706-12.
7. Government of Ontario, *Personal Health Information Protection Act, 2004*, S.O. 2004, c. 3, Schedule A.
8. Cancer Care Ontario website, http://www.cancercare.on.ca (accessed 26 October 2009).
9. Government of Ontario, *The Cancer Act*, R.S.O. 1990, c. C-1, s. 7.
10. Government of Ontario, *Personal Health Information Protection Act, 2004*, S.O. 2004, c. 3, Schedule A, s. 1a.
11. Cancer Care Ontario, "ColonCancerCheck" (2008), http://www.cancercare. on.ca/pcs/screening/coloscreening/cccprivprogram/ (accessed 26 October 2009).
12. Government of Ontario, *Public Hospitals Act*, R.S.O. 1990, c. P-40, s. 23(a).
13. A. Gershon and J. Tu, "The Effect of Privacy Legislation on Observational Research," *Canadian Medical Association Journal* 178, no. 7 (2008): 871-73. Observational research refers to studies that examine a defined population and do not have intervention administered, including cohort, cross-sectional, and case-control studies.
14. Cancer Care Ontario, "Privacy" (2008), http://www.cancercare.on.ca/about/ who/privacy/ (accessed 26 October 2009).
15. Cancer Care Ontario, "Data Use and Disclosure Policy" (2008), http://www. cancercare.on.ca/about/who/privacy/privdocs/ (accessed 26 October 2009).
16. T. Sullivan, W. Evans, H. Angus, and A. Hudson (eds.), *Strengthening the Quality of Cancer Services in Ontario* (Ottawa: Canadian Healthcare Organization Press, 2003).
17. Canadian Cancer Society/National Cancer Institute of Canada, *Canadian Cancer Statistics 2008* (Toronto: Canadian Cancer Society, 2008).

18 Ibid., 2.
19. L.D. Marrett and M. Chaudhry, "Cancer Incidence and Mortality in Ontario First Nations, 1968–1991 (Canada)," *Cancer Causes and Control* 14 (2003): 259-68.
20. Cancer Care Ontario, "Aboriginal Cancer Strategy" (2009), http://www.cancercare.on.ca/about/programs/aborstrategy/aboriginal/.
21. J. Smylie and M. Anderson, "Understanding the Health of Indigenous Peoples in Canada: Key Methodological and Conceptual Challenges," *Canadian Medical Association Journal* 175 (2006): 602-5.
22. Cancer Care Ontario, "First Nations Cancer Research and Surveillance Priorities for Canada" (Toronto, 2003), http://www.cancercare.on.ca/common/pages/UserFile.aspx?fileId=13688 (accessed 20 November 2009).
23. Cancer Care Ontario, "Cancer in Young Adults in Canada" (Toronto, 2006), http://www.phac-aspc.gc.ca/publicat/cyac-cjac06/index-eng.php (accessed 20 October 2009).
24. R. Doll, "Progress against Cancer: An Epidemiologic Assessment. The 1991 John C. Cassel Memorial Lecture," *American Journal of Epidemiology* 134 (1991): 675-88.
25. Government of Ontario, "Ontario Cancer-PET Study," http://www.health.gov.on.ca/english/providers/program/ohip/bulletins/4000/bul4464_2.pdf (accessed 20 October 2009).
26. A. Laupacis, W. Levinson, F. Merali, D.K. Martin, R. Chafe, B. Evans, T. Sullivan, A. Cuyler, and University of Toronto Citizens' Council, "PET Scanning in Ontario: Deliberations of the University of Toronto Citizens' Council – Recommendations and Lessons Learned" (Toronto, 2008), http://www.canadianprioritysetting.ca/html/documents/cc_PET_report.pdf (accessed October 20, 2009).
27. Cancer Care Ontario, "Wait Time Information System" (2009), http://www.cancercare.on.ca/ocs/wait-times/wtio/ (accessed 26 October 2009).
28. Canadian Information Productivity Awards, "Cancer Care Ontario: Wait Time Information System," http://www.cipa.ca/award_winners/winners_07/CancerCare254.html (accessed 4 February 2009).
29. S. Sundaresan, B. Langer, T. Oliver, F. Schwartz, M. Brouwers, H. Stern, and the Expert Panel on Thoracic Surgical Oncology, "Standards for Thoracic Surgical Oncology in a Single-Payer Healthcare System," *Annals of Thoracic Surgery* 84 (2007): 696-701.
30. S. Sundaresan, B. Langer, T. Oliver, F. Schwartz, M. Brouwers, H. Stern, and the Expert Panel on Thoracic Surgical Oncology, *Thoracic Surgical Oncology Standards* (Cancer Care Ontario's Evidence-Based Series, 2005).
31. Cancer Care Ontario, "Completeness of Pathology Reporting," http://www.cancercare.on.ca/qualityindex2007_old/download/Pathology%20reporting%20completeness.pdf (accessed 20 October 2009).
32. M. Agha, B. Dimonte, M. Greenburg, C. Greenburg, R. Barr, and J.R. McLaughlin, "Incidence Trends and Projections of Childhood Cancer in Ontario," *International Journal of Cancer* 188, no. 11 (2006): 2809-15.
33. S.M. Alibhai, M. Leach, G. Tomlinson, M.D. Krahn, N. Fleshner, E. Holowaty, G. Naglie, "30-Day Mortality and Major Complications after Radical Prostatectomy: Influence of Age and Comorbidity," *Journal of the National Cancer Institute* 97, no. 20 (2005): 1525–32.

34. W.K. Evans, B.P. Will, J-M. Berthelot, and M.C. Wolfson, "The Economics of Lung Cancer Management in Canada," *Lung Cancer* 14 (1995): 19-29.

35. M.M. Finkelstein, "Cancer Incidence among Ontario Police Officers," *American Journal of Industrial Medicine* 34, no. 2 (1998): 157-62.

36. R.E. Gray, M. Fitch, V. Goel, E. Franssen, and M. Labrecque, "Utilization of Complementary / Alternative Services by Women with Breast Cancer," *Journal of Health and Social Policy* 16, no. 4 (2003): 75-84.

37. E. Simunovic, M. Rempel, E. Theriault, A. Coates, T. Whelan, E. Holowaty, B. Langer, and M. Levine, "Influence of Hospital Characteristics on Operative Death and Survival of Patients after Major Cancer Surgery in Ontario," *Canadian Journal of Surgery* 49, no. 4 (2006): 251-58.

38. B.W. Zanke, C.M. Greenwood, J. Rangrej, R. Kustra, A. Tenesa, S.M. Farrington, J. Prendergast, et al., "Genome-wide Association Scan Identifies a Colorectal Cancer Susceptibility Locus on Chromosome 8q24," *Nature Genetics* 39, no. 8 (2007): 989-94.

39. Godard et al., "Guidelines for Disclosing Genetic Information," see note 3.

40. Hudson, Holohan, and Collins, "Keeping Pace with the Times," see note 4.

41. M.A. Harris, A.R. Levy, and K.E. Teschke, "Personal Privacy and Public Health," *Canadian Journal of Public Health* 99, no. 4 (2008): 293-96.

42. *Personal Health Information Protection Act*, s. 44(6)(e).

43. L. Beskow, R. Sandler, and M. Weinberger, "Research Recruitment through US Central Cancer Registries: Balancing Privacy and Scientific Issues," *American Journal of Public Health* 96 (2006): 1920-26.

44. G. Barrett, J.A. Cassell, and M.P. Coleman, "National Survey of British Public's Views on Use of Identifiable Medical Data by the National Cancer Registry," *British Medical Journal* 332 (2006): 1068-72.

WHAT MAKES US SICK? WHAT MAKES US BETTER? DATA AND DISEASES

METHODS FOR ASCERTAINING CHRONIC DISEASE CASES FROM ADMINISTRATIVE DATA

LISA M. LIX

Research about the epidemiology of chronic disease, disease management, and treatment outcomes is now routinely conducted using administrative data. Many jurisdictions are pursuing the development of population-based surveillance systems using case ascertainment algorithms based on diagnosis codes in hospital discharge and medical services data. For some conditions, like diabetes, these algorithms can accurately classify individuals as disease cases or non-cases. For other conditions, like osteoporosis, substantial misclassification may result from relying solely on diagnosis codes to distinguish disease cases from non-cases. This chapter will focus on the technical issues as well as the data confidentiality and security issues to address when ascertaining cases of chronic disease from administrative data, including choice of data sources, external and internal validation techniques, and statistical models to adjust for misclassification. The challenges of comparing case ascertainment results across time and space will also be discussed. Illustrative examples will be drawn from recent studies about osteoporosis, Parkinson's disease, and hypertension.

Concerns about the increasing morbidity and mortality associated with chronic disease have sparked interest in using population-based administrative health data to identify and investigate cases of chronic disease. These data have been used to describe demographic, socioeconomic,

Data Data Everywhere: Access and Accountability? ed. C.M. Flood. Montreal and Kingston: Queen's Policy Studies Series, McGill-Queen's University Press. © 2011 The School of Policy Studies, Queen's University at Kingston. All rights reserved.

and temporal variations in estimates of chronic disease prevalence and incidence, detect geographic clusters of disease cases, and compare the health service use and costs of chronic disease cases with those of healthy controls. All of these data are critical for formulating public health policy on chronic disease prevention and treatment, and for evaluating the effectiveness of population-based health promotion and disease management strategies.[1]

Using administrative data for chronic disease surveillance has several advantages: (a) administrative data are population-based and are therefore unlikely to miss or underrepresent important subgroups within the population, (b) the data are relatively inexpensive to process, (c) the data are collected on a routine basis, and (d) most jurisdictions possess multiple years of administrative health datasets, which facilitates the conduct of longitudinal studies.

Health survey and clinical registry data have also been used to identify and investigate cases of chronic disease, but these data sources have some limitations. For example, while disease-specific clinical registries can usually provide accurate estimates of disease prevalence and incidence, registries are expensive and time consuming to establish and maintain. Moreover, registries that are specific to particular geographic areas, clinical groups, or health-care facilities do not provide estimates of disease prevalence or incidence that can be generalized to the larger population. Surveys suffer from problems of self-report bias, and the results of longitudinal surveys are sensitive to respondent attrition, which can result in inaccurate estimates of prevalence and incidence. As well, health surveys are not always conducted on a regular basis, which may limit their usefulness for monitoring trends. Some of these limitations can be overcome by using administrative data to identify and investigate cases of chronic disease.

Many different chronic diseases have been studied using administrative health data, including diabetes, hypertension, arthritis, osteoporosis, and gastrointestinal conditions such as inflammatory bowel disease.[2] In Canada, some investigations of chronic disease using administrative data have been led at the national level. For example, the National Diabetes Surveillance System (NDSS) provides one model for using administrative data from provinces and territories to provide information about the population burden of diabetes.[3] Other investigations have been initiated at provincial and regional levels. In Manitoba, the Ministry of Health has shown a high level of interest in investigations about methods to ascertain cases of chronic disease. In 2006, Lix et al. completed an extensive report on this topic that investigated the validity of multiple case ascertainment definitions for several different chronic diseases.[4] Manitoba has a long history of conducting research about methods for studying chronic disease using administrative data.[5] This research has contributed to the development of the public health system in Manitoba.

Underpinning the many developments surrounding the use of administrative health data for studying chronic disease is the recognition that there are technical issues as well as privacy and confidentiality issues that must be addressed. This chapter reviews these issues as they apply to the following topics: (a) linking databases, (b) constructing case ascertainment algorithms, (c) assessing data quality, and (d) comparing case ascertainment over time and across jurisdictions. Examples based on recent research from Manitoba are used to illustrate some of the challenges that have emerged. The chapter concludes with specific recommendations to address these challenges.

DATABASE LINKAGE

In some studies, individual administrative datasets have been used to ascertain cases of chronic disease. For example, hospital discharge data are widely used for case ascertainment because they are available in most countries and because they include accurate diagnosis data.[6] Cricelli et al. investigated the utility of pharmaceutical data for identifying cases of 31 chronic diseases, including Alzheimer's disease, cardiovascular disease, and osteoporosis and used the data to produce national estimates of disease prevalence for Italy.[7]

Most studies, however, recognize that accurate case ascertainment requires the use of multiple, linked administrative datasets. Hospital discharge data, while containing accurate diagnostic information, have limited value on their own because hospitalization is an infrequent event; only the most advanced forms of disease are likely to result in a hospital stay. While hospital discharge data have been the sole source of stroke case ascertainment in a number of studies,[8] a recent paper by Moore et al. that focused on stroke case identification in hospital, physician, and pharmaceutical data has confirmed that substantial under-ascertainment may result from exclusive reliance on hospital discharge data.[9]

Medical services data are another common source for chronic disease case ascertainment because (a) individuals who are ill are highly likely to visit a doctor in order to manage their conditions and (b) most medical services datasets contain diagnostic information. Many jurisdictions maintain records of prescription drug dispensations under drug insurance plans, either for the entire population or a portion of the population (e.g., 65 years of age and older),[10] and these data have also been used to ascertain disease cases.[11] Other administrative sources that have been used for case ascertainment include laboratory test results, electronic medical records, and records of contacts with public health professionals such as public health nurses. All of these data sources have the potential to improve the accuracy of case identification.

There can be tension between the goals of accurately ascertaining cases of chronic disease and maintaining confidentiality and privacy of personal health information. On the one hand, linkage of databases is required to achieve the goal of accurate case ascertainment. On the other hand, as the number of linkages among administrative sources increases, so does the potential for individuals to be identified in the data, even when these data are stripped of personal identifiers as required under privacy legislation.

Most chronic disease case ascertainment research in Manitoba has been conducted within a privacy-conscious environment. To begin with, most of the research takes place within the secure physical environment of the Manitoba Centre for Health Policy (MCHP). The Population Health Research Data Repository housed at MCHP contains anonymized administrative health data (i.e., no names or addresses), and datasets are linked via an anonymized unique personal health identifier. Furthermore, all research conducted using the repository must receive approval from the University of Manitoba Health Research Ethics Board. The Manitoba Health Information Privacy Committee must also provide its approval before data can be accessed.

Data validation, a scientifically necessary step in the process of using administrative health data for chronic disease case ascertainment, is undertaken by anonymously linking administrative data to sources such as clinical records or chart review results. The linked data are used to derive estimates of sensitivity (i.e., ability to identify true disease cases in administrative data) and specificity (i.e., ability to avoid detecting false disease cases). Because administrative data were collected for purposes of health system management and provider payment and not for studies about chronic disease, data validity assessment is imperative.

However, concerns about confidentiality may also arise when linking administrative data to a validation source. Clinical registries are typically established to monitor disease treatment and management, not for research purposes. Consequently, consent for data linkage may not have been obtained from individuals who comprise a clinical registry. Data trustees may be reluctant to approve requests to link clinical registry data with administrative data, or linkage may not be allowed under current interpretations of privacy legislation. Even where data linkage is allowed, it may be subjected to a high level of scrutiny if consent has not been obtained.

As with all data linkage processes, a strict protocol must be followed if linkage is allowed, to ensure data confidentiality. Personal identifying information must be stripped from the validation data source prior to its linkage to administrative data, and this anonymized linkage must be conducted only within a secure physical environment.

CONSTRUCTING A CASE ASCERTAINMENT ALGORITHM

A case ascertainment algorithm is the set of rules used to identify disease cases from administrative data. The elements of an algorithm include the type of data source, number of years of administrative data, diagnostic/ pharmaceutical drug code(s), and number of contacts in administrative data records with the relevant code(s). Different algorithms have been used to identify cases of different types of disease. For example, Bernstein et al.[12] found that five or more diagnosis codes in medical claims over a two-year period were required to accurately identify individuals with Crohn's disease or ulcerative colitis in Manitoba's administrative data. Lix et al.[13] compared a number of different ascertainment algorithms for identifying cases of arthritis, asthma, heart disease, hypertension, and stroke and found that no single algorithm performed best for all chronic diseases. The NDSS relies on a validated case ascertainment algorithm of one or more hospital discharge records or two or more medical service claims in a two-year period to identify cases of diabetes.

Using multiple sources and years of administrative data may be necessary to construct accurate case ascertainment algorithms for some diseases, as the likelihood of detecting disease cases in any one dataset or over short periods of time may be low. For example, an individual with rheumatoid arthritis may not have regular contact with the health system and may not use prescription drugs to manage pain and inflammation. Such individuals will be difficult to identify in administrative data. For other diseases, such as hypertension, individuals may have consistent and sustained contact with the health system and may therefore appear in medical claims or pharmaceutical data on a regular basis. Accordingly, these individuals will be easier to identify in administrative data.

Diagnosis codes are the primary tool for ascertaining cases of chronic disease in hospital discharge and medical services data. The Ninth Revision of the International Classification of Diseases (ICD-9) was adopted in Canada in 1979. A second classification system, the ICD-9-Clinical Modification (ICD-9-CM), was also used in Canada prior to the adoption of the tenth revision (ICD-10-CA), which was introduced in a phased-in approach in hospital discharge data beginning in 2001. Medical services data, however, continue to use ICD-9 or ICD-9-CM codes. These changes in diagnosis classification systems are a challenge to the accurate ascertainment of chronic disease cases because results may not be comparable across these systems. Moreover, the ICD system has been criticized because it looks at disease from the perspective of systems of organisms and pathophysiology rather than from the perspective of prevention and treatment.[14] Medical services data and hospital data do not capture information about symptoms, which could be useful for ascertaining some types of chronic disease. For example, irritable bowel syndrome is one chronic condition that has no biological markers. Diagnosis is achieved only by the identification of a pattern of symptoms that is consistent with the occurrence of the condition.[15]

For the classification of prescription drugs, many Canada researchers have adopted the Anatomical Therapeutic Chemical (ATC) Classification System. Using pharmaceutical data to ascertain cases of chronic disease requires the identification of one or more ATC code(s) that correspond to the prescription drugs used in the treatment or management of a specific chronic disease. One limitation is that some prescription drugs have multiple indications. Consequently, it may not be possible to identify a single disease diagnosis associated with an ATC code. Moreover, in using pharmaceutical data for case ascertainment, one must evaluate whether disease indications and prescribing practices have changed over time in order to ensure validity of the results. For example, Guttman et al. proposed a case ascertainment algorithm for Parkinson's disease based on diagnosis codes in hospital, physician data, and pharmaceutical dispensations for Levodopa.[16] Guttman applied this case ascertainment algorithm to Ontario's administrative health data in a longitudinal study of disease prevalence for the period from 1993 to 1999. In Manitoba, however, attempts by the author and clinical collaborators to apply Guttman's methodology to more recent years of administrative data have resulted in inflated estimates of Parkinson's disease prevalence and incidence. Moreover, the magnitude of this inflation appears to be increasing over time. This is likely due, in part, to an increase in recent years in the prescribing of Levodopa for the management of restless leg syndrome, a condition characterized by an irresistible urge to move one's body parts (commonly the legs) to stop uncomfortable or odd sensations.[17]

In summary, while several technical challenges arise when constructing a case ascertainment algorithm, the process tends not to be affected by concerns about data privacy and confidentiality. This component of case ascertainment, however, depends heavily on working relationships between clinicians and methodologists in order to identify relevant data sources and diagnosis/prescription drug codes to detect disease cases in administrative data. Detailed documentation from data providers is also needed to ensure that the case ascertainment algorithm reflects any changes in the coding classification system. Finally, all elements of the algorithms must be carefully documented by the investigator; this includes inclusion and exclusion criteria and the rationale for the choice of algorithm elements. Such documentation is essential to maintain comparability of case ascertainment results within or across jurisdictions.

ASSESSING DATA QUALITY

The quality of the administrative data can significantly impact the ability to accurately identify and investigate cases of chronic disease. Quality is a broad concept that is measured by indicators of (a) completeness or comprehensiveness (i.e., Are any records missing or are any parts of the population not included?), (b) reliability (i.e., Are the data reproducible?), and (c) temporal consistency (i.e., Are the data elements standardized over time?).[18] Concerns about the quality of administrative data abound. For example, completeness of physician data has been shown to vary with the method of provider payment. An Ontario report found that reduced incentives for salaried physicians to shadow bill have resulted in gaps in that province's administrative data.[19] Completeness of physician data has also been questioned in Manitoba as a result of the introduction of alternate payment plans.[20] Inaccuracies in the diagnoses recorded in medical services data have also been documented using Quebec data.[21]

Quality of administrative data has primarily been viewed from a scientific perspective. Poor-quality administrative data can result in biased estimates of disease prevalence and incidence, erroneous conclusions about health-care utilization and costs for disease cases, and misclassification of disease cases and non-cases.[22] The magnitude of misclassification varies across diseases. For example, Lix et al. found evidence of substantial misclassification of osteoporosis cases in administrative data.[23] Specifically, the diagnosis of osteoporosis is likely to be underreported in administrative data, resulting in much lower estimates of disease burden than have been reported using primary data. Data quality can also be viewed from the perspective of efficiency in resource utilization.[24] Large amounts of time and energy may be spent collecting documentation about changes in the form and content of administrative datasets over time, checking for gaps in the data, and evaluating the accuracy of individual fields in datasets.

A number of statistical tools are available to evaluate data quality and to address deficiencies.[25] Data visualization techniques, including frequency distributions and bivariate plots of the data, are useful for identifying gaps in the data or potential errors in diagnoses.[26] Lix et al. proposed the use of statistical and machine-learning models, such as neural networks and classification and regression trees, to account for potential misclassification of osteoporosis cases in administrative data.[27] These models use multiple pieces of information in administrative data, including demographic, socioeconomic, diagnosis, and prescription drug codes to improve the sensitivity and specificity of case ascertainment algorithms. Missing data models have also been proposed to address problems of incomplete reporting of diagnoses in administrative data.[28]

One concern that arises when identifying chronic disease cases from administrative data is the quality of the data source(s) used in the validation process. Ideally, a gold standard exists, that is, a data source that can provide unbiased information about disease diagnosis. Medical charts or diagnostic tests are often accepted as the gold standard. However, these sources may contain errors. For example, while bone mineral density test results are recognized by the World Health Organization as the gold standard for the diagnosis of osteoporosis, test results may not be error-free. Several factors affect test accuracy, including failure to follow the manufacturer's protocol for machine operation, position of the body during the scan, and physical characteristics of the body. Errors in the validation data source can result in erroneous conclusions about the "best" case ascertainment algorithm.

Another concern is that the validation data source may miss select segments of the population, and may therefore not produce estimates of sensitivity and specificity that can be generalized to the entire population. While bone mineral density testing is not limited to specific groups within the Manitoba population, males who are referred for bone mineral density tests are unlikely to be representative of the male population in Manitoba. Accordingly, a biased assessment of the sensitivity and specificity of an osteoporosis case ascertainment algorithm for males will result from using these testing data to validate administrative data.

The need for further investigations into administrative data quality and development of methods to assess quality is highlighted by a recent study that found only 6 percent of published studies that used Manitoba and Saskatchewan administrative data reported results of assessments of validity and reliability of these data.[29] This is a surprising finding given the widespread concerns about the quality of administrative data.

In summary, poor data quality represents a challenge to the accurate identification of disease cases in administrative data. Again, these issues are largely technical in nature and tend not to have implications for maintaining the security and confidentiality of administrative data.

COMPARING CASE ASCERTAINMENT OVER TIME AND ACROSS JURISDICTIONS

There is significant interest in using administrative data in longitudinal studies about chronic disease. Such studies can provide evidence about the effectiveness of population-based treatment and intervention strategies, and assist in establishing new priorities. Many of the challenges that arise in the identification and investigation of cases of chronic disease over time are technical in nature. These include changes in coding classification systems, dates of availability of administrative data sources, and changes in data collection systems. For example, in Manitoba pharmaceutical data for case ascertainment are captured from the Drug Program Information Network (DPIN), an electronic, online, point-of-sale prescription drug database connecting all retail pharmacies in the province to a central database. Because the DPIN system was not initiated until 1995, it is not possible to define a case ascertainment algorithm based on pharmaceutical data prior to this date. This can result in discrepancies in the number of identified cases before and after the start of DPIN. The introduction of, or changes to, alternative payment programs for physicians may also have an impact on case ascertainment from medical service claims.

A few projects have examined the feasibility of developing national chronic disease surveillance systems that combine administrative data from multiple provinces and territories. For example, the Public Health Agency of Canada's NDSS provides one model for national surveillance that is based on the collection of aggregate data. Provinces extract their administrative data using a common case ascertainment algorithm and then summarize these data. The data summaries are compiled in a central location, further summarized, and then distributed. An alternate model involves compiling each jurisdiction's anonymized person-level administrative data in a central location and employing a single analyst/analytic team to summarize the data and disseminate the analysis results. There are multiple privacy and confidentiality issues associated with the latter model. Provinces and territories may be reluctant to transfer their administrative data to an out-of-province location for analysis. Indeed, under some interpretations of privacy legislation, this type of transfer may not be allowed. However, the advantage of this model is that it minimizes the possibility that differences in cross-jurisdictional results are due to differences in the analysts' approach to the data. The Hypertension Outcomes and Surveillance Team (HOST), which is composed of health services and population health researchers from across Canada, is pursuing the latter model to investigate trends in hypertension incidence, prevalence, and health outcomes. HOST members have adopted a case ascertainment algorithm based on diagnoses for hypertension in one or more hospital discharge records or two or more medical service claims in three years of data. Several provinces have provided data for this study, but the process of finalizing data-sharing agreements and ensuring the security of the physical environment in which the data will be housed may slow the process of data acquisition.

In summary, while cross-jurisdictional studies of chronic disease can provide valuable information, significant time and energy must be invested in acquiring and analyzing data from multiple sources. As well, because of differences in data collection systems across jurisdictions and limited ability to conduct validation studies that use a common national validation data source, it may be difficult to draw accurate conclusions about differences in chronic disease prevalence, incidence, and outcomes across jurisdictions.

CONCLUSIONS AND RECOMMENDATIONS

There is little doubt that administrative data are an important resource for chronic disease research. Many important studies from across Canada have been conducted about chronic disease prevalence and incidence, health outcomes, and health-care utilization and costs while operating in a privacy-conscious environment. The challenges that exist in acquiring and using administrative health data to accurately identify and investigate cases of chronic disease can be addressed in a number of ways.

First, to ensure ongoing access to administrative health data, it is important to maintain dialogue with data trustees/providers. Increased emphasis on evidence-informed decision-making means that data trustees are often keenly interested in the methods and results of case ascertainment studies. By engaging in knowledge transfer sessions and communicating the health system benefits to be achieved by extracting knowledge from administrative data, the process of data access may be facilitated for future studies.

Furthermore, strict protocols must be established to ensure that administrative data are housed in a secure physical environment and confidentiality of anonymized data is not compromised. Security breaches could result in restricted data access or complete cessation of data access.

Collaborating with the developers of new or redesigned administrative data systems can help to facilitate access to data for chronic disease case ascertainment studies. In Manitoba, provincial and regional planners have been engaged in a process to redesign the province's public health statistics system, which records patient contacts with public health personnel. These data may be useful for studying health service use and costs associated with chronic disease.

Careful attention to data documentation is essential to address concerns about data quality as well as to ensure ongoing access to data. Researchers should become familiar with the environment in which administrative data are collected, including any legislation that governs the collection process, the overall program objectives, and the frequency and timeliness of data collection. While data collected over multiple years provide a rich resource for monitoring trends, longitudinal data are particularly difficult to include in case ascertainment studies, because (for example) individuals may have more than one anonymized personal health identifier over time, or the same identifier may be assigned to more than one individual. Careful documentation and correction of these anomalies is important to ensure a high level of data quality.

Further research on statistical methods for case ascertainment should result in increased sensitivity and specificity of administrative data. The growing body of research about methods to address problems of misclassification of disease cases is currently being applied in chronic case ascertainment studies with promising results.[30]

Finally, because administrative data systems may change over time, it is important to conduct regular assessments of data validity. Sensitivity and specificity of case ascertainment algorithms may change over time as a result of changes in assignment of diagnoses or prescribing patterns. This may require modifications to the case ascertainment algorithm to ensure consistency and validity in the identification of disease cases.

NOTES

1. S.B. Thacker, D.F. Stroup, and R.B. Rothenberg, "Public Health Surveillance for Chronic Conditions: A Scientific Basis for Decisions," *Statistics in Medicine* 14, no. 5-7 (1995): 629-41.
2. J.E. Hux, V. Flintoft, F. Ivis, and A. Bica, "Diabetes in Ontario: Determination of Prevalence and Incidence Using a Validated Administrative Data Algorithm," *Diabetes Care* 25, no. 3 (2002): 512-16. See also G. Maskarinec, "Diabetes in Hawaii: Estimating Prevalence from Insurance Claims Data," *American Journal of Public Health* 87, no. 10 (1997): 1717-20; T.K. Young, N.P. Roos, and K.M. Hammerstrand, "Estimated Burden of Diabetes-Mellitus in Manitoba according to Health-Insurance Claims – A Pilot Study," *Canadian Medical Association Journal* 144, no. 3 (1991): 318-24; J.F. Blanchard, S. Ludwig, A. Wajda, H. Dean, K. Anderson, O. Kendall, and N. Depew, "Incidence and Prevalence of Diabetes in Manitoba, 1986–1991," *Diabetes Care* 19, no. 8 (1996): 807-11; N. Muhajarine, C. Mustard, L.L. Roos, T.K. Young, and D.E. Gelskey, "Comparison of Survey and Physician Claims Data for Detecting Hypertension," *Journal of Clinical Epidemiology* 50, no. 6 (1997): 711-18; C.N. Bernstein, J.F. Blanchard, P. Rawsthorne, and A. Wajda, "Epidemiology of Crohn's Disease and Ulcerative Colitis in a Central Canadian Province: A Population-Based Study," *American Journal of Epidemiology* 149, no. 10 (1999): 916-24; L.R. Harrold, R.A. Yood, S.E. Andrade, J.I. Reed, J. Cernieux, W. Straus, M. Weeks, B. Lewis, and J.H. Gurwitz, "Evaluating the Predictive Value of Osteoarthritis Diagnoses in an Administrative Database," *Arthritis and Rheumatism* 43, no. 8 (2000): 1881-85; and L.M. Lix, M.S. Yogendran, W.D. Leslie, S.Y. Shaw, R. Baumgartner, C. Bowman, C. Metge, A. Gumel, J. Hux, and R.C. James, "Using Multiple Data Features Improved the Validity of Osteoporosis Case Ascertainment from Administrative Databases," *Journal of Clinical Epidemiology* 61, no. 12 (2008): 1250-60.
3. Health Canada and Health Surveillance Coordination Division, *Chronic Disease Surveillance in Canada: A Backgound Paper* (Ottawa: Centre for Surveillance Coordination Population and Public Health Branch, 2007).
4. L.M. Lix, M. Yogendran, C. Burchill, C. Metge, N. McKeen, D. Moore, and R. Bond, *Defining and Validating Chronic Diseases: An Administrative Data Approach* (Winnipeg: Manitoba Centre for Health Policy, University of Manitoba, 2006).
5. Young, Roos, and Hammerstrand, "Estimated Burden of Diabetes-Mellitus in Manitoba," see note 2. See also J. R. Robinson, T.K. Young, L.L. Roos, and D.E. Gelskey, "Estimating the Burden of Disease: Comparing Administrative Data and Self-Reports," *Medical Care* 35, no. 9 (1997): 932-47.
6. Maskarinec, "Diabetes in Hawaii," see note 2.
7. C. Cricelli, G. Mazzaglia, F. Samani, M. Marchi, A. Sabatini, R. Nardi, G. Ventriglia, and A.P. Caputi, "Prevalence Estimates for Chronic Diseases

in Italy: Exploring the Differences between Self-Report and Primary Care Databases," *Journal of Public Health Medicine* 25, no. 3 (2003): 254-57.

8.   D.L. Tirschwell and W.T. Longstreth, "Validating Administrative Data in Stroke Research," *Stroke* 33 (2002): 2465-70. See also A. Wigertz and R. Westerling, "Measures of Prevalence: Which Healthcare Registers Are Applicable?" *Scandinavian Journal of Public Health* 29, no. 1 (2001): 55-62.

9.   D.A. Moore, L.M. Lix, M. Yogendran, P. Martens, and A. Tomayo, "Stroke Case Ascertainment in Administrative Data," *Chronic Disease Canada* 29, no. 1 (2008): 22-30.

10.   E. Miller, B. Blatman, and T.R. Einarson, "A Survey of Population-Based Drug Databases in Canada," *Canadian Medical Association Journal* 154 (1996): 1855-64.

11.   M. Guttman, P.M. Slaughter, M.E. Theriault, D.P. DeBoer, and C.D. Naylor, "Burden of Parkinsonism: A Population-Based Study," *Movement Disorders* 18, no. 3 (2003): 313-19. See also W.M. Vollmer, E.A. O'Connor, M. Heumann, E.A. Frazier, J. Breen, J. Villnave, and A.S. Buist, "Searching Multiple Clinical Information Systems for Longer Time Periods Found More Prevalent Cases of Asthma," *Journal of Clinical Epidemiology* 57, no. 4 (2004): 392-97.

12.   Bernstein et al., "Epidemiology of Crohn's Disease," see note 2.

13.   Lix et al., *Defining and Validating Chronic Diseases*, see note 4.

14.   Thacker, Stroup, and Rothenberg, "Public Health Surveillance for Chronic Conditions," see note 1.

15.   A.P. Legoretta, J.-F. Ricci, M. Markowitz, and P. Jhingran, "Patients Diagnosed with Irritable Bowel Syndrome: Medical Record Validation of a Claims-Based Identification Algorithm," *Disease Management and Health Outcomes* 10 (2002): 715-22.

16.   Guttman et al., "Burden of Parkinsonism," see note 11. See also Vollmer et al., "Searching Multiple Clinical Information Systems," see note 11.

17.   C.F. Conti, M.M. de Oliveira, R.G. Andriolo, H. Saconato, A.N. Atallah, J.S. Valbuza, L.B.C. de Carvalho, and G.F. Prado, "Levodopa for Idiopathic Restless Legs Syndrome: Evidence-Based Review," *Movement Disorders* 22, no. 13 (2008): 1943-51.

18.   K. Iron and D.G. Manuel, *Quality Assessment of Administrative Data (QuAAD): An Opportunity for Enhancing Ontario's Health Data* (Toronto: Institute for Clinical Evaluative Sciences, 2007).

19.   Institute for Clinical Evaluative Sciences, *Improving Health Care Data in Ontario* (Toronto: Institute for Clinical Evaluative Sciences, 2005).

20.   L.L. Roos, S. Gupta, R.A. Soodeen, and L. Jebamani, "Data Quality in an Information-Rich Environment: Canada as an Example," *Canadian Journal of Aging* 24, Suppl. 1 (2005): 153-70.

21.   M. Wilchesky, R.M. Tamblyn, and A. Huang, "Validation of Diagnostic Codes within Medical Services Claims," *Journal of Clinical Epidemiology* 57, no. 2 (2004): 131-41.

22.   H. Brenner and O. Gefeller, "Use of the Positive Predictive Value to Correct for Disease Misclassification in Epidemiologic Studies," *American Journal of Epidemiology* 138 (1993): 1007-15.

23.   Lix et al., "Using Multiple Data Features," see note 2.

24.   A.F. Karr, A.P. Sanil, and D.L. Banks, "Data Quality: A Statistical Perspective," *Statistical Methodology* 3 (2006): 137-73.

25. H. Zheng, R. Yucel, J.Z. Ayanian, and A.M. Zaslavsky, "Profiling Providers on Use of Adjuvant Chemotherapy by Combining Cancer Registry and Medical Record Data," *Medical Care* 44, no. 2 (2004): 1-7. See also M. Ladouceur, E. Rahme, C.A. Pineau, and L. Joseph, "Robustness of Prevalence Estimates Derived from Misclassified Data from Administrative Databases," *Biometrics* 63, no. 1 (2007): 272-79.

26. Karr, Sanil, and Banks, "Data Quality," see note 24.

27. Lix et al., "Using Multiple Data Features," see note 2.

28. R.M. Yucel and A.M. Zaslavsky, "Imputation of Binary Treatment Variables with Measurement Error in Administrative Data," *Journal of the American Statistical Association* 100 (2005): 1123-32.

29. A.C. Tricco, B. Pham, and N.S. Rawson, "Manitoba and Saskatchewan Administrative Health Care Utilization Databases Are Used Differently to Answer Epidemiologic Research Questions," *Journal of Clinical Epidemiology* 61 (2008): 192-97.

30. Ladouceur et al., "Robustness of Prevalence Estimates," see note 25. See also R. J. Prosser, B.C. Carleton, and M.A. Smith, "Identifying Persons with Treatment Asthma Using Administrative Data via Latent Class Modelling," *Health Services Research* 43, no. 2 (2008): 733-54.

GAINING TRUST, ENSURING SECURITY: THE EVOLUTION OF AN ONTARIO HIV COHORT STUDY

DALE MCMURCHY, LAUREL CHALLACOMBE,
MEGAN EDMISTON, MARK FISHER, DAVID KERRY,
CAROL MAJOR, PEGGY MILLSON, SEAN B. ROURKE,
AND DARIEN TAYLOR

This chapter will review the issues related to the privacy and confidentiality of the health information of people living with HIV and the evolution of an Ontario HIV cohort study, highlighting the cohort study's governance, key accomplishments, and best practices, as well as the challenges it encountered during its evolution.

PRIVACY AND CONFIDENTIALITY FOR PEOPLE LIVING WITH HIV/AIDS

While privacy and confidentiality are pertinent to all patients, people living with HIV and AIDS often face systemic barriers in everyday life activities because of their positive status. As a result of unauthorized disclosure of their HIV status to third parties, some have been deprived of housing, lost their jobs, and had social relationships compromised.[1] People living with HIV/AIDS are unlikely to qualify for life, health, and mortgage insurance and may be restricted in travelling on the basis of

Data Data Everywhere: Access and Accountability? ed. C.M. Flood. Montreal and Kingston: Queen's Policy Studies Series, McGill-Queen's University Press. © 2011 The School of Policy Studies, Queen's University at Kingston. All rights reserved.

their HIV status. These insurance and travel policies have the effect of reinforcing prejudice and myths about HIV/AIDS. Concern about third-party disclosure without consent to employers, insurance companies, the government, friends, and relatives means individuals with HIV are wary and distrustful about disclosing details of their health and HIV status, even for research purposes.

To provide context for the privacy and confidentiality concerns of participants in the HIV Cohort Study, we interviewed insurance agents and managers of AIDS service organizations about insurance coverage and travel restrictions for people living with HIV/AIDS. Insurance companies oftentimes do not state their policies explicitly and publicly, but some industry sources were willing to disclose their policies anonymously. The information below about travel restrictions is available to the general public.

Life Insurance

Depending on health status, medication, habits, and lifestyle, applicants with HIV/AIDS might be eligible for life insurance, but their premiums could increase up to 400 percent. However, it appears that companies will not insure people with HIV/AIDS at any price. An agent from a prominent insurance company stated that someone living with HIV/AIDS seeking individual life insurance was "wasting time." While the agent first indicated he could get anybody insurance and it was "only a question of how much you'll pay," he later stated that life insurance was unavailable to someone with HIV. He advised, "Go to Timmy's and get a job. I don't care if you hate it—work there until you are eligible for benefits. The best case scenario is for you then to convert to individual coverage and not be required to make any personal health disclosures. You didn't hear this from me."[2] It is clear that once diagnosed or treated for HIV, individuals become categorically ineligible for individual life insurance and may only obtain coverage through group policies, which do not require health disclosure.

Health Insurance

The key to health insurance, according to insurance agents, is that "you can't need it." Like individual life insurance, health insurance applications require disclosure of HIV status. People living with HIV/AIDS are unlikely to be offered health insurance because insurers view expensive medications and treatment as a certainty.[3]

Those with HIV are also not able to get critical illness insurance coverage (which covers conditions like heart attack, stroke, and life-threatening cancer). By contrast, individuals with pre-existing heart and other chronic conditions are not categorically excluded, and there is a special price for smokers. Health insurance companies may send their own nurses to examine applicants.

Long-Term Disability Insurance

Long-term disability insurance is usually provided through employers as group insurance on a non-medical basis, which means the only requirement for eligibility is employment. Group long-term disability policies normally do not categorically exclude coverage of particular pre-existing conditions. These policies may, however, require that a certain period of time pass once the plan begins before they will pay out. This means the policy may initially disallow claims for pre-existing medical conditions.[4]

Mortgage Insurance

Mortgage insurance applications include health questions similar to other insurance applications, and HIV status disclosure is required. At a large provider company, both an agent and an underwriter stated up front that they "imagined" someone with HIV would be declined, which would be consistent with what another underwriter called the "general industry practice"[5] of declining coverage to people living with HIV / AIDS. By contrast, those with diabetes or a history of heart disease or cancer will not automatically be declined—the success of these applications will depend on the severity and specifics of the individual's condition. Like health insurers, mortgage insurers may require that a company nurse complete physical examinations of applicants, including taking blood samples.

Travel

The UNAIDS International Task Team on HIV-Related Travel Restrictions, established in 2008, reported that a minimum of 67 countries denied entry, stay, or residence to those with HIV / AIDS solely because of their seropositive status.[6] At that time, nine of these countries completely barred any entry to people living with HIV,[7] another five countries denied applications for entry for stays from 10 days up to 90 days,[8] and 30 countries deported foreign nationals if their HIV status was discovered.[9] The UNAIDS position is that these practices are discriminatory, contrary to human rights, not based on rational connections to public health or the spread of disease, and have a negative impact on and represent unjustified restriction of people living with HIV / AIDS.

Since 1987, an HIV positive status has been a ground for exclusion under the US *Immigration and Nationality Act*. Under this legislation, waivers are required on either an individual or a categorical basis for travel to the United States. In 2007, the Senate introduced Bill S. 2486, which would remove the provision from the *Immigration and Nationality Act* that prohibits individuals with HIV from travelling to the United States. The Obama administration repealed the ban in late 2009, and this came into effect in January 2010. Some other countries have followed suit.

THE HIV ONTARIO OBSERVATIONAL DATABASE (HOOD)

Gaining Trust

Despite the concerns about privacy and confidentiality discussed above, the Ontario HIV community, health-care providers, researchers, and Ministry of Health and Long-Term Care formed a partnership in the early 1990s to develop a cohort study of people living with HIV/AIDS. The study involved data extraction from medical charts and the potential for linking these data to administrative datasets (e.g., physician billing and hospital discharge databases) for research purposes. The cohort study was designed to collect clinical data retrospectively (to the date of the first HIV positive test result or first visit to the recruiting physician) and then prospectively (data collection every six months). There was also a one-time collection of sociodemographic and behavioural data at enrolment. The database was housed at Sunnybrook Health Sciences Centre in Toronto under the direction of Dr. Anita Rachlis, an infectious disease specialist who worked with two researchers, Dr. Greg Robinson and Dr. Peggy Millson, and an ethicist, Jim Lavery.

The HIV Ontario Observational Database (HOOD) was formed in response to a challenge from people living with HIV/AIDS. The initiative stemmed from community activists like James Thatcher of AIDS ACTION NOW! and others at the Ontario AIDS Network and the HIV/AIDS Legal Clinic of Ontario, who felt that important information on the treatment and progression of HIV was being lost. They challenged the provider and research community to pursue research that would improve the health care and outcomes of those living with HIV/AIDS, *and* respect the privacy of these individuals.

From the beginning, the cohort study had full partnership among all stakeholders, including people living with HIV/AIDS. The HOOD executive committee included representation from the community, government, HIV providers, and researchers. This cohort study was unique in the extent of community consultation and involvement in its conception, development, and evolution. Community input was ongoing and could be seen through collaborative research, majority community membership on the governance committee, and community input on research priorities and projects.

The initiation of the cohort database entailed extensive community consultation and involvement, offering the HIV community a chance to take ownership of the process. Key to this process was gaining people's trust and support. In the first two to three years, the focus was on laying the foundation and achieving buy-in. The community is described by one researcher present at the project's conception as having been "positive, but skeptical" at the initial meetings. People wanted to know what information would be used and how, who would benefit, and whether participation might improve their access to clinical trials. Their greatest concern was that a security breach could release confidential information about their HIV and health status to insurance companies, employers, or government. The cohort study was funded by the Positive Action Fund, created with contributions from the AIDS Bureau at the Ministry of Health and Long-Term Care and from Burroughs Wellcome (the company donated 25 percent of its provincial profits from the HIV drug zidovudine or AZT). The community also wanted assurances about the nature of the "arms-length" involvement from these funders.

The onus was on the researchers to allay the community's concerns about security and confidentiality, convey the benefits of research, and develop a system with which both groups would be comfortable. The researchers and community members had to determine where their interests overlapped and strike a mutually agreeable balance between privacy and confidentiality, and the requirements for quality research. Given that many community members were not researchers and did not have the technical knowledge related to consent and database security procedures, additional time and effort was needed to describe and build confidence in these areas. According to those present at the time, the tipping point may have been the "infectious excitement" for the project by one of the physician/research leaders who had HIV and was able to instill "faith" in others who were more skeptical.

The impacts of this level of community involvement were (a) increased community literacy on privacy and confidentiality issues, (b) stakeholder choice of a model that included a majority community representation on the executive committee, and (c) the institution of a policy of accountability to the community about data collection and storage and the production of research, including community representation on the research review committee. The extensive consultative process delayed the initial start-up of the cohort database, but it enhanced buy-in and later enrolment.

Physicians were recognized as the gateway to patients and their data, as providers were the ones who would need to gain the trust of patients and encourage them to consent to participation. Thus, it was necessary to reach out and involve the majority of physicians who provided health-care services to people living with HIV/AIDS to ensure their patients' buy-in and participation. As a result, several physicians participated in the development and governance of the database, and they continue to be extensively involved.

Another important partner in the development of the database was the provincial government. Key government officials, like Jay Browne and Frank McGee, helped to secure funding and overcome obstacles. Christine Henderson, a lawyer for the Ministry of Health and Long-Term Care, worked diligently on the regulation, and later legislation, that would enable the collection of participants' OHIP (Ontario Health Insurance Plan) numbers.

HIV Ontario Observational Database (HOOD) Privacy Measures

The HOOD database was a non-nominal database that contained limited personal and extensive medical information on people living with HIV/AIDS in Ontario. Enrolment into the database was strictly voluntary and conducted primarily through specialty care clinics and primary care physicians in the province.

The enrolment and consent processes were initiated and administered by the staff or physicians at clinical sites. Data were extracted from the medical charts of consenting patients and housed in the database using unique, coded identifiers. The consent and data collection processes entailed several steps. Patient consent to be included in the cohort was sought and obtained at the point of care. Patients also had the option to consent to the provision of their health card number (to facilitate linkages with external databases), to be contacted for the purposes of collecting additional information not routinely collected in the cohort database, and to be included in a trials access registry. Once they consented, participants could opt out at any time and have their data removed completely from the database.

Patients who agreed to participate signed a consent form, witnessed by their provider, that remained at the clinic. A second patient "assurance of consent" form, which held no personally identifying information, was completed at the physician's office and forwarded to the cohort study to provide documentation of consent.

Patients also completed an enrolment form that included their date of birth, initials, and mothers' maiden initials. As well, enrollees completed a background information form that included basic demographic information such as gender, education level, country of origin and race, and some additional information, such as their date of diagnosis and use of complementary therapies. (The variables collected at enrolment can be found in Appendix A.)

Manual chart extraction was conducted by trained data extractors across the province. Baseline data extraction from charts was extensive and included relevant background and medical data. Follow-up clinical data extraction occurred every six months thereafter. (See Appendix B for data elements collected.)

The information collected on the enrolment form was used to create a patient identifier. As well, a unique numeric identifier was randomly generated for each patient in the database and was the main patient relational variable used in the database and by researchers. This ensured that no identifying information about the participant was shared with researchers accessing the dataset.

A Research Example

Several research studies were undertaken under the auspices of the cohort study. One study, funded by Health Canada, looked at the utilization and cost of health services and prescription medications in Ontario. Using the HIV cohort as a sampling frame, the study developed health service utilization and cost profiles of those living with HIV based on their demographic and socioeconomic characteristics, risk factors, clinical markers, and disease stage by linking their clinical data with other data sources.

This cross-sectional examination of the economic costs of HIV in Ontario was conducted using a number of study components, including primary and secondary data. Data were obtained from the HIV Ontario Observational Database, a patient survey, the Ontario Drug Distribution and Monitoring Database, the Ontario Health Insurance Plan, three hospital sites, and two HIV specialty clinics. The extent of this data triangulation is rare in Canada, and the ability to link these data allowed for a more comprehensive and robust analysis. The linked data sources used are illustrated in Figure 1.

Rates of service use and resource consumption were estimated using the data sources shown in Figure 1. There was often more than one data source for the various services and resources used, allowing for the internal validation of results. The use of multiple data sources also allowed for the determination of utilization and costs that could not be determined by any one source. For example, as a result of the triangulation of the data, the study was able to determine the number and proportion of people on antiretroviral therapy, the number and combination of drugs they were taking, and the total and per patient cost of therapy, disaggregated into costs covered by government, insurance companies, and out-of-pocket expenditure. Table 1 shows the variables for which utilization rates and costs were calculated and the multiple data sources.

FIGURE 1
Information for Costing HIV

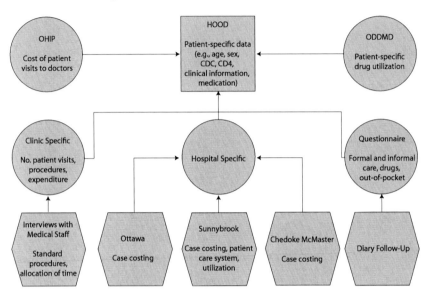

Note: OHIP = Ontario Health Insurance Plan. HOOD = HIV Ontario Observational Database. ODDMD = Ontario Drug Distribution and Monitoring Database. CDC = CDC categorization of disease stage. CD4 = T4-cell counts.

Source: D. McMurchy, M. Millson, K. Leeb, R.W. Palmer, G. Robinson, A. Rachlis, and R. Wall, "Costing HIV Using an Observational Database" (paper presented at the 12th World AIDS Conference, Geneva, Switzerland, 28 June–3 July 1998).

THE ONTARIO HIV TREATMENT NETWORK (OHTN)

Introducing New Technology

In 1998, the Ontario HIV Treatment Network (OHTN) was created by the Ontario Ministry of Health and Long-Term Care. The HIV Ontario Observational Database was moved from Sunnybrook Health Sciences Centre to the OHTN in Toronto and became part of the HIV Information Infrastructure Project. The vision of the project was to develop and implement electronic medical records (or clinical management systems) in all participating HIV physicians' offices in order to improve the quality of care to people living with HIV and AIDS *and* to improve the efficiency of data gathering for research purposes through electronic data extraction. The project was to provide all HIV clinics participating in the cohort study with servers, work stations, other hardware, clinical management software and licenses, and technical support. The use of a completely electronic system would remove the necessity for manual chart extraction, since the

TABLE 1
Linked Data Sources for Service Use and Resource Consumption

Data Source	Inpatient Stays	Outpatient Visits	Drugs	Physician Encounters	Nursing Activities	Tests	Procedures	Diagnoses	Informal Care	Complementary Remedies
HOOD	X					X		X		X
OHIP		X		X		X	X			
Patient survey	X	X	X	X		X	X		X	X
Ontario Drug Distribution and Monitoring Database			X							
Hospitals	X				X	X	X	X		
HIV clinics		X		X	X	X	X			
Ontario Public Health Laboratory						X				

Note: HOOD = HIV Ontario Observational Database. OHIP = Ontario Health Insurance Plan.

Source: D. McMurchy, M. Millson, K. Leeb, R.W. Palmer, G. Robinson, A. Rachlis, and R. Wall, "Costing HIV Using an Observational Database" (paper presented at the 12th World AIDS Conference, Geneva, Switzerland, 28 June–3 July 1998).

medical data could be electronically transferred to the cohort database. The previous cohort data were to be archived into the new system so that the historical data would not be lost.

However, the project ran into a number of implementation challenges. Overall, it was difficult to get buy-in from physicians, as migrating from paper to electronic patient records was a new concept for many at that time. Some physicians were not interested in or comfortable with adopting computerized systems, some already had an electronic system, and others were concerned about security and patient privacy. Changing the attitudes of physicians to accept electronic charting was difficult, and so few HIV clinics implemented the system initially chosen for the project. In hospital settings, restrictions on the software that could be used within the institution and integration with hospital information systems presented obstacles to implementation. Other initiatives underway both federally (Canada Health Infoway) and provincially (Ontario MD) trying to implement analogous systems at the time met with similar challenges.

As with many such efforts to develop comprehensive electronic clinical management systems and convert physicians' offices to support electronic health records, the system encountered technical challenges at start-up. The system had not been deployed in clinics as large as the beta site and required redesign to reflect particular aspects of the delivery of HIV care. Moreover, the complexity of including unstandardized electronic data from a variety of sources hindered the development of an interoperable system.

The challenges experienced were even greater given that the system was to be designed to support *both* patient management and research. For example, some data in the clinical management system were contained in text or memo fields and therefore could not be transmitted to the cohort database for fear of disclosing identifying data. Even if it were transferred, the data would not be useful for research purposes in free text form. Moreover, the nature of the structure and coding in the system made integration with other data challenging.

The system initially chosen for the project went through the challenges associated with early adoption and subsequently (as is sometimes the case) was surpassed by other electronic systems. Consequently, some sites chose to adopt other clinical management systems instead, while others decided against moving forward at that time.

Ultimately, in spite of its potential, the project went too long without concrete results in terms of research outputs and without exploration of other options. Several lessons were learned:

- such initiatives need constant reappraisal of goals and objectives;
- achieving provider buy-in can be difficult, and the focus should be on those who have capacity and are engaged;

- it is difficult not to take past investments into account; and
- the introduction of electronic medical records in the health sector can entail unanticipated technical challenges.

The OHTN now finances two clinical management systems at selected and engaged clinics, and more clinics are interested in implementing these systems. The systems' functionality includes electronic laboratory results, drug interaction alerts, and patient fact sheets. Three sites that have implemented an electronic clinical management system provide their patient data to the database electronically. The HOOD data have been merged with data extracted from the sites with clinical management systems into the OHTN cohort study. Manual data collection by chart extractors has recommenced at other participating sites to ensure data from original cohort participants are up-to-date. Recent advances in manual data collection include the development of a platform for data collection directly onto laptops for secure, electronic transfer to the database, removing the need for manual entry and reducing the chance of error.

Maintaining Trust and Stakeholder Involvement

With the transition to the Ontario HIV Treatment Network in 1998 and the adoption of new technologies, significant efforts were made to consult with and inform the community about the changes and to gain its support. Several focus groups, consultations, and meetings were conducted with community members prior to the transition. There was somewhat more skepticism and mistrust about the HIV Information Infrastructure Project than the HIV Ontario Observational Database (HOOD) among HIV community members, even though the staff working with the cohort study had done much to engender trust in the preceding years. The community was initially wary about moving to a more technologically sophisticated system—a system that was more virtual, where data were transmitted electronically rather than on paper (and therefore no longer on a closed network), and where digital security, which is harder to grasp, was substituted for physical security. This apprehension may have reflected a growing concern on the part of the public and patients about the security of electronically housed personal information in general, as well as limited understanding of the technology.

Presentations were made to the community by the data manager and a security specialist about the new technology, but key to gaining the community's support was the input from a champion from within the community who understood the technology, could explain it in plain language, and vouch for its security. Overall, this process led to a heightened community awareness of issues related to technology, privacy, and methods used to prevent the breach of confidentiality during data linking and electronic transfer. While this process was time consuming, community representatives on the governance committee endeavoured to understand the issues at hand, and gained a heightened technical literacy and increased comfort level with the new technology that they could convey to others.

In the transition, the former governance committee migrated into a new advisory committee that continued to have representation from all stake-holders—HIV community members, researchers, health-care providers, and government officials—as well as members with expertise in ethics, HIV research, legal, and other areas. It was chaired by an HIV physician, Dr. Don Kilby, and had a majority representation by people living with HIV/AIDS. The shift to majority representation of people living with HIV/AIDS (rather than simply community representation) meant that the overall project was firmly under the control of the population being studied, which strengthened the level of trust. The mandate of the new governance committee included overseeing the development of the clinical management system and policies related to security, confidentiality, and management of the cohort data. The governance committee was also responsible for the cohort study research activities, including developing research priorities and approving research proposals.

In 2005, with a reduced focus on technology, the OHTN introduced four new subcommittees to advise on and shape a new direction: the Research Network Advisory Committee, the Community Network Advisory Committee, the Health-Care Provider Network Advisory Committee, and the OHTN Cohort Study Governance Committee (which assumed oversight of the cohort study). Those living with HIV maintained majority representation on the study's Governance Committee and are represented on all subcommittees.

These subcommittees provide advice in their respective areas of expertise to the OHTN Board of Directors. The Research Network Advisory Committee is made up of researchers from basic science, clinical science, epidemiology, socio-behavioural science, and community-based research, as well as community members. Its role is to provide advice on research priorities and investment. The Community Network Advisory Committee includes individuals working in research, advocacy, housing, and AIDS service organizations; several members are living with HIV. Drawing on its network of individuals and organizations, the committee advises the OHTN on issues facing those with HIV and identifies issues related to people who are disproportionately affected by HIV. The committee also advises on building research literacy in the community and promotes collaborative models between researchers and community agencies in order to improve public policy and clinical care through research, particularly research that focuses on social justice and the social determinants of health.

The Health-Care Provider Network Advisory Committee includes HIV-treating physicians, nurses, pharmacists, social workers, and people living with HIV/AIDS. Its role is to encourage students in the health-care professions to consider a career that includes HIV treatment and care; to support those treating HIV in the field through continuing education, accreditation, and practice aids; and to advocate for the needs of health-care providers and their patients. The committee's first initiative was to establish the Ontario Society of Physicians in HIV Care, which currently has 50 members. Based on recommendations from this committee, the OHTN also provides scholarships for health-care providers, supports residencies in HIV care, and promotes capacity-building initiatives for interdisciplinary education and health-care delivery.[10]

Improving Data Quality

Following the transition, the staff at the OHTN worked to update the database. Records on approximately 3,000 patients were migrated to the OHTN. One of the greatest accomplishments during this time was updating the data. With rapid expansion of the database in the late 1990s, the ability to extract data had exceeded available resources. Thus, at the beginning of 2000, there was little follow-up/prospective cohort data. With an aggressive push on data collection and processing, staff quadrupled the patient-years of data in the cohort by the spring of 2001.

The data platform and formats were updated to current technology and database platforms. The data were initially housed in DOS-based FoxPro, and their structure was more like a series of spreadsheets than a relational database. Moreover, data were not easily entered and could only be entered at one station. Over the course of a year and a half, the existing database was extensively redesigned. Data were cleaned and migrated to a Windows-based system. As well, additional critical variables—for example, all prescription medications (rather than HIV-related only), drug start and stop dates, and adverse clinical events—were improved and back-entered. Data were recoded in a manner to improve ease of queries and analysis. As well, international coding standards were introduced for prescription medications and adverse drug reactions. ICD-9 coding was also introduced, which improved the integrity of the database and enabled the potential for international comparative work. While some data quality issues remain, the data are much improved. Given that the cohort study mainly relies on manual data collection, vigilance is required to ensure data quality, completeness, accuracy, and consistency across sites.

One ongoing question regarding the cohort data is representativeness; as with other voluntary cohorts, there is a potential for bias. While the data are generally representative, some populations are underrepresented, including Canadians from endemic countries, women, people with un-stable housing, and intravenous drug users. There is also evidence that those who have been infected or have come to know their HIV status more recently, and those who are drug naïve, are underrepresented. As well, the overall cohort was found to have a somewhat better health status than the HIV positive population in Ontario generally, based on standard clinical markers.[11] A new recruitment push is currently underway to strategically target groups underrepresented in the cohort; 1,000 individuals were recruited over the course of a year.

Maintaining Privacy and Security

In response to significant changes in federal and provincial privacy legislation, the OHTN underwent an ethics review and revisioning process, and altered its policies and procedures. While to date the HIV Information Infrastructure Project has seen limited success in terms of uptake of clinical management systems that provide data to the cohort study, it has been very successful in setting high privacy and security standards for the database. The project helped in reforming procedures in adherence with the federal *Personal Information Protection and Electronic Documents Act (PIPEDA)*, enacted in 2000, and with Ontario's *Personal Health Information Protection Act 2004*. The project also helped to educate staff and the governance committee about security procedures, which increased the comfort and confidence of the community in the security of its data.

Internal data access and utilization procedures were changed. As well, the HIV cohort study's staff and researchers continue to be required to sign confidentiality agreements, and staff now undergo privacy awareness training. There is an official complaints and dispute resolution process in place should it ever be required. The cohort study has research ethics board (REB) approval for all participating sites, and the OHTN now has approval to conduct internal ethics reviews and approvals for submitted proposals.

A critical change has been the introduction of one-way encryption of patient identifiers (e.g., health care number, social insurance number, name, and date of birth) based on international standards. Thus, personally identifying information is now removed before data are transferred to the database, and patient identifiers such as health card numbers are not held on site as they are encrypted using a mathematical algorithm. As well, all data sent to the database are encrypted during transmission. Public-Key Infrastructure (PKI) technology is used.

Figure 2 was used by the OHTN to communicate the data collection, transfer, and storage processes to cohort participants and the public.

The OHTN is also undergoing a process of re-consent for all former HIV Ontario Observational Database enrollees. All enrollees will be approached to reaffirm their agreement to be in the cohort study or, if they wish, to have their data permanently removed. After re-consenting, they will no longer be able to have their retrospective data removed if they later decide to opt out of the study; rather, their data will simply cease to be collected going forward.

FIGURE 2
The OHTN's Use of Anonymization and Encryption

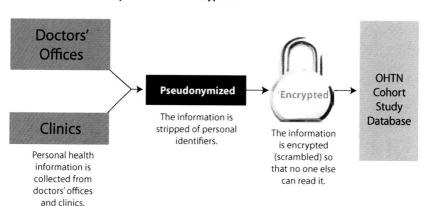

Source: Ontario HIV Treatment Network, *The Thatcher Report* (newsletter, Winter 2006), http://www.googlesyndicatedsearch.com/u/ohtn?q=Thatcher+Report&sa=Go.

With the new process, participation is contingent on the use of the patient's health card number and other personal information to create an encrypted identifier. As such, it is now possible to link all participants' data to administrative databases—like the Ontario Health Insurance Plan (OHIP) or the discharge abstract database (DAD)—based on their health card numbers. Linkage entails the use of an algorithm within the administrative database to recreate the one-way encryption code in memory and then extract and link the administrative data with the cohort data using system-generated generic identifiers.

The cohort database is linked regularly with the Ontario Public Health Laboratory to obtain enrollees' data on viral load, as well as documented CD4 cells counts and antiretroviral use. If available, laboratory genotype testing data, including viral clades and resistance patterns, are also linked to participants' files. Data linkage has also been beta tested with the Institute for Clinical Evaluative Sciences, which houses OHIP data. All data linkage agreements are consistent with the provisions of the *Personal Health Information Protection Act, 2004*.

Related to data transfer and linkage, community representatives insisted that the technical details be presented and discussed in a way that they could understand so that they could make informed decisions on behalf of their constituents and not simply rubber stamp proposals. For example, there were extensive discussions before Virtual Private Network (VPN) and electronic data transfer technology were approved to ensure that community members understood and were confident in the new technology. Community representatives also provided extensive input on the revised consent form.

While this level of community representation in the governance of a research database may require additional time and effort to develop policy and implement change, this participation has ensured that the HIV community's interests are served. People living with HIV / AIDS who sit on committees are expected to communicate with the community, and their majority vote on the governance committee is meant to provide cohort participants with confidence that they are effectively represented and that their confidential health information is secure.

Moving Forward with Research

Research at the OHTN was conducted under the direction of Dr. Peggy Millson and Dr. Ahmed Bayoumi, and later, Dr. Sean Rourke. In 2005, with the reassessment of the implementation of the clinical management systems, Dr. Rourke led the development of a new strategic plan entitled Advancing HIV Policy and Practice through a Network of Excellence. The plan renewed the focus on research, and continued to support HIV health-care providers who used or who were interested in using clinical management systems. The plan also supported providers through education and networking opportunities.

As mentioned earlier, the OHTN Cohort Study Governance Committee was formed as a result of the new direction. It has a mandate to guide and advise the OHTN on strategies to maintain and develop the cohort database; recommend strategies and policies on conduct of the research; recommend standards for research activities; establish benchmarks for research activities; monitor research activities; review applications requesting data for research; make recommendations on which protocols to approve, reject, or request revision; and review research outputs to ensure that manuscripts are consistent with the values and principles of the OHTN and that study participants' confidentiality has not been compromised.

Additionally, the Scientific Steering Committee was formed to develop, refine, and oversee the program of research. Membership includes a representative from each data collection site, the chair of the OHTN Cohort Study Governance Committee, and two community representatives. Each member sits on one of three working groups—social-behavioural, health services, and population health; clinical and health outcomes; and genotyping analyses and health outcomes—that provide input on the scope of specific research questions covered under the research program. Membership in working groups is extended to HIV researchers, physicians, community service providers, and community members.

During the time that the emphasis was on implementing new technology through the HIV Information Infrastructure Project, the data in the database were used infrequently by external researchers. Researchers were waiting for the new data from the initiative to come online. Given the delays, instead of working with what was available, potential research projects were put on hold. Once the focus shifted from technical issues to research and a renewed effort to manually collect data at clinics with paper-based charts, research efforts were renewed. Fifteen studies using the cohort data are currently underway, ranging from trends in HIV RNA suppression, comorbidities, and adverse drug events to social and demographic determinants of diagnosis and disease progression, and quality of life. Recent publications have covered such topics as utilization rates of viral load testing and trends in antiretroviral use and drug interactions.

A recent initiative to build on the data in the cohort database includes a patient survey that will be linked to cohort participants' clinical data. The patient survey is administered in the participating clinics and includes extensive social and demographic data, as well as behavioural, functional, health, and mental status information. (The variables are shown in Appendix C.) These data can be compared to patient treatment patterns and clinical outcomes.

Along with individual research projects, the OHTN is participating in national and international initiatives to build clinical cohorts with large sample sizes. The OHTN is collaborating nationally with the BC Centre for Excellence and cohort studies in Quebec as part of a Canadian Institutes of Health Research (CIHR) Emerging Team Grant—the Canadian Observational Cohort (CANOC) Collaboration. This also includes the training of new investigators in cohort and population-based HIV research. The international initiative brings together HIV cohorts from across North America to share data under the North American AIDS Cohort Collaboration on Research and Design (NA-ACCORD), funded by the US National Institutes of Health. The NA-ACCORD is a collaboration of 15 HIV cohorts and study groups with more than 50,000 participants. These initiatives with other cohort studies allow researchers to address questions that require large numbers of participants—for example, determining the most appropriate drugs for commencing antiretroviral therapy and for subsequent treatments, and identifying adverse clinical events related to antiretroviral use.

The OHTN, along with the Ontario AIDS Network, has launched a knowledge transfer and exchange initiative. The OHTN works with AIDS service organizations to assess and enhance their capacity to use research evidence in their work, and has held sessions on housing, mental health and addictions, and best practices in knowledge transfer. As well, the OHTN provided funding to support the development of a community-based proposal for a longitudinal study on HIV, housing, and health. The study, entitled Employment and Health Outcomes in HIV/ AIDS: A Prospective Mixed Methods Cohort Study, was funded by CIHR and examined the relationship between quality of housing and people's physical and mental health, and their ability to access care, treatment, and other services.

The level of community involvement has led to an Ontario cohort study that is sanctioned by participants, but some community members feel that it has not yet achieved the "full cycle of engagement." While the OHTN requires that there be a knowledge translation and exchange component to research proposals and holds an annual research conference, research findings are not systematically communicated to the community. Opportunities to better engage the community in ways that are meaningful for the delivery of HIV programs and services include involving people living with HIV/AIDS in the development of research questions, improving the dissemination of research findings, and illustrating how these findings directly affect their lives. Greater research-related linkages with community-based AIDS service organizations, and with the Canadian AIDS Treatment Information Exchange (CATIE) in its role as the national knowledge broker, could allow for improved dissemination of research findings at the community level and more community linkage between researchers and community-based research initiatives.

Research capacity is needed to increase research quality and quantity. It is the in-house analytical capacity that supports and drives the output of research. One of the challenges with such an initiative is that of ensuring outreach to and education of potential data users, while building up and financing in-house training and research capacity. A core set of technical data analysis skills is required to conduct analyses with a dataset such as this—including recoding data, merging and linking datasets, constructing drug and other treatment regimes, and performing longitudinal analyses—and the data custodians need time and resources to support external users in this regard. The Research Network Advisory Committee has addressed this issue and has advised on how to achieve balance in the types of research and capacity enhancements that the OHTN supports, and make sure these efforts respond to current and emerging needs. This committee also provides advice on how to ensure OHTN research dollars are having an impact.

LESSONS LEARNED

Introducing New Technology

In Canada, there is recognition of the importance of clinical management systems or electronic health records in supporting improved health-service quality and outcomes.[12] Moving from paper-based to electronic records is said to be "essential to modernizing and transforming the health-care system."[13] In its October 2002 report, the Standing Senate Committee on Social Affairs, Science and Technology, chaired by Senator Michael Kirby, summarized the benefits of electronic health records:

> An EHR system can make patient data available to health care providers and institutions anywhere on a need-to-know basis by connecting interoperable

databases that have adopted the required data and technical standards. Not only can a system greatly improve quality and timeliness in health care delivery; it can also enhance health care system management, efficiency and accountability. Moreover, the data collected ... can provide very useful information for the purpose of health research.[14]

However, many physicians in Canada lag behind in the use of technology and clinical information systems. For example, a 2007 Commonwealth Fund survey revealed that only 23 percent of the primary care physicians in Canada used electronic health records compared with 79 percent or more of the primary care physicians in Australia, the Netherlands, New Zealand, and the United Kingdom. Use of electronic health records within Canada is highest in Alberta, where approximately 60 percent of family physicians use computerized medical records.[15] Yet the extent to which the functionality of these records is used in Canada is inferior to that in New Zealand, Australia, and the United Kingdom.

Introducing new technology is challenging at the best of times, but even more so if one is ahead of the curve as was the case with the HIV Information Infrastructure Project. Technology presents many promising opportunities for health-care delivery, but there can be several implementation challenges. There is evidence that the major challenges to implementation are just as related to psychological and behavioural issues as they are to technical concerns;[16] users must be convinced of the value of technology and feel "ownership" in the system.[17] Successfully introducing new systems into health-care organizations requires good technical and organizational skills, as well as effective leadership and change management. An effective implementation process should include stakeholder involvement, an implementation team, defined roles and responsibilities, external financial and technical resources, a needs assessment and environmental scan, an implementation work plan, and comprehensive training and support programs.[18] The OHTN initiative had some, but not all, of these features, and the technological challenges did not allow for full implementation as planned.

The initiative suffered from being an early adopter. The system had not been sufficiently pre-tested for the environment in which it was implemented, nor had it been designed with attention to human process engineering. One key lesson learned was that the choice of vendor is critical, especially with regard to initial and ongoing customer support. As well, when innovating and developing a system while launching a new product, vendors must be prepared to incorporate feedback and make the requisite modifications.

Three HIV clinics and practices in Ontario are now using electronic clinical management systems that transmit their data to the cohort database electronically. All successfully link with laboratories and include electronic laboratory data in the patient charts and downloads to the research database. Some data—those collected in text fields—are not downloaded. In some cases, additional data collection is required. Manual data collection continues at other sites. Notably, the new electronic clinical management systems are more difficult to implement in (and link with) hospitals than in stand-alone HIV clinics, because the systems need to be integrated into existing hospital platforms. Thus, additional considerations are required when integrating hospital-based services in such a cohort database.

It is anticipated that more clinics will come online in the future and that clinics with existing systems will soon require upgrades. The continued growth and evolution of the cohort study will require additional investment in the electronic systems, as well as longer-term resources for support and upgrades.

Initiatives such as these also require investments beyond the hardware and software costs. Budgets need to account for the resources required to convert paper charts into electronic records.[19] In addition, time and resources are required for ongoing data entry training and refresher workshops to ensure consistency in the manner in which data are entered within a clinic and across all sites so that data are accurate and comparable for research purposes.

The HIV Information Infrastructure Project was ultimately hindered by the technology itself. But few places in Canada have implemented an interoperable, co-functional electronic patient data collection system such as was envisioned without challenges and setbacks. In essence, the Ontario HIV Treatment Network beta tested an electronic, chronic disease clinical management and research system that, at launch, was not sufficiently stable, interoperable, and "ready for prime time." Nonetheless, eight clinics are now operating electronic systems funded by the OHTN, with three of those sites supplying downloaded data into the database. This represents about 10 percent of the participants in the cohort. Moreover, approximately 5,500 people in Ontario living with HIV/AIDS—about one-third of the 16,000 diagnosed with HIV in the province—now have electronic health records funded by the project (whether or not they have been recruited into the cohort).

Stakeholder Involvement

The inclusion of the HIV community in the conceptualization, development, and management of this HIV cohort study has been its defining feature. The involvement of people living with HIV/AIDS—gaining their trust, securing their ongoing involvement, and having their leadership and ownership of the process—has led to the availability of one of the richest sources of information on a chronic disease among an affected population in Canada and has ensured that the research priorities are a better reflection of the patient experience.

Some stakeholders believe that the extent of community involvement has slowed progress and led to some misdirected decisions. This may be somewhat true. Working in a truly collaborative manner takes time and compromise, and requires additional effort to ensure buy-in and the understanding of new approaches proposed. Any such effort will need to find a balance between expediency for researchers and comfort for the community, and address the trade-offs between delays and potential misstarts and full partnership. Trust is the basis upon which patients (through their providers) will make their data available. The greater the trust, the more extensive the data that are likely to be made available and the greater the likelihood of consent to data transfer and linkage. Moreover, this model has fostered a more informed health-care consumer, and has led to the creation of several plain language tools to explain research. It has also sparked useful discussions on health information privacy standards and the concept of altruism in research participation.

Another important group in this process has been the HIV health-care providers, predominantly the physicians who provide HIV services in the province. They are the gatekeepers to the patient data and the ones who will gain patients' trust in the research initiative. Thus, they must have full confidence in the cohort study. Physicians have been involved in this study from its initiation. The cohort database was first housed at Sunnybrook Health Sciences Centre under the directorship of Dr. Anita Rachlis, an infectious disease physician, and health-care providers have always been represented on the governance committee and now have a stand-alone committee. This does not mean that relations have always gone smoothly. There have been areas of contention along the way, particularly around the adoption of new electronic clinical management systems. Nonetheless, effective partnerships with providers have greatly facilitated the successful recruitment of participants and the ensuing research activities.

The Ontario government has also been at the table throughout and was instrumental in getting the cohort study off the ground through financial, administrative, and legal support. Because of the level of support from government at the beginning, the cohort study was able to have the legislation changed in order to collect health card numbers for the purposes of linkage. The government of Ontario continues to provide funding for the OHTN and to be represented at the table. Support from the Ontario Public Health Laboratory has also been invaluable.

Numerous researchers have been involved over the years, many of whom also wear other professional hats. Their input has been important to the design, content, and format of the cohort database and to ensuring that the data are adequate for conducting quality research. Using the cohort study data, several researchers have conducted multiple studies, which have been presented at conferences and published.

In spite of the challenges along the way, it has been the consistent involvement and perseverance of all these stakeholders together that accounts for the nature of the OHTN cohort study today. The cohort study is now well positioned to make a valuable contribution to HIV research, as well as to health services, population health, and clinical research in general.

Making the Best Use of the Data for Research

Today the Ontario HIV Treatment Network Cohort Study has data on more than 4,000 people living with HIV / AIDS, approximately one-quarter of those diagnosed in Ontario, providing a solid research sample. One of the challenges of administering a research cohort such as this is determining the main model for data analysis. With some research databases, the data are collected, managed, and analyzed internally; with some, data analysis is predominantly internal with some external access to the data; and other databases have a custodial function and release the data based on research proposal submissions. Over its evolution, this cohort study has wavered between an emphasis on internal research capacity and a reliance on external researchers. The OHTN is currently investing in more research staff.

Internally based researchers often have the greatest understanding of data and tend to have higher research production rates, but it is resource intensive to develop and maintain high quality, in-house research capacity. Thus, the HIV cohort study promotes external research among university, participating clinic, and community-based researchers. When data are available for external use, outreach and education are critical, and extensive internal resources are required to support external users. The core technical knowledge related to the data and algorithms for recoding data, merging and linking datasets, constructing treatment regimes, performing longitudinal analyses, and so on needs to be conveyed.

The most efficient approach to analysis might be to concentrate resources and activity within the central organization. However, from the beginning there has been a commitment to building an Ontario-wide research database that can be used by researchers from all participating data collection sites and research-based institutions. As well, participating clinics that are funded by the OHTN are required to conduct a certain amount of research annually using the cohort data. Given its mandate, the OHTN also has opportunities to promote more knowledge exchange and community-based research. This allows for a wider range of research ideas and expertise than would be available at the OHTN alone, while at the same time providing researchers with a highly developed database, including a much larger number of participants than any individual clinic would have.

Researcher and community leadership on current and new initiatives is a critical success factor for high quality, relevant, and more prolific research that is responsive to the needs of people living with HIV/AIDS in Ontario. The patient survey, the CIHR Emerging Team Grant, and the North American AIDS Cohort Collaboration on Research and Design (NA-ACCORD) are promising new initiatives for the use of the cohort data. These initiatives may also present opportunities for the innovative involvement of all stakeholders.

NOTES

We would like to acknowledge the contribution of the following individuals to the development of this chapter: Ahmed Bayoumi, University of Toronto, St. Michael's Hospital; Loralee Gillis, Rainbow Health Ontario; Jim Lavery, McLaughlin-Rotman Centre for Global Health; Anita Rachlis, University of Toronto, Sunnybrook Health Sciences Centre; Robert Remis, University of Toronto; and Greg Robinson, former director of the HIV Ontario Observational Database (HOOD).

1. Canadian HIV/AIDS Legal Network, "HIV/AIDS and the Privacy of Health Information," Info Sheets (2004), www.aidslaw.ca/publications/publications-docEN.php?ref=187.
2. Personal interview with Megan Edmiston, September 2008.
3. Consumers Council of Canada, "Can Anyone Get Private Health Insurance?" Consumer – General Information section, www.insurance-canada.ca/consinfogeneral/uaskus/uaskusMore.php?uaskus=26&zoom_highlight=HIV.
4. Canadian HIV/AIDS Legal Network, "Income Security for People Living with HIV/AIDS in Canada," Info Sheet 1 (2005), http://www.aidslaw.ca/publications/publicationsdocEN.php?ref=107.
5. Personal interview with Megan Edmiston, September 2008.
6. UNAIDS, "Third Meeting of the International Task Team on HIV-Related Travel Restrictions" (18 July 2008), http://www.unaids.org/en/KnowledgeCentre/Resources/FeatureStories/archive/2008/20080718_travel_restrictions.asp; International AIDS Society, *Denying Entry, Stay and Residence Due to HIV Status: Ten Things You Need to Know*, http://www.iasociety.org/Web/WebContent/File/Entry%20denied%2010%20things%20you%20need%20to%20know.pdf.
7. Brunei, China, Oman, Qatar, the Republic of Korea (South Korea), Sudan, the United Arab Emirates, Yemen, and the United States of America.
8. Egypt, Iraq, Singapore, Tunisia, and the Turks and Caicos Islands.
9. Armenia, China, Equatorial Guinea, Kazakhstan, Moldova, Turkmenistan, the Democratic People's Republic of Korea (North Korea), Singapore, the Republic of Korea, Bahrain, Bangladesh, Kuwait, Sudan, Brunei, Malaysia, Syria, Mongolia, Taiwan, Egypt, Oman, the United Arab Emirates, Hungary, Qatar, the United States of America, Iraq, the Russian Federation, Uzbekistan, Jordan, Saudi Arabia, and Yemen.
10. Ontario HIV Treatment Network, *The OHTN Exchange* 1, no. 1 (Autumn 2005).
11. T. Forte, A.M. Bayoumi, R.S. Remis, C. Swantee, A. Andrews, C. Goia, P. Millson, A. Rachlis, and G. Robinson, "Representativeness of the HIV Ontario

Observational Database (HOOD)" (paper presented at 12th Annual Canadian Conference on HIV / AIDS Research, Halifax, Nova Scotia, 10–13 April 2003).

12. Standing Committee on Social Affairs, Science and Technology, *The Health of Canadians – The Federal Role. Interim Report,* vol. 6, *Recommendations for Reform* (October 2002), chap. 10, para. 10.2, www.parl.gc.ca/37/2/ parlbus/commbus/senate/com-e/soci-e/rep-e/repoct02vol6part4-e. htm#CHAPTER%20TEN.

13. Canada Health Infoway, "Senate Committee Endorses Infoway Strategy," Press release (28 October 2002).

14. Standing Committee on Social Affairs, Science and Technology, *Recommendations for Reform,* chap. 10, para 10.2, see note 14.

15. D. Protti, S. Edworthy, and I. Johansen, "Adoption of Information Technology in Primary Care Physician Offices in Alberta and Denmark, Part 1: Historical, Technical and Cultural Forces," *Electronic Healthcare* 6, no. 1 (2007): 95-102.

16. N.M. Lorenzi and R.T. Riley, "Managing Change: An Overview," *Journal of the American Medical Informatics Association* 7, no. 2 (2000): 116-24.

17. Ibid.

18. College of Family Physicians of Canada, "Primary Care Toolkit for Family Physicians" (2007), http://toolkit.cfpc.ca/en/information-technology/ (accessed September 2008); Health Canada, "Implementing Electronic Medical Records in Primary Health Care Settings," www.emrtoolkit.ca/ (accessed September 2008); B. Gamble, "Using IT to Make Primary Care Reform Work for You," *Future Practice* (11 April 2006), www.cma.ca/multimedia/ CMA/Content_Images/Inside_cma/Future_Practice/English/2006/April/ using_IT.pdf.

19. The OHTN provides funds to support this for physicians who have patients with HIV in their practices and who have implemented electronic health records.

APPENDIX A: VARIABLES PROVIDED BY ORIGINAL HOOD ENROLLEES AT ENROLMENT

Demographics

- gender
- educational level
- geographic area (first three characters of postal code)
- country of birth/country of parents' birth
- ethnic background/language preference
- number of children under 18 living with respondent
- current spouse/partner

HIV-Related

- date of first positive HIV test
- date of last negative HIV test (if any)
- site of first HIV test
- date of HIV exposure (if known)
- risks for exposure to HIV
- HIV status of partner
- community resources currently used (family, friends, family doctor, HIV specialist doctor, office nurse, social worker, psychologist, occupational therapist, physiotherapist, AIDS service organization, services in the home)
- (open-ended) categories of alternative therapies used, currently and in past
- dietary supplements: multivitamins, antioxidants, vitamin supplements, mineral supplements, other supplements
- medicines from plants (e.g., herbal medicines)
- physical therapies, body-mind therapies
- alternative therapies (e.g., ozone, hydrogen peroxide, DNCB)
- complementary therapists and practitioners (e.g., Chinese medicine, homeopathy)

APPENDIX B: VARIABLES EXTRACTED FROM CLINICAL RECORDS

These data were collected retrospectively at first enrolment, going back to the inception of the patient's clinical care in that setting, and then updated every six months.

- date of first HIV positive test
- date of last HIV negative test
- presumptive exposure date (if known)
- p24 antigen and antibody status
- CD4 and CD8 counts (if available)
- B2 microglobulin (if available)
- Hepatitis B and C antibody, Hepatitis B antigen
- CMV antibody
- cryptococcus antigen
- VDRL
- toxoplasma antibodies
- TB skin test result; anergy test results
- history of non-AIDS defining conditions related to HIV and their date of onset
- history of AIDS-defining conditions and their date and method of diagnosis
- past and present use of medications for treatment of HIV or related conditions
- clinical symptomatology / adverse effects experienced
- current CDC classification
- current Karnofsky score
- hospitalization history
- current weight
- occurrence of pregnancy for females

APPENDIX C: VARIABLES PROVIDED BY SURVEYS OF COHORT STUDY PARTICIPANTS

Core Survey Variables (all participants)

- gender
- sexual orientation
- relationship status
- household composition
- usual language spoken at home
- country of birth
- citizenship status
- year first came to Canada to live
- racial background (with specifics of group and status for Aboriginal persons)
- ethnicity of ancestors
- employment status and occupational category
- work situation
- impact of HIV on work in past month
- personal and household income
- income sources
- highest level of education
- cigarette smoking history
- alcohol use
- non-medicinal drug use
- HIV risk factors
- health-related quality of life (SF-12)
- depression

Extended Survey Variables (subset of participants)

All of the variables in the core questionnaire plus the following:

- psychosocial variables: coping, social support, mastery, HIV-related stigma
- clinical variables: health-related quality of life, depression, lipodystrophy, symptom distress

Survey Instruments Used in the Questionnaire, by Variable

- alcohol use (AUDIT)
- symptom distress (ACTG)
- body change and distress (ACTG)
- health-related quality of life (SF-36 or SF-12, and the EQ5D)
- adherence (ACTG)

- mental health (K10 or CES-D)
- social support (MOS-SSS or ACTG)
- stigma (HIV Stigma Scale)
- stress (Recent Life Events, Chronic Stress Measure, Early Childhood Activities)
- mastery (Pearlin Mastery Scale)
- coping (Brief COPE)
- neuropsychological ability (Spatial Span, Digit Symbol, Grooved Pegboard, and Hopkins Verbal Learning Test)
- health-related quality of life Health Utilities Index

Three mechanisms were used to develop additional questions: (1) use or modification of questions from existing national surveys, including the National Population Health Survey; (2) consultation with experts in the field; and (3) use or modification of questions currently being used in HIV research studies, including the Canadian Cardiovascular Study.

MAKING THE MOST OF THE CURRENT ENVIRONMENT: SECONDARY USES OF DATA FOR CANCER RESEARCH AND SYSTEM MANAGEMENT

SIMON B. SUTCLIFFE

THE BC CANCER AGENCY AND ITS MANDATE

The BC Cancer Agency (BCCA) provides a comprehensive, population-based cancer control program for British Columbia's 4.3 million citizens. As a publicly funded institution, the BCCA's process for undertaking interventions, demonstrating clinical benefit, and allocating resources must be based in fact, evidence, and readily interpretable analytic logic. To fulfill its mandate, the BCCA uses—and must use—data from many sources to enhance its knowledge and understanding of cancer control, and to improve individual and population outcomes. The BCCA's cancer control planning involves population-based registries and databases with distinctive, well-defined standards for comprehensiveness, relevance, accuracy, and timeliness. As a result, the data acquired are usually more useful than information obtained from self-reports or surveys requiring consent.

In general, the BCCA uses the information for public, patient, health provider, health administration, and political/policy purposes. More

Data Data Everywhere: Access and Accountability? ed. C.M. Flood. Montreal and Kingston: Queen's Policy Studies Series, McGill-Queen's University Press. © 2011 The School of Policy Studies, Queen's University at Kingston. All rights reserved.

specifically, the information is used for identification of cancer risk, early detection, care system planning, survivor issues, and projecting change in medical practice through applied research.

This chapter presents three examples of the BCCA's use of linked datasets: planning service capacity and performance for radiation therapy; planning service capacity and performance for systemic therapy, including the management of the provincial drug budget; and examining health services utilization by adult survivors of childhood and adolescent cancer. In each case, interpretation of information in linked datasets is essential not only for planning service capacity and system performance, but also for projecting future needs and identifying opportunities for enhancement.

The BC Cancer Agency comprises five cancer centres, two cancer research centres, and numerous community cancer clinics and provincial networks. Its mandate is to provide a population-based cancer control program for the citizens of British Columbia. Cancer control comprises the ability to reduce the incidence and mortality of cancer, and to enhance the quality of life of those affected by cancer, through an integrated and coordinated approach to primary prevention, early detection, treatment, rehabilitation, and palliation.

Accordingly, cancer control has many components. It is directed toward those who do not have cancer as well as those who do, and toward those who survive cancer as well as those who will not. It is based in population health as well as disease management; it applies what we know and investigates what we do not. The purpose of cancer control is to improve outcomes by addressing the needs of the population for interventions and services, and to improve the quality of life during, and after, cancer.

PRINCIPLES OF POPULATION-BASED CANCER CONTROL

Good population-based programs of cancer control, whether in British Columbia or in any other global jurisdiction, are based on several widely agreed-upon principles or standards. Good programs are

- *comprehensive.* They provide interventions across the spectrum of cancer control from primary prevention, through care and treatment, to palliation and end-of-life care. By so doing, the programs are directed toward the entire population—whether people are healthy, at high risk for cancer, acutely ill with cancer, chronically ill, cured, or dying of cancer.
- *equitable.* They are "fair." In fact, they address (mitigate) disparities that give rise to poorer outcomes.
- *well defined.* They provide services to meet population needs using defined standards and measures of quality and safety.

- *evidence based.* They provide services based on evidence for benefit, through use of accessible, available, valid data.
- *internally coordinated.* They are integrated with services across the continuum of cancer control that are delivered from public, patient, provider, and health system perspectives.
- *externally coordinated.* They support and facilitate interventions to address other non-communicable diseases.
- *flexible.* They adapt to changing standards, innovations, regulations, and so on.
- *accountable.* They are appropriately governed, administered, and operated.
- *responsive.* They are broadly engaging and responsive to stakeholders.

BC CANCER AGENCY'S USE OF POPULATION-BASED REGISTRY AND SURVEILLANCE DATA

To exercise its mandate in a way that meets these standards, the BCCA needs to use population-based registry and surveillance data, because these data can be applied to population-wide cancer control in a way that surveys, self-reports, and questionnaires requiring consent cannot. Table 1 compares the attributes of population-based registries with those of datasets that require consent.

TABLE 1
A Comparison of Datasets

Attribute	Population-Based Registry and Surveillance	Surveys, Self-Reports, Questionnaires by Consent
1. Comprehensive	1. Defined by population dataset	1. Defined by survey dataset
2. Relevance to population served	2. Population data	2. Defined subpopulations
3. Accuracy	3. Built into process	3. Individually determined
4. Timeliness (relevance to need)	4. Constantly collected	4. Collected as needed
5. Susceptibility to bias(es)	5. Population derived and representative	5. Dependent on study design
Ability to acquire	Not consent-determined (legislated access)	Consent required
Deceased populations	Registry information available to time of death	Not contactable if deceased

Source: BC Cancer Agency.

The BCCA relies on a number of linked databases containing population information. These databases are held either by the agency, by the provincial government, or by national (federal) agencies. The BCCA's ability to manage and operate a cancer control program for the population is totally dependent upon certain key data in these databases:

- population censuses and key demographics
- cancer incidence and mortality (age standardized), and cancer prevalence ("prevalence" refers to the total number of cases in a population, while "incidence" refers to the number of new cases in a time period)
- disease outcomes (e.g., mortality, five-year survival)
- allocation of resources to interventions
- program performance and outcome measures
- measures of quality and safety of services

The BCCA uses these data to

- manage cancer (control incidence, mortality and disease outcomes)
- manage the performance of interventional services (the health system)
- ensure safe, accessible, effective services
- align resources to support the most effective, evidence-based interventions
- identify opportunities for cancer research or for services/system enhancements
- demonstrate clinical, operational, and fiscal accountability

EXAMPLES OF USING DATA TO PROVIDE CANCER CONTROL

While all aspects of the agency's programs are based on data, the following three examples highlight why the BCCA requires population-based registry and surveillance data, and how the BCCA uses these data to provide cancer control at a population level.

Service Capacity and Performance Planning for Radiation Therapy

Radiation therapy is a therapeutic modality used to treat cancer within a defined anatomical location, either to achieve local control, cure, or palliation of symptoms. For the majority of patients it is delivered by a machine external to the body; for a discrete minority it involves insertion of the radioactive material into tissue or a body cavity (internal to the body).

Delivering radiation therapy to the population who need it requires multiple types of information:

- The clinical "case"
  - Who needs it? How many people?
  - What are the relevant standards (access, wait time, quality, safety)?
  - Is the intent curative or palliative? What are the courses and fractionation? (Fractionation is the dividing of a large dose of radiation into smaller doses, delivered over time, in order to facilitate normal tissue repair.)
  - What is the interrelationship with other therapeutic modalities?

- The operational "case"
  - What are the operating standards?
  - What are the operational days and hours?

- The personnel
  - Radiation therapy involves radiation oncologists, clinical physicists, dosimetrists, radiation therapists, radiation therapy nurses, and electronic technologists. What are their recruitment, retention, training, and development needs?
  - What patient support services are required?

- The system/provincial program
  - What are the capital renewal and replacement requirements?
  - What are the system performance measures and standards?

Radiation therapy need is most closely related to cancer incidence; most patients receive radiation once during the cancer experience. Data from many jurisdictions, or individually derived and aggregated across disease sites, indicate that approximately 60 percent of people newly diagnosed with cancer require radiation in "westernized" (high income) countries. Of this 60 percent, approximately 90 percent receive "radical" radiation through a protracted, fractionated course of radiation; the remaining 10 percent receive brief duration, single, or limited fractionation therapy. Radiation therapy has evolved through experience to once daily treatments, five days per week over a number of weeks.

Other than for internal treatments or unique fractionation protocols, radiation services in British Columbia operate on a 250-day working year, and usually within an eight- to ten-hour operational day. Staff workloads, schedules, and performance derive from this template.

On average, approximately four patients are treated per hour per radiation machine. The life cycle of a radiation unit performing in this manner is approximately ten years. Each radiation unit is technologically complex, requiring regular attention as to performance output specifications and maintenance. One of these units costs about $2 million. Thus, for a distributed provincial system, the capital investment is substantial, both for replacement (based on machine life cycle) and for new machines (based on increasing incidence).

Figure 1 shows the relationship between incident cases per annum, the number of radiation therapy courses required to meet the need at 55 percent coverage of the incident population, and the number of linear accelerators, both new and replacement, required over the period 2004–2015.

Using the data shown in Figure 1, the BCCA has drawn up a plan under which system capacity meets the need for radiation therapy at defined standards. The system can meet, or exceed, the provincial radiation therapy performance standard of more than 90 percent of patients receiving therapy within four weeks of being ready to treat with radiation therapy (see Figure 2).

FIGURE 1
Incidence Cases Per Annum, Number of Radiation Therapy (RT) Courses, and Number of Linear Accelerators Required

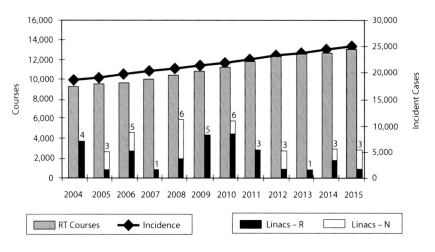

Note: Linacs = linear accelerators. R = replacement. N = new.
Source: BC Cancer Agency.

FIGURE 2
Percentage of Patients Receiving Radiation Therapy with Four Weeks of Being Ready to Treat

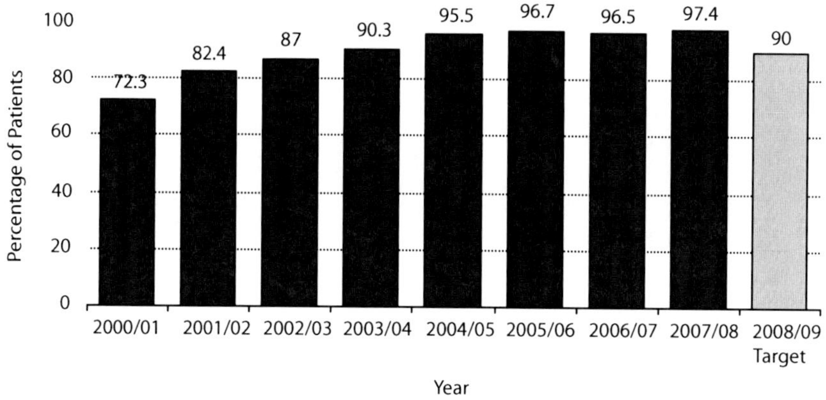

Source: BC Cancer Agency.

Service Capacity and Performance Planning for Systemic Therapy

Even though the treatment modality differs, similar principles apply to this chapter's second example: the planning of systemic therapy. Systemic therapy is directed at advanced and/or disseminated cancer, either alone or in combination with surgery and/or radiation. Systemic cancer agents comprise cytotoxic drugs, hormones, biological agents, and "targeted" drugs directed to highly specific targets. They may be administered either orally or parenterally (that is, by means other than the alimentary tract—for example, by intravenous injection). Systemic therapies can be administered singly or in combination, and in a variety of schedules or cycles.

Figure 3 illustrates the trends in incidence of cancer, prevalence of patients receiving drug therapy, and average drug cost per patient. The increase in prevalence of patients receiving drug therapy (as well as prevalence rate, not shown) is primarily due not to increasing incidence of cancer, but rather to increased utilization of systemic therapy—more patients, living for longer, and eligible, repeatedly, for more systemic therapies.

Systemic therapy need and capacity, within defined parameters of service quality and safety, has an impact on

- operational parameters
  - days and hours of operation
  - chemotherapy units, chemo chairs, beds, pumps, supplies
  - pharmacy services (inpatient, ambulatory, and chemo units)

- personnel
  - medical oncologists, hematologic oncologists
  - pharmacists
  - oncology nurses
  - patient support services

- system / provincial program
  - cancer centres
  - community cancer centres and clinics
  - tertiary / community / primary care networks and data
  - clinical practice guidelines, protocols, and so on

- drugs (systemic therapies)
  - selection
  - acquisition
  - distribution
  - usage
  - compliance

The acquisition costs of new drugs have risen steeply over the last seven years; typical prices are now in the range of $10–50,000 per year per patient. Moreover, the number of patients accessing systemic therapy increases approximately 6 percent per year. As discussed above and shown in Figure 3,

FIGURE 3
Incidence of Cancer, Prevalence of Patients Receiving Drug Therapy, and Average Drug Cost Per Patient

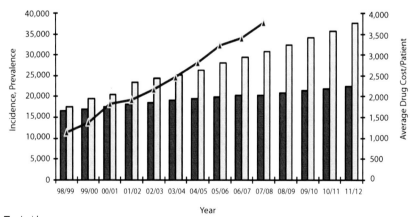

- ■ Incidence
- □ Prevalence (each patient counted only once even if received care in more than one centre)
- ▲ Average drug cost/patient

Source: BC Cancer Agency.

this is primarily due not to increasing incidence of cancer, but rather to increasing utilization of systemic therapy. Provincial cancer agencies and drug benefit plans have experienced 15–20 percent annual growth in cancer drug budgets over the past several years. For British Columbia, with a population of 4.3 million people and 20,000 new cancer cases per year, the provincial cancer drug budget for 2008–09 was approximately $130 million.

The process for managing the provincial cancer drug budget (Figure 4) involves

- the evaluation and ranking of new therapeutics (singly or in combination), based on evidence for effectiveness in curative, life prolongation, and palliation situations
- estimation of costs of acquisition based on assumptions of uptake, compliance, and toxicity
- health economic assessments based on cost-effectiveness analysis
- approval of agents for usage through the publicly funded budget
- development of clinical practice guidelines, protocols, and pre-printed orders for approved drugs and
- utilization management to ensure correct utilization according to approved guidelines as a basis for payment of drug costs (including "online" adjudication, direct utilization reporting by all users, and periodic audits to confirm accuracy of submitted data)

FIGURE 4
Schematic Representation of the Process for Cancer Drug Budget Management

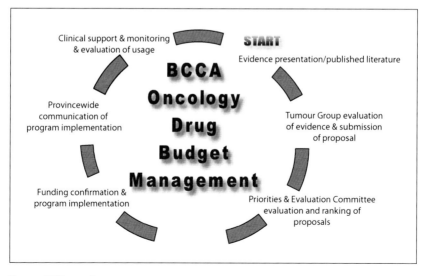

Source: BC Cancer Agency.

Through this data-intensive process, actual drug costs have been very closely aligned to annual drug budgets over the past decade. In addition, there has been a high level of satisfaction with access to new effective agents through the publicly funded system. Moreover, as shown in Figure 5, the system has been able to administer chemotherapy to new patients within 14 days of their being "ready to treat" at (or very close to) the provincial target of 90 percent.

FIGURE 5
Percentage of New Patients from "Ready to Treat" to Chemotherapy Treatment within 14 Days

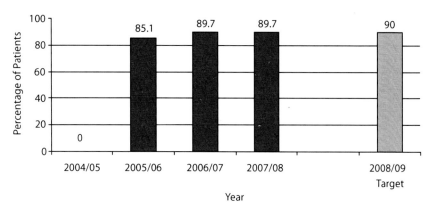

Source: BC Cancer Agency.

Adult Survivors of Pediatric Cancer – Health Implications

Advances in management have resulted in a substantial increase in survival among children diagnosed with cancer over the last three decades. Notwithstanding the relatively small incidence rate of pediatric cancer, therapeutic advances have resulted in a progressively increasing prevalence of survivors of child and adolescent cancer (see Figure 6).

Long-term survivors are known to be at risk for late effects—including second malignancies—often resulting from their cancer therapy. These late effects are expected to lead to increased use of health-care services; however, little is known about hospital utilization and use of physician services (general practitioner, oncologist, and specialist physician) in this population of adult survivors of child and adolescent cancer. The third example of the use of linked datasets is a study that tried to fill this knowledge gap.

As in so many other cases, multiple data sources were needed in order to examine health utilization impacts. A population-based cohort and

FIGURE 6
Prevalence of Cancer Survivors Diagnosed under Age 25 in BC

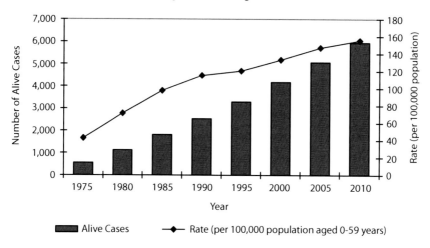

Source: BC Cancer Agency.

case-control study design was employed, using data linkage from the BC Cancer Registry (for case ascertainment), the BC Ministry of Health Client Registry (for control ascertainment), hospital discharge data, and physician services claim data. All data were linked through unique personal health identifiers.[1]

The study group comprised survivors meeting the following eligibility criteria:

- first diagnosed with cancer before 20 years of age, between 1970 and 1995
- resident in BC at the time of diagnosis
- survived five years or more after diagnosis
- alive, resident in BC, and registered with the Client Registry of the provincial health insurance plan of the BC Ministry of Health on 1 January 1998 and 31 December 2000

An age- and sex-matched "control" cohort from the general population was selected randomly, ten times the size of the study cohort, from the Ministry of Health Client Registry. The control cohort comprised individuals meeting the following eligibility criteria:

- born in the same range of years as the survivors in the study group
- survived to at least age five
- alive, resident in BC, and registered with the Client Registry on 1 January 1998 and 31 December 2000

In the three-year period 1998–2000, 97 percent of the childhood cancer survivors visited a physician at least once, compared to 61 percent of controls. The survivors were significantly more likely to visit all types of outpatient health practitioners over the three-year period, including general practitioners (GPs), specialist physicians, and non-physician practitioners. Relative risks for a visit (as compared to the control group) ranged from 1.87 (GPs) to 2.4 (specialists) to 9.15 (pediatricians). The frequency of physician visits by survivors after five years of survival, shown in Figure 7, indicates that 40 percent of survivors visited a GP between one and nine times, and 55 percent visited a specialist between one and nine times.

FIGURE 7
Frequency of Physician Visits after Five Years' Survival, 1970 to 1992

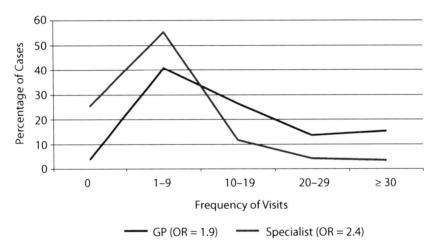

Note: OR = odds ratio as compared to controls.
Source: BC Cancer Agency.

Among those with at least one GP visit, female survivors had more GP visits than males. Age at diagnosis, disease type, and potential barriers to access (socioeconomic status, urban/rural residence, and region of residence) did not appreciably affect the frequency of physician visits.

With regard to hospitalizations, 24 percent of survivors versus 13 percent of controls were hospitalized at least once, as shown in Table 2. Survivors had a significantly higher probability of hospitalization, more admissions per hospitalized person, and longer duration in hospital than controls, both overall and for each type of hospital admission. Rehabilitation and extended care admissions accounted for less than 1 percent of overall hospital admissions for survivors and controls. Females, older survivors, and survivors of central nervous system tumours were more likely to be hospitalized at least once, and survivors of central nervous system tumours spent more days in hospital (both overall and in acute care).

TABLE 2
Hospitalization in a Population-Based Cohort of Young Cancer Survivors, 1998–2000

	% Hospitalized		*Mean No. of Admissions*		*Mean No. Days in Hospital*	
	Survivors	*General Population*	*Survivors*	*General Population*	*Survivors*	*General Population*
All	24.4	13.3	2.0	1.4	10.3	5.5
Females	32.2	19.3	4.2	1.5	7.2	5.3
Males	17.3	6.2	1.9	1.5	15.5	6.5

Source: BC Cancer Agency.

As a direct result of these findings indicating a greater utilization of inpatient and ambulatory services by survivors of childhood and adolescent cancer, the BC Registry and Surveillance program has been proposed. Its proponents argue that, for this high-risk group, there is a legal and ethical responsibility to identify and mitigate health risks, and improve health awareness, promotion, and monitoring.

DISCUSSION

Three examples of the use of data derived from various datasets, internal and external to the agency, have been presented. They are representative of many other potential examples and illustrate the absolute necessity of this information to plan, manage, and operate the provincial cancer control system according to principles of optimal population-based care.

Within a publicly funded system with expectations of transparency, accountability, and sustainability of evidence-based, effective care, these data are relevant to many stakeholders.

The Public

The public becomes more aware of the incidence and mortality of cancer, as well as the steps being taken in the areas of primary prevention, early detection, rehabilitation, and palliation. Because the information the public receives is scientifically valid and evidence based, people can be more confident in that information. This includes, for example, claims that a certain amount of money must be budgeted to provide radiation therapy for the population (as discussed in the first of the three examples above).

Patients

Cancer patients receive high-quality, up-to-date information about their cancer and their treatment, rehabilitation, and palliation options. From a larger health policy perspective, the flow of resources to patients will presumably be more efficient when driven by valid, evidence-based research results, so that patients will receive more benefits from each public dollar than would be the case otherwise.

Health-Care Providers

Correct practice is validated. Health-care providers can be confident that their practices—and the priorities of the health system—are evidence based. Health services can be better integrated and coordinated. Moreover, protocols and procedures can be transferred and compared across populations because common standards are adopted for capturing information. Future health needs can be better predicted, as research yields results in both population health and disease management.

Health Administrators

Health administrators can allocate resources in an evidence-based manner, optimizing cost-efficiency and effectiveness. They can also predict and plan for the population's future health needs.

Politicians

Politicians can align their policies with public opinion. They can set public policy, establish priorities, and allocate funds based on solid information.

CONCLUSIONS

The BC Cancer Agency has a mandate—and an ethical duty—to follow the principles of good population-based cancer control. To meet its obligations, the BCCA must access the information in population datasets, because

- this information is not available through other routes (e.g., surveys, self-reports, questionnaires, and other consent-based studies), and yet
- this information is absolutely essential to plan, manage, and operate the health system.

In addition to supporting optimal evidence-based care at the health-care provider level—that is, care that is effective, appropriate, and safe—these data can also be used to identify opportunities to improve clinical services and health system performance; risks associated with disparities of performance or hitherto unrecognized health impacts; and areas or topics for knowledge generation through research to enhance clinical or health system function.

The future will bring an even greater need for access to population datasets due to increasing incidence of non-communicable diseases (including cancer); more opportunities for early detection of asymptomatic disease; novel diagnostic and imaging technologies; enhancements to the safety, precision, and performance of interventional services; and the introduction of "targeted" therapies for populations selected by molecular attributes. This last item suggests that our existing demographic and health databases will have to change to incorporate molecular information, at both the personal and population levels.

NOTES

The following individuals contributed to and/or provided information for this chapter: Mary McBride, Mark Elwood, Ivo Olivotto, Susan O'Reilly, Mario Lorenzi, Jacqueline Page, Zenaida Abanto, John Spinelli, Karen Goddard, and Barbara Poole of the BC Cancer Agency; Chris Fryer, Paul Rogers, and Susan Pritchard of the BC Children's Hospital; Ann-Marie Brow of the Centre for Health Policy and Research, University of British Columbia; and Sam Sheps of the Department of Health Care and Epidemiology, University of British Columbia.

1.   BC Cancer Agency, "Childhood, Adolescent, and Young Adult Cancer Survivors Research Program," http://www.bccrc.ca/ccr/mmcbride_cayacs.html (accessed 19 November 2009).

WALKING THE TALK: A ROADMAP FOR ACTION AND EXCELLENCE

A ROADMAP TO RESEARCH USES OF ELECTRONIC HEALTH INFORMATION

DON WILLISON, ELAINE GIBSON, AND KIM MCGRAIL

Electronic health information, whether from administrative databases or electronic health records, holds potential as an extremely rich resource for researchers. In 2000, Dalhousie University researcher George Kephart and a number of colleagues undertook a research study that required linking the National Population Health Survey, held by Statistics Canada, with hospital discharge abstracts and physician administrative billing records from five provinces to examine socioeconomic differences in access to health care across Canada.[1] The logistical, organizational, and political barriers they encountered stymied their work so badly that, despite years of attempts, they failed to gain the cooperation of one of the provinces. To the frustration of the researchers, the dataset used for undertaking the planned examination was ultimately only partial. This seriously diminished the value of the study.

This complex research proposal involved multiple data providers and jurisdictions, but it is emblematic of barriers still encountered by researchers today. Why are the data not flowing to researchers as anticipated? This chapter examines several reasons and makes suggestions for addressing these challenges that we hope will stimulate discussion and debate among researchers and policy-makers.[2] Our specific lens for this paper

Data Data Everywhere: Access and Accountability? ed. C.M. Flood. Montreal and Kingston: Queen's Policy Studies Series, McGill-Queen's University Press. © 2011 The School of Policy Studies, Queen's University at Kingston. All rights reserved.

is Canada, but the issues identified are common to many countries, and the suggestions are general enough to be widely relevant.

THE CHALLENGES

In this section, we identify and describe a number of technical or procedural challenges affecting access to personal information[3] for health research. Before turning to these, a few introductory comments are in order.

First, many parties are involved in or affected by the research uses of personal information, including those who draft and revise legislation and ethical codes; those who ensure those laws and codes are followed (chiefly research ethics boards, data custodians/stewards, and privacy commissioners); researchers; and those whose data are being used. Because there are multiple parties, primarily functioning at the provincial and local levels, policies are often inconsistent, and attempts to harmonize policies involve inherently slow and complex multilateral discussions.

Second, while some argue that personal information simply should not be accessed for health research,[4] we believe the greater stumbling block is the uncertainty and disagreement among those who support research use of that information regarding how to interpret or operationalize some commonly agreed-upon fundamental overarching principles about how to collect, use, and process individuals' information.[5]

Third, the distinction between research and other secondary uses of data has blurred over time. It is uncontroversial that health information collected in the course of providing health care to an individual is to be used for purposes directly related to care provision. Historically, any secondary use of this information by a care provider or an institution for purposes of service planning, quality improvement, or risk management was assumed to fall within the scope of the intended use for the data. This assumption does not usually extend to research uses of that information. However, it is often difficult to distinguish health research uses from health services planning and quality improvement because of common analytic methods and the shift toward multi-institutional quality improvement activities.[6] Indeed, this distinction becomes even more difficult to make because it is often the same individuals who function both as service providers and as academic researchers. Similar blurring occurs between public health practice and public health research.

Finally, newer approaches to collection of personal information for health research purposes challenge existing assumptions about the conditions under which exemptions from requiring consent may be granted. Single time-limited studies are being replaced with registries and biobanks, for which one cannot articulate, in advance, all the intended uses of the data. Electronic health record (EHR) systems are being developed, and some institutions are considering how best to glean data from these systems for research purposes. EHR systems are also being heralded as avenues to screen patients for phase 3 and phase 4 trials.[7] These developments break down existing distinctions between research, clinical care, and other system uses. This in turn creates major challenges in regulating research use of personal information using existing norms and tools.

Confusion and Uncertainty Regarding Law and Policy

There has been rapid change in Canadian information laws over the past decade. The federal government has enacted the *Personal Information Protection and Electronic Documents Act*.[8] One province has enacted general private-sector legislation that does not discriminate between health and non-health information.[9] Five provinces have brought in legislation focusing specifically on issues of personal health information,[10] and in two provinces such legislation is under development.[11] Add to this the pre-existing legislation covering the private sector in Quebec,[12] plus federal and provincial public-sector legislation, along with the common law, and we witness a smorgasbord of laws governing personal information. Also in the past decade, and directly relating to research uses of information, the *Tri-Council Policy Statement* (*TCPS*) was implemented by the major federal research funding agencies in Canada: the Medical Research Council (now Canadian Institutes of Health Research), Social Sciences and Humanities Research Council, and National Sciences and Engineering Research Council.[13] Researchers are required by research ethics boards to follow the *TCPS*, but it is a policy statement and not legislation, and therefore carries lesser status in law.

Along with these developments has come a high degree of uncertainty and concern on the part of researchers, research ethics boards, health records departments, and other custodians of personal health information about interpretation of the applicable laws and policies in specific circumstances of research uses. Following the enactment of legislation, there usually follows a period of education, discussion, and the launching of test-case lawsuits seeking clarification as to judicial interpretation of the legislative provisions. This period is still in progress. Add to this the fact that most individuals striving to respect the new laws are not legally trained, and the result is confusion and, at times, misinterpretation or inaccurate implementation of legal provisions in the resulting policies and procedures. Nobody wants to be on the wrong side of the law, so initial policy interpretations of the legal requirements have tended to err on the side of restricting access.

An additional complicating factor for health researchers and data custodians is the lack of consistency in the legislation. No two pieces of legislation are entirely alike, and the applicability and interactivity between the federal and provincial legislation are at times opaque. Health research is frequently conducted in multiple jurisdictions, and the regional differences and difficulty in meeting the varying requirements may be jarring or, indeed, may render aspects of comparative research impossible.[14]

Absence of Clarity Regarding Consent for Research Use of Personal Information

One particularly vexing concern within law and ethics is the question of health research uses of personal information without consent. A substantial and increasing amount of research is conducted utilizing database information that was originally collected for treatment or administration. In most circumstances, the individual patient is not notified that the information collected might be used for research.

Understandably, researchers have a keen interest in gaining access to such information in order to conduct their research. Additionally, the risks associated with this breach of confidentiality often appear minimal, and the value of the proposed health research high. Further, the seeking of consent for secondary use of the information may be unmanageable or may give rise to a range of further issues, including the need to re-identify the data to contact the individual for permission to use the data, the risk of introducing bias into the sample, and cost concerns.[15]

On the other hand, the privacy interests of individuals should not get lost in the mix.[16] The problem is exacerbated by the stark and limited options utilized at present: project-specific consent versus exemption from requiring consent (or sometimes even notification) as to research use of the information. Options such as prior authorization or "broad consent"[17] have been suggested, but their status in law is unclear[18] and there has not been a great deal of examination of the ethics of such approaches.

Additionally, current models of consent for research participation are heavily influenced by the clinical trials paradigm and do not translate well to the secondary use of data. The risks to individuals associated with secondary use of personal information are very different from the risks associated with participation in a trial of a new drug, device, or surgical procedure. The former are more concerned with potential breaches of confidentiality whereas the latter are potentially physically invasive.[19]

When consent is sought—for example, if enrolling patients prospectively into a disease registry that will be used for research—an unresolved challenge is how much information to provide patients. It may be impossible for consent to be fully informed, as many of the future research uses may not yet be fully articulated. Even if it were possible to articulate all the potential users and uses, limitations on these uses, risks, and safeguards to mitigate those risks, most individuals would likely encounter decision overload, which could lead to arbitrary decision-making, refraining from making any decision, or post-decision regret.[20] At the other extreme, some institutions have implemented blanket consent processes indicating to patients, on admission to the hospital or registration with a clinic, that their information might be used for research purposes. The legal status of such practices is unclear and their meaningfulness to patients is questionable.

Polls of public opinion do not point to easy policy solutions. Recent survey research suggests that people generally support their health information being used for research, but most wish to retain some control over use of their information, even if that consists only of a reliable system of notification and opt-out.[21] No single approach to consent in the use of personal information for health research receives majority support: about one-third of the population choose conventional project-specific consent, another one-third prefer a broad authorization (opt-in), one-quarter choose a notification and opt-out system if researchers want to use their information for health research, and the remaining 12 percent are unconcerned if researchers use their information without notification.

Heterogeneity in Institutional Policies and Procedures and in Ethics Review Processes

Research ethics boards (REBs) vary in composition, training of their members, outlook, and application of the *Tri-Council Policy Statement*. Policies and practices therefore differ: research that is readily allowed in one place might be strictly circumscribed or disallowed in another location.[22] While recent years have witnessed substantial progress in these matters,[23] there is still considerable variation in policies and procedures for managing privacy, confidentiality, and security. This variation leads to challenges of inconsistency in execution of multisite studies and considerable frustration on the part of researchers.

Complicating the problem is the fact that many research studies making secondary use of personal health information draw upon data from multiple jurisdictions. In these circumstances, multiple REBs may need to review the research protocol. In some cases, there may also be a separate review by the data custodian's privacy officer. There are two challenges here. First, the process of obtaining REB approval can be very time consuming, sometimes delaying commencement of research by months while incurring substantial up-front costs.[24] Second, there may be substantial variation in judgments over whether consent is required for particular research, or the conditions under which the research may be exempted from requiring consent.[25] If REB requirements differ substantially, there is a risk that the data collected across sites might be incommensurate, which could threaten the validity of the data. The challenge is compounded further when multiple data custodians have different requirements.

"Anonymous" Data and the Challenge of Re-identification

Virtually all privacy laws apply only to data that identify individuals either directly or indirectly. It is difficult, if not impossible, to declare definitively that non-aggregated data are truly "anonymous" because it may remain possible to use combinations of the remaining data to indirectly re-identify individuals through matching these variables with other files that contain identifying information. The classic example was that of a graduate student at the Massachusetts Institute of Technology who was able to identify the Governor of Massachusetts from an "anonymized" dataset by matching the combination of sex, date-of-birth, and full postal code with information available on a public voters' registry.[26] It becomes more difficult to prevent re-identification when one is dealing with a rich dataset with dozens of variables about, for example, health care services use, especially if the dataset includes multiple dates like admission, discharge, and when specific procedures were conducted.

One can minimize the risk of re-identification using statistical or other technological procedures, such as switching values of variables.[27] These methods, however, are designed for producing high-level statistical tables. Their impact is unknown if more complicated analyses, such as statistical modelling of cause-and-effect associations, are undertaken.

Insufficient Capacity for Secure Management of Data

Several large data repositories are exemplary in their secure management of data for research purposes.[28] In these cases, there has been significant investment in the physical plant to ensure that "intruders" are identified and stopped before there is any possibility of access to data.[29] Security systems can be custom built, managed, and controlled, ensuring adherence to high standards and adaptability even as those standards change. However, this requires ongoing investment in highly skilled staff who are capable of developing these systems, keeping up with technology and privacy standards, linking and de-identifying data, and analyzing data. Costs of infrastructure development and ongoing compliance, which are substantial, are often not covered through operating grants available to researchers.[30]

Currently, these kinds of laboratories are not available at every university in the country. In fact, much academic research is done by small research teams that lack equivalent structures available to researchers who work in secure data enclaves. However, powerful personal computers and the gradual expansion of clinical electronic health records in the inpatient and outpatient settings make the development of smaller ad hoc research databases both easy and inexpensive to assemble.

The result is heterogeneity in the level of safeguards for personal information used in research. A researcher at a large data repository may expect to encounter a high level of data protection, including formalized training in privacy policies and procedures, and constant checks and balances on activities. In contrast, access to similar data in a smaller research unit may involve a researcher putting data onto a laptop with few or no safeguards in place. The result can be a substantial security breach, as was the case with the theft of a researcher's computer containing the fully identifiable records of thousands of patients participating in several research studies.[31] This is not to impugn the best intentions of researchers regardless of their work locations. Instead, it raises the question of how best to extend or ensure secure research environments for all researchers.

Low Comparability of Data

The *Canada Health Act* provides a federal framework for the provision of health-care services, but the management of the health-care system falls primarily under provincial or territorial jurisdiction. This structure has provided a natural "laboratory" for the comparative evaluation of health-care policies across provinces and territories; indeed, the deployment of different health-care policies across the country has been called the "great experiment."[32] Despite this obvious natural laboratory for comparative analysis, relatively little comparative research has actually been done. In some cases this is because of the difficulty of gaining access to data from multiple jurisdictions, but in other cases proposals are not even developed because of current challenges in comparing data generated in different provincial/territorial health-care systems.

The Canadian Institute for Health Information has made substantial progress in improving comparability of hospital data[33] and is working on developing other data sources, for example a National Ambulatory Care Reporting System and a National Pharmaceutical Drug Utilization Information System. But there are obvious challenges in such development. For example, some data are problematic because of variations between provinces (and, over time, within provinces) in who and what is covered by public programs. This is particularly the case with coverage for pharmaceuticals provided out-of-hospital and home health-care services because these services fall outside of the *Canada Health Act.* There are also challenges with interjurisdictional and interinstitutional variation in the operationalization of certain policy-critical statistics such as "wait times."

Perhaps the biggest challenge, however, rests with physician data. Fee schedules across jurisdictions are incommensurate, fee negotiations use different processes, the diagnostic codes used for billing have questionable validity for research purposes, and the mix of remuneration methods varies. And all of these things have been shifting—sometimes substantially—within jurisdictions. To date, little has been done to respond to these challenges, even though physician data are fundamental to understanding health status and health-care services use.

Failure to Design Research Use into the Common Interoperable Electronic Health Record (EHR) Infrastructure

Many people have put a great deal of stock in the emergence of a common interoperable electronic health record system for Canada, implicitly (or explicitly) assuming that the development of the EHR will replace administrative data sources for conducting research.[34] Certainly, the EHR is *an* answer, and in many respects a positive development, for reasons of patient care as well as the extraordinary research possibilities. However, it is not *the* answer for health services and policy research. In the best-case scenario, the EHR will still take many years to roll out, and there will still likely be administrative datasets that provide information useful for research (e.g., on characteristics of providers).

There will be many challenges encountered on the road to accessing data from the EHR for research purposes. Not least of these challenges is that, to date at least, researchers have had little involvement in the development of the EHR or the systems that house it. Without some influence on development, it is quite likely that the ultimate value of the data may not be what it could be, at least in terms of research.

More fundamentally, however, without researcher input, the issues of *how* and under *what conditions* researchers might have access to these data are unlikely to be addressed. It is looking more and more that the approach taken will be to develop the information systems for patient care, and then retrofit to make the data usable for research.[35] This is problematic for addressing the interests of both researchers (as discussed above) and those whose information will be accessed for research. Kosseim and Brady have labelled this "policy by procrastination."[36]

Political Hurdles

Even if the above issues of data privacy, quality, and comparability could be resolved, there would still remain several political challenges. For example, there have been long-standing sensitivities over federal-provincial sharing of data. Provinces are sensitive to increasing unilateral efforts at the federal level to effect health policy changes while cutting back on federal funding for health. As health care is primarily the purview of the provinces and territories, they have resisted federal government requests for data, direction on uses of additional funds, and federally initiated comparisons among provinces.[37]

Provincial governments are also reticent to allow more open access to researchers. There are three principal reasons behind this. First, governments are accountable to their citizens to ensure the safe handling of information that has been entrusted to them—including data made available to researchers. Thus, governments must ensure that researchers have the capacity to manage the data securely, understand the requirements of the law and why certain safeguards need to be maintained, and understand how to use the data to draw reasonable inferences.

Second, governments are also keenly aware of the potential for political embarrassment every time a report is produced with findings that speak to some aspect of the quality, distribution, or amount of services provided in their province. Indeed, substantial time goes into briefing ministers and preparing for media responses when a new research report or paper is issued. The amount of work involved in responding to a new report is not necessarily related to the quality or reliability of the research. If independent researchers were to gain easier access to data, the time spent in responding to reports (and the corresponding risk of issues management fatigue) would increase proportionately. This would certainly increase governments' reluctance to provide more open access to these data.

Finally, as more and more data are created, various parties demand access to the data for a myriad of secondary purposes. The expansion in uses of data over time is called "information usage creep" or "function creep." A challenge for any regulator is limiting access to health information for these secondary purposes. Governments may restrict access for research due to concern that they not set a precedent for accessing data for other secondary uses.

MOVING FORWARD

We have identified numerous challenges that are both complex and intertwined: confusion and uncertainty regarding law and policy; absence of clarity regarding consent for research use of personal information; heterogeneity in institutional policies and procedures and in the ethics review processes; insufficient capacity for secure management of data; low comparability of data; failure to design research use into the common interoperable electronic health record infrastructure; the proliferation of electronic databases; and political hurdles. Given these daunting challenges, a comprehensive solution for increasing researcher access to data may not be within our grasp at the present time. However, we offer a number of suggestions that may provide at least a partial roadmap for getting to that ultimate destination. At minimum, we anticipate that our comments will stimulate discussion and debate among researchers and policy-makers as to possible directions forward.

Rethinking the Place of Research Vis-à-vis Other Secondary Uses of Personal Health Information

As research becomes increasingly blurred with quality improvement, systems planning, and public health, it has been argued that we should be evaluating *all* secondary data uses—including research, quality improvement, systems planning, and public health—proportionate to the risks associated with accessing, processing, and disclosing that information.[38] This would help to dissolve the artificial distinction between research and other non-research secondary uses as discussed and even raise the ethical bar for quality improvement and similar activities. Clear guidance would be needed as to when research might be exempted from requiring consent for use of personal information.[39]

A more radical approach would be to expand the definition of *permitted* uses of health information to encompass management of (a) the care of individuals, (b) the health-care system, and (c) the health of populations. This option acknowledges more formally what have been, for decades, implicitly sanctioned uses of health information. Insofar as research provides evidence integral to decision-making, research that supports these permitted uses—clinical care, systems management, and public and population health—would then also be considered a permitted use.

This approach would provide a more coherent conceptual framework for the integration of data infrastructures into the interoperable EHR blueprint to support research[40]—a conceptualization that is consistent with the original recommendations of the Advisory Council on Health Infostructure, wherein the electronic health record would empower the general public, strengthen and integrate health-care services, create the information resources for accountability and continuous feedback on factors affecting the health of Canadians, and improve privacy protection within the health sector.[41] It would also provide the justification for researchers to participate in the design of the necessary research databases and the specifications for the data fields.

Formal integration of research uses into the EHR infrastructure would shift the debate from asking "*Should* health research be considered a permitted use of health information?" to asking "What *types* of research would qualify, and under what conditions?" In particular, questions would necessarily arise if, for example, the research had some commercial element or was ethically problematic (e.g., by stigmatizing some minority group). This is a proposal for shifting the line, but there is no escaping the hard fact that a line must be drawn.

Formal integration of research into permitted EHR uses may relieve the need for consent for each and every intended research use, but it does not entirely eliminate any role for consent. Depending on a variety of factors, including the type of research, the invasiveness, and the sponsor of the research, different research uses may allow for opting-in or opting-out.

Promulgate Consensus, and Clarify and Harmonize Laws and Policies Regarding Conditions for Research Use of Health Information

Regardless of whether certain types of research are conceptualized as legitimate uses of health information, we need to promulgate public consensus on the role of consent for different types of research and the necessary safeguards and conditions for those uses. Following this, we need to clarify and harmonize laws, and to educate REB members and data custodians. Finally, we need to educate the public about how their health information is being used. Each of these steps will be discussed in turn.

First, it would be beneficial to promulgate consensus across the multiple affected parties on acceptable circumstances for use of health information for research purposes, including (a) the place for individual consent,[42] (b) the necessary infrastructures for secure data management, (c) governance over and accountability for data use, and (d) the role of the commercial sector in research and how this affects consent. This consensus could be developed via a series of stakeholder consultations along with analysis of Canadian values on these topics through public dialogues. These consultations and dialogues might revolve around a series of case studies that represent the key archetypical types of research approaches that are likely to be utilized over the next couple of decades. One possible outcome of these consultations would be a series of suggestions as to appropriate conditions for use of health information, including the role of consent, with the understanding that different types of research may well require different types of consent.

Second, once areas of convergence across affected parties have been determined, guiding documents such as the *CIHR Best Practices for Protecting Privacy in Health Research*[43] and the *Pan-Canadian Health Information Privacy and Confidentiality Framework*[44] should be revised. These revisions should contain sufficient detail to reflect this consensus. Ideally, revisions would include the case studies developed for the consultations and would illustrate critical features of these cases that affect consent considerations. It may be anticipated that these steps—development of consensus and reflection of this consensus in key documents—will in turn lead to gradual revision of the relevant laws.

An additional route to be considered is to refer this matter to the Uniform Law Conference, which develops draft legislation for Canadian jurisdictions to consider adopting in those areas of primarily provincial jurisdiction that cry out for harmonized legislation. The use of health information by researchers would appear to be one such topic.

As identified above, a necessary and integral step is education of research ethics boards and data custodians. The process of education is already underway with the development of the CIHR best practices document[45] and the *Pan-Canadian Health Information Privacy and Confidentiality Framework*,[46] and with the CIHR-sponsored educational opportunities occurring across Canada. Education is an ongoing, iterative process as laws and standards develop over time.

There will also be a need to educate the public as to how their health information is being used for research and what are the options and mechanisms for participating or opting-out. To date, public education has been largely absent from discussions.

Developing Infrastructures, Policies, and Procedures

Even once privacy legislation, a fuller understanding of how to work through consent issues, and consensus on governance are in place, there will still be practical issues of data stewardship and management. We need to develop transparent and consistent policies and procedures that ensure secure and confidential management of these data. If there is no confidence in the physical and technical capabilities for appropriate data stewardship and management, the amount and type of data available for research purposes are unlikely to increase, and may even shrink.

A set of "best practices" for data management has been developed that could be the basis for future certification of data repositories.[47] As well, these best practices could be adapted for use with smaller, clinical databases that may or may not end up in larger data repositories. This might give assurance to research ethics boards, and provide protection for researchers, where they can show their practices conform with accepted best practices in the field. The challenge is that meeting these standards requires a substantial investment in human resources and infrastructure, beyond the capacity of many smaller institutions. Therefore, infrastructures need to be developed to meet privacy and security requirements, and also to extend access to researchers who work outside of data enclaves.

Some steps have been made in this direction. CIHR resource grants, for example, acknowledge the "equipment-type" costs of health services research. Another possibility is setting up provincial or regional research centres that can serve as brokers for researchers wishing to access data. The challenge here is that many existing research centres are built as data enclaves, meaning that researchers have to travel to them and/or be affiliated with them to gain access to data. Some efforts are being made to expand the number of enclaves available through satellite centres.[48] An alternate approach is the development of virtual as well as physical structures.[49] All of these efforts to improve access to data must ensure that appropriate data protection measures are in place. Regardless of the particular approach to developing a secure research repository, long-term stable funding is necessary to ensure ongoing operating capacity for the organizations providing these services.

More effort could be made to facilitate the use of statistical disclosure control methods to reduce the risk of re-identification of data. This direction, while technically complex, could potentially facilitate greater access to microdata from administrative datasets, thereby increasing the amount of data available for research uses while minimizing risk to individual confidentiality. Also, the adaptation of these tools to the kinds of epidemiologic analyses employed by health services and policy researchers needs to be explored.

Finally, a necessary part of the infrastructure for the interoperable EHR is some mechanism for determining and managing individuals' consent choices for different types of research use. This will not be a simple or quick process. However, substantial inroads are being made toward providing patients with portals into their electronic health files. One possibility is to incorporate the ability of patients to monitor research uses of their health information and to opt in or out of certain research uses. These and other mechanisms for notification and control should be explored.

Designing Research Uses into the Electronic Health Record

Some efforts are currently underway to address the incorporation of research uses into the EHR. One example is the joint funding by CIHR's Institute of Health Services and Policy Research and Canada Health Infoway of a chair in evaluating the EHR; however, it is not clear that there will be a specific focus on researcher uses of data. In addition, Infoway has launched a series of consultative sessions, including one on secondary uses of information from the interoperable EHR.

Even in the presence of a pan-Canadian interoperable EHR, we anticipate there will be an ongoing need for access to other data sources— complementary sources of information that can help improve the quality of research and research evidence. In addition, population health research looks beyond the medical determinants of health, and so these researchers will seek information not found in the EHR.

Improving Resources for Researchers

Ultimately, researchers need more than access to data. They need to have training, data documentation, and other resources available to them to optimize their analyses of data. Helping researchers produce more sound research has the added benefit of responding to the political imperative of limiting data stewards' need to respond to misuse or misinterpretation of data—a great deal of which is based not on mischief but on insufficient understanding of the limitations of the data.

One response to the requirement for detailed understanding may be to limit access to users who either have proven their knowledge or who have an association with users (for example with a research centre) who are known to have relevant knowledge. This would provide some assurance that detailed knowledge is passed on, and that data stewards are not solely responsible for ensuring that new researchers are sufficiently trained in the complexities of administrative data. However, some researchers may regard this as a limiting and perhaps even draconian method, as it privileges individuals and organizations that are already established.

Another approach is to invest in documentation of data, not just at the level of individual variables, but also at the level of datasets and data systems. This documentation, often referred to as metadata, exists in some cases but is limited in others. Much could be done not only to improve this sort of documentation but also to ensure that research findings build on previous work by developing detailed information on new concepts, new ways of analyzing data, and ways of working with data that are available outside a limited circle of researchers. The pre-eminent example of this sort of effort is the "concept dictionary" developed by the Manitoba Centre for Health Policy.[50]

A third suggestion is to improve the educational and training resources available to researchers who wish to use data. Statistics Canada does this, for example, through seminars and training opportunities offered through its Research Data Centres. Population Data BC has a mandate in this area as well, with the intent of building a broad and virtual "community of researchers" who will encourage sharing of expertise and a broad-based building of research knowledge.

Improving the Efficiency of the Research Ethics Review Process

While harmonization of laws and education of REBs and data custodians will go a long way toward improving consistency in decision-making across sites, management of large multicentred studies remains challenging due to administrative delays. The *Tri-Council Policy Statement* does permit a research ethics board to accept the review conducted by another REB (Article 1.2), but in practice this is the exception rather than the rule. Initial research on this topic has been conducted by a working committee of the Interagency Advisory Panel on Research Ethics, and a series of recommendations developed.[51] However, the committee stopped short of recommending specific revisions to the policy statement, so much work remains to be done on this issue.

Securing the Trust of Governments

Some of the most important health services and policy research requires interprovincial comparisons of service delivery—for example, pharmaceutical benefits and home care services. The Canadian Institute for Health Information is continuing to develop databases, but the potential to link datasets is currently limited. Statistics Canada is working with jurisdictions to develop its holdings of administrative data, which can then be linked to population surveys. Plans include allowing researcher access to these data through Research Data Centres.[52] These efforts should be supported for cross-national comparative research, but will take some time to develop, and do not currently include key files like pharmaceuticals and physician services.

Some joint efforts have been conducted between pairs of provinces.[53] These kinds of project-specific analyses may lead to both greater comfort with and greater facility for interprovincial analyses.

CONCLUDING STATEMENT

All of the efforts described above would work toward securing the trust of all parties involved, including governments and other agencies who are data stewards. There is much to be done to improve access to data for research purposes in Canada. The primary need is to develop a plan for action. The issues involved are complex, touching on the interests of many stakeholders. Piecemeal developments have proven effective in some cases, but we need now to think about the larger endeavour. Variations in health-care systems across Canada provide a natural laboratory that has the potential to make enormous contributions to our understanding of what makes and keeps people healthy. It is our challenge to find a way to develop and use this laboratory that is consistent with privacy legislation and acceptable to everyone involved.

NOTES

1. G. Kephart, *Barriers to Accessing and Analyzing Health Information in Canada* (Ottawa: Canadian Institute for Health Information, 2002).
2. Throughout this chapter, our framing of "research uses" is restricted to those approaches consistent with health services/health policy research and population and public health research. Other uses—for example, for recruitment for clinical trials or translational bioinformatics—fall outside the scope of this discussion.
3. "Personal information" refers to information that either directly identifies an individual (e.g., name, address, social insurance number) or contains some combination of elements that allows indirect identification of an individual (e.g., date of birth combined with sex and postal code). This definition is adapted from Canadian Institutes of Health Research (CIHR) Privacy Advisory Committee, *CIHR Best Practices for Protecting Privacy in Health Research* (Ottawa: Public Works and Government Services Canada, 2005), http://www.cihr-irsc.gc.ca/e/documents/pbp_sept2005_e.pdf. In this chapter, we discuss both use of personal information for *health* research and use of personal *health* information for research. The former makes broad reference to research that includes the effect of non-medical factors (e.g., income and education) on the health of populations. The latter refers specifically to research uses of health sector holdings and electronic sources of health information.
4. D.J. Willison, L Schwartz, J Abelson, C. Charles, M. Swinton, D. Northrup, and L. Thabane, "Alternatives to Project-Specific Consent for Access to Personal Information for Health Research: What Is the Opinion of the Canadian Public?" *Journal of the American Medical Informatics Association* 14, no. 6 (2007): 706-12.
5. These "fair information principles" are the foundation of most privacy laws and policies in Western industrialized nations. See the Canadian Standards Association, *Model Code for the Protection of Personal Information: A National Standard of Canada*, CAN/CSA-Q830-96 (Mississauga, ON: Canadian

Standards Association, 1996). These principles have been developed, in large part, out of recognition by regulators that individuals will permit the use of their personal information only if they are confident that it is being reasonably protected. Central to these fair information principles are the following:

(a) Information about individuals is to be collected, used, or disclosed to others with a clear and finite purpose in mind.

(b) Unless impracticable, this collection, use, or disclosure should be done with the express consent of the individual. Exceptions may apply to this consent requirement, but these exceptions should be for specific purposes and should not go on for an indefinite time.

(c) Personal information collected for one purpose should not be used for another purpose unless consent is obtained from the individual, again with exemptions.

6. W.E. Thurston, A.R. Vollman, and M.M. Burgess, "Ethical Review of Health Promotion Program Evaluation Proposals," *Health Promotion Practice* 4, no. 1 (2003): 45-50. See also Alberta Research Ethics Community Consensus Initiative, *Protecting People While Increasing Knowledge: Recommendations for a Province-wide Approach to Ethics Review of Knowledge-Generating Projects (Research, Program Evaluation, and Quality Improvement) in Health Care* (Edmonton: Alberta Heritage Foundation for Medical Research, 2005).

7. National Center for Research Resources, Agency for Healthcare Research and Quality, and FasterCures, "Ensuring the Inclusion of Clinical Research in the Nationwide Health Information Network," Meeting Report (Washington, May 2006), http://www.fastercures.org/objects/pdfs/meetings/FC_AHRQ-NCRR_report.pdf. See also *UKCRC R&D Advisory Group to Connecting for Health: Report of Research Simulations* (UK Clinical Research Collaboration, 2007), http://www.ukcrc.org/pdf/CfH report June 07 full.pdf.

8. *Personal Information Protection and Electronic Documents Act*, S.C. 2000, c. 50.

9. British Columbia, *Personal Information Protection Act*, S.B.C. 2003, c. 63.

10. The five provinces are Alberta (*Health Information Act*, R.S.A. 2000, c. H-5), Manitoba (*Personal Health Information Act*, C.C.S.M. c. P33.5), Ontario (*Personal Health Information Protection Act, 2004*, S.O. 2004, c. 3, Sch. A.), Saskatchewan (*Health Information Protection Act*, S.S. 1999, c. H-0.021), and most recently Newfoundland and Labrador (*Personal Health Information Act*, S.N.L. 2008, c. P-7.01 (to be proclaimed).

11. Nova Scotia (http://www.gov.ns.ca/health/phia/default.asp) and New Brunswick (http://www.gnb.ca/0051/personal_health_information/index-e.asp).

12. Quebec, *Act Respecting the Protection of Personal Information in the Private Sector*, R.S.Q. c. P-39.1.

13. Canadian Institutes of Health Research, Natural Sciences and Engineering Research Council of Canada, Social Sciences and Humanities Research Council of Canada, *Tri-Council Policy Statement: Ethical Conduct for Research Involving Humans, 1998 (with 2000, 2002, 2005 amendments)* (Ottawa: Public Works and Government Services Canada, 2005).

14. Kephart, *Barriers*, see note 1. See also Subgroup on Procedural Issues for the TCPS (ProGroup): A Working Committee of the Interagency Advisory Panel on Research Ethics (PRE), "Ethics Review of Research in Multiple Settings and/or Involving Multiple REBs (Previously Multicentred Ethics Review): A

Discussion Paper and Recommendations" (Interagency Panel and Secretariat on Research Ethics, Ottawa, 2008).

15. CIHR Working Group on Case Studies, *Secondary Use of Personal Information in Health Research: Case Studies* (Ottawa: Public Works and Government Services Canada, 2002), http://www.cihr-irsc.gc.ca/e/pdf_15568.htm.

16. E. Gibson, J. Downie, G. Kephart, L. Schwartz, and D. Willison, "Conceptual Paradigms Responding to Privacy and Access Challenges in Health Research," submitted to the CIHR Ethics Office (2007).

17. The terms *prior authorization* and *broad consent* refer to authorization for use of one's information beyond a single application, to encompass a range of potential uses. This type of consent may come with restrictions, such as "use for stroke-related research." This is distinct from the term *blanket consent*, which does not include restrictions on those uses. An example here would be consent "for research" with no qualifiers. The legal status of all these alternatives to project-specific consent is unclear.

18. T. Caulfield, R.E.G. Upshur, and A. Daar, "DNA Databanks and Consent: A Suggested Policy Option Involving an Authorization Model," *BMC Medical Ethics* 4 (2003): 1-4. See also T. Caulfield, N. Ries, and T.C. Bailey, "Consent, Privacy and Confidentiality in Longitudinal, Population Health Research: The Canadian Legal Context," *Health Law Journal Supplement* (University of Alberta Law Institute, 2004).

19. N.C. Manson and O. O'Neill, *Rethinking Informed Consent in Bioethics* (New York: Cambridge University Press, 2007).

20. N. Ram, "Tiered Consent and the Tyranny of Choice," *Jurimetrics* 48, no. 3 (2008), ssrn.Com/Abstract=1112364 (accessed 10 November 2009).

21. Willison et al., "Alternatives to Project-Specific Consent," see note 4.

22. D.J. Willison, C. Emerson, K.V. Szala-Meneok, E. Gibson, L. Schwartz, K.M. Weisbaum, F. Fournier, K. Brazil, and M.D. Coughlin, "Access to Medical Records for Research Purposes: Varying Perceptions across Research Ethics Boards," *Journal of Medical Ethics* 34, no. 4 (2008): 308-14.

23. CIHR, *Best Practices*, see note 3. See also P.M. Slaughter, P.K. Collins, N. Roos, K.M. Weisbaum, M. Hirtle, J. Williams, P.J. Martens, and A. Laupacis, *Harmonizing Research & Privacy: Standards for a Collaborative Future. Privacy Best Practices for Secondary Data Use (SDU)* [CD-ROM] (Manitoba: Institute for Clinical Evaluative Sciences and Manitoba Centre for Health Policy, 2006).

24. C. Metcalfe, R.M. Martin, S. Noble, J.A. Lane, F.C. Hamdy, D.E. Neal, and J.L. Donovan, "Low Risk Research Using Routinely Collected Identifiable Health Information without Informed Consent: Encounters with the Patient Information Advisory Group," *Journal of Medical Ethics* 34, no. 1 (2008): 37-40.

25. Willison et al., "Access to Medical Records," see note 22.

26. L. Sweeney, "Weaving Technology and Policy Together to Maintain Confidentiality," *Journal of Law Medicine & Ethics* 25, no. 2&3 (1997): 98-110.

27. Statistical Policy Office, "Report on Statistical Disclosure Limitation Methodology," Statistical Policy Working Paper 22 (Statistical Policy Office, Office of Information and Regulatory Affairs, and Office of Management and Budget, Washington, May 1994). See also G.T. Duncan and S. Mukherjee, "Optimal Disclosure Limitation Strategy in Statistical Databases: Deterring Tracker Attacks Through Additive Noise," *Journal of the American Statistical Association* 95, no. 451 (2000): 720-29; and K. El Emam, E. Jonker, S. Sams,

E. Neri, N. Neisa, T. Gao, and S. Chowdhury, *Pan-Canadian De-identification Guidelines for Personal Health Information* (report prepared for the Office of the Privacy Commissioner of Canada, Ottawa, 2007), http://www.ehealthinformation.ca/documents/OPCReportv11.pdf.

28. Slaughter et al., *Harmonizing Research & Privacy*, see note 23.
29. For example, the Institute for Clinical Evaluative Sciences, the Manitoba Centre for Health Policy, the Centre for Health Services and Policy Research, and Population Data BC have all used awards from the Canada Foundation for Innovation to build secure physical premises with state-of-the-art server rooms, moated areas for programmers, and surveillance and security systems protecting the perimeters.
30. Slaughter et al., *Harmonizing Research & Privacy*, see note 23.
31. A. Cavoukian, *Order H0-004* (Toronto: Information and Privacy Commissioner of Ontario, 2007), http://www.ipc.on.ca/images/Findings/up-3ho_004.pdf.
32. M.J. McGregor, R.B. Tate, K.M. McGrail, L.A. Ronald, A.-M. Broemeling, and M. Cohen, "Care Outcomes in Long-Term Care Facilities in British Columbia, Canada: Does Ownership Matter?" *Medical Care* 44, no. 10 (2006): 929-35.
33. Canadian Institute for Health Information, *Quality Assurance Processes Applied to the Discharge Abstract and Hospital Morbidity Databases* (Ottawa: Canadian Institute for Health Information, 2007).
34. R.J. Romanow, *Building on Values: The Future of Health Care in Canada – Final Report* (Ottawa: Commission on the Future of Health Care in Canada, 2002), http://www.hc-sc.gc.ca/hcs-sss/alt_formats/hpb-dgps/pdf/hhr/romanow-eng.pdf. See also M.J.L. Kirby and M. LeBreton, *The Health of Canadians – The Federal Role, Final Report*, vol. 6, *Recommendations for Reform* (Ottawa: Standing Committee on Social Affairs, Science and Technology, 2002), http://www.parl.gc.ca/37/2/parlbus/commbus/senate/com-e/soci-e/rep-e/repoct02vol6-e.htm.
35. Infoway revised its Blueprint document in 2006 to include uses of the data for public health surveillance (see Canada Health Infoway, "EHRS Blueprint," http://knowledge.infoway-inforoute.ca/en/knowledge-centre/ehrs-blueprintv2.aspx). However, the capacity to conduct more sophisticated population-level analyses is, as yet, unclear.
36. P. Kosseim and M. Brady, "Policy by Procrastination: Secondary Use of Electronic Health Records for Health Research Purposes," *McGill Journal of Law and Health* 2 (2008): 5-45.
37. T. McIntosh, "Intergovernmental Relations, Social Policy and Federal Transfers after Romanow," *Canadian Public Administration* 47, no. 1 (2004): 27-51.
38. Alberta Research Ethics Community Consensus Initiative, *Protecting People*, see note 6.
39. A good starting point may be found in Section 3 of the CIHR privacy best practices document, see note 3.
40. Canada Health Infoway, "EHRS Blueprint," see note 35.
41. Advisory Council on Health Infostructure, *Canada Health Infoway: Paths to Better Health* (Final Report) (Ottawa: Health Canada Publications, 1999).
42. As noted above, there are consent options beyond the traditional dichotomy of conventional project-specific consent versus exemption from requiring consent. Other options include "broad opt-in to a range of research

with restrictions" and "notification with opt-out." See P. Singleton and M. Wadsworth, "Consent for the Use of Personal Medical Data in Research," *British Medical Journal* 333, no. 7561 (2006): 255-58. See also D.J. Willison, M. Swinton, L. Schwartz, J. Abelson, C. Charles, D. Northrup, J. Cheng, and L. Thabane, "Alternatives to Project-Specific Consent for Access to Personal Information for Health Research: Insights from a Public Dialogue," *BMC Medical Ethics* 9, no. 18 (2008), doi:10.1186/1472-6939-9-18.

43. Canadian Institutes of Health Research, *Best Practices*, see note 3.

44. Health Canada, *Pan-Canadian Health Information Privacy and Confidentiality Framework* (Ottawa, 2005), http://www.hc-sc.gc.ca/hcs-sss/pubs/ehealth-esante/2005-pancanad-priv/index-eng.php.

45. Canadian Institutes of Health Research, *Best Practices*, see note 3.

46. Health Canada, *Confidentiality Framework*, see note 44.

47. Slaughter et al., *Harmonizing Research & Privacy*, see note 23.

48. The Institute for Clinical Evaluative Sciences in Toronto, for example, is creating satellite centres in Ontario, so that researchers can have access without travelling to Toronto.

49. See, for example, the Population Data BC website, www.popdata.bc.ca. Population Data BC is developing a different hybrid model where data are held centrally, but access is allowed (to approved research datasets) through "virtual private network" type facilities over the Internet. In this model, researchers are not bounded by geography (within Canada), university, or research centre affiliation.

50. Manitoba Centre for Health Policy, "Research Tools: Concept Dictionary," http://umanitoba.ca/faculties/medicine/units/mchp/resources/concept_dictionary.html.

51. Subgroup on Procedural Issues for the TCPS, "Ethics Review," see note 14.

52. "The Research Data Centres Program" (2009), available on the Statistics Canada website, http://www.statcan.gc.ca/rdc-cdr/index-eng.htm.

53. J.M. Paterson, G. Carney, G. Anderson, K. Bassett, G. Naglie, and A. Laupacis, "Case Selection for Statins Was Similar in Two Canadian Provinces: BC and Ontario," *Journal of Clinical Epidemiology* 60, no. 1 (2007): 73-78. See also M. Mamdani, L. Warren, A. Kopp, J.M. Paterson, A. Laupacis, K. Bassett, and G.M Anderson, "Changes in Rates of Upper Gastrointestinal Hemorrhage after the Introduction of Cyclooxygenase-2 Inhibitors in British Columbia and Ontario," *Canadian Medical Association Journal* 175, no. 12 (2006): 1535-38. See also notes 39 and 40.

SECURING A BRIGHT HEALTH INFORMATION FUTURE: CONTEXT, CULTURE, AND STRATEGIES

STEVEN LEWIS

This chapter is intended as a challenge to the belief that the open and highly diffused use of health information for research and other non-clinical purposes is inherently sensitive and dangerous. It examines the rationale for restrictive policies and addresses the privacy and related concerns that feature prominently in the debates about policy, access, and use. The premise of the chapter is that Canadian health care will not improve unless and until its practices are driven by high-quality, real-time data analyses. Both scientific discovery and quality improvement will be impeded by a restrictive approach to data use. In the current Canadian climate, for the most part prospective users of health data have to argue why this information should be made available and under what circumstances; in an advanced health information culture, the onus would be on policy-makers and stewards to justify why it should not.

Canada is at a crossroads in the evolution of its health information agenda. As a country we have a long history of accumulating and analyzing administrative data. While a great deal of insight has emerged from these data and their uses, there are limits to what they can reveal and, more importantly, to what improvements they can support. The information

Data Data Everywhere: Access and Accountability? ed. C.M. Flood. Montreal and Kingston: Queen's Policy Studies Series, McGill-Queen's University Press. © 2011 The School of Policy Studies, Queen's University at Kingston. All rights reserved.

revolution currently underway has the potential to improve practice, resource allocation, social justice, and health outcomes. But the potential is at risk on several grounds, which is why it is important to identify the challenges to data access and address them transparently and cogently.

Debates surrounding the design of health information systems and their use are grounded in culture. Health information is contested ground. Coming from different cultures, policy-makers, practitioners, and researchers often have different views on the balance between opportunity and risk, and intended and unintended consequences of data use.[1]

Citizens are by and large bystanders in these cultural clashes, but from time to time various constituencies conduct surveys or polls to coat their perspectives in the sheen of democratic legitimacy. However, it is both easy and tempting to engineer the desired results of a public consultation.

Unfortunately, too often the prospect of an honest and transparent debate is thwarted by the failure to disclose ulterior motives, and by the use of language that conceals rather than illuminates one's true position. Usually, those opposed to a liberal policy of data access use the language of privacy, consent, legitimacy, potential harm, and rights.[2] Rarely are the issues cast in terms of interests, power, clinical autonomy, accountability, and control—yet these factors are as integral to the debate as the real and nuanced concerns about privacy and potential harm.

CANADA'S HEALTH INFORMATION ENVIRONMENT

When medicare began and spread across Canada in the 1960s and 1970s, one of the great benefits was the development of administrative databases that—largely as an unintended consequence—created opportunities for population-based health services research and analysis. These databases, collected mainly for physician billing and financial management purposes, also contained considerable lodes of mineable clinical data. As a result, for 20 or 30 years Canada was at or near the head of the pack in terms of the quality and comprehensiveness of its data, and their use in health services research.

Times have changed and our position has become more tenuous. The use of these data for research purposes has always been constrained. It typically takes a long time and considerable cost to assemble and clean data for research purposes, so the findings from most studies are several years old. Governments collect and are the ultimate stewards of the data, and they set the terms and conditions for third party use. Access is uneven but generally restricted, even for agencies fully in the public sector. For example, in many regional health authorities, even senior public officials and managers cannot access physician-specific utilization data.

Canada now ranks last in the seven countries studied by the Commonwealth Fund in the rollout of the electronic medical record (EMR).[3] One of the consequences is that much practice continues to be unsupported by modern information technology. Interprofessional communication is uneven. Patients endure both inconvenience and quality defects. We know little in real time about the results of health-care interventions, the root causes of either excellent or poor quality, or the pathways to improved practice. Quality improvement initiatives remain voluntary, local, and labour intensive. What we do know about the system is sobering: error abounds, the morbidity and mortality toll is high, and a 60 percent real increase in health-care spending in the last decade has not been sufficient to ensure timely, reliably high quality, responsive person-centred care.

Because care is not primarily driven by real-time, relevant, comprehensive information, it is driven by other forces. While there have been laudable efforts to refashion funding and payment systems to address needs and support quality, by and large the system pays for volume and activity, and in many cases we pay more for bad quality and mistakes than for excellence.[4] Figure 1 illustrates the dominant approach to funding in Canada.

This approach to funding is not merely of theoretical interest. Those cultures that seek out and rely on health information to inform decisions at all levels have driven the most highly cited system-transformation successes. In high-performing health systems such as the Veterans Affairs

FIGURE 1
Canadian Health-Care Financing Method

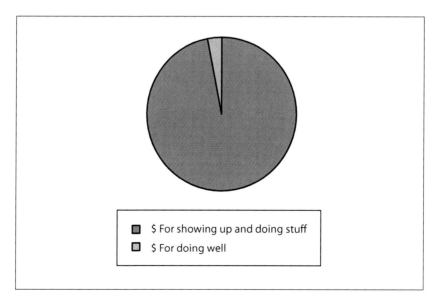

Source: Author's illustration of how health budgets flow in Canada—not empirically derived.

system in the United States and Jönköping County in Sweden, the collection, standardization, and widespread use of health information has been integral to large-scale improvement. Imagining that Canada can dramatically improve its health system performance without a widely accessed, first-rate health information system is a delusion. So, too, is the notion that a multibillion dollar investment in health information technology will yield optimal returns absent good design and a public interest–oriented policy on data use.

The remainder of this chapter proposes an approach to thinking about the health information policy agenda, and raises a number of questions that need to be answered to inform public policy. A precondition for sound public policy is a full exploration of the issues underlying the policy debates.

UNPACKING THE QUESTIONS

Privacy: Getting to the Heart of the Matter

Health information about identifiable people can be misused and cause harm: about this there should be no dispute. There is an obligation to protect privacy and mitigate both the potential to violate it and the harms that ensue when and if a violation occurs. Privacy is a heavily weighted concept, so it is important to ascertain whether it or something else is at the heart of disputes about the collection and use of health information for research. A number of questions emerge in the current context:

Who has a right to privacy? Citizens and health system users clearly do. In the Canadian context the more contentious issue is whether providers, both institutional and individual, are entitled not to disclose identified performance data. There has been a long history of producing reports and analyses that code organizations and individual providers to conceal identity (e.g., hospital A, B, C). There appears to be no solid ethical or legal justification for withholding such information, and there is a substantial literature advocating an obligation to disclose, for instance, surgeon-specific outcomes.[5] This perceived obligation exists even though it is precisely providers who are potentially the most affected by the revelations inherent in the use of health information to report on performance in various dimensions. There are many cogent *methodological challenges* to the validity of performance data at both the facility and individual levels, but these challenges should not be confused with *ethical principles*.

What types of health information require vigilant stewardship? There are three general categories of personal health information:

(a) data that include the actual name or other obvious identifiers of a person;

(b) data that are about *an* individual but not an individual whose identity is known ("these data pertain to person X" is critically different from "these data pertain to Alice Smith of 123 Wilson Road in Brampton"); and

(c) data that are fully anonymized, with no potential to re-identify.

Each category has a commensurate level of sensitivity and risk. Few would argue that category (a) information use should not be subject to strict criteria. There is some dispute about category (b), hinging on the matter of potential identifiability. If the risk for practical purposes is non-existent or immaterially low—ultimately an empirical question—then category (b) becomes, essentially, category (c).[6] And since the vast majority of proposed uses of health information by governments, health-care organizations, and researchers fall into category (c), the central question is whether there is significant risk inherent in the use of definitively anonymized health data. By definition, privacy is not at risk here, so objections would have to be made on other grounds.

Is public expression of concern about the use of information in general sufficient to put a chill on the extensive use of anonymized health information? In other domains, person-specific information (gleaned from commercial trans-actions, subscriptions, websites, etc.) is widely and often annoyingly used without incurring huge public opposition or behavioural change. It seems inconsistent to object to the use of anonymized information to improve a system to which the public is deeply attached. Public opinion (for what it's worth) strongly supports such use. It can be argued that consistency is too high a standard to apply to public sentiment: the citizenry has a right to policy eclecticism. Others will argue that some public policies and practices should not depend merely on public sentiment because that would jeopardize the public interest.[7]

Is health information inherently sensitive if it is not personally identifiable? Reflexively, many would say "yes" because health is a deeply personal issue. But on closer examination it is not at all clear why anonymized health information is more sensitive than income distribution data or the air quality index. "There are 32 HIV cases in Red Deer" is an epidemio-logical fact of an entirely different order than "Alice Smith of 123 Wilson Road is HIV positive." Aggregate and anonymous data are simply facts; they are, by definition, not facts about anyone in particular.

Is there any defensible right or entitlement for an individual to keep personal but fully anonymized information out of public databases? If so, what is the ethical or other basis for exercising this entitlement? What is the balance between the public interest and individual interests in this case?

Qualifications, Legitimacy, and Misuse: What Are the Issues?

One of the arguments against a liberal policy on access to data is potential misuse, which can take several forms, including misunderstanding what the data mean, misinterpreting the data intentionally or inadvertently, and using the data for purposes not considered in the public interest. These forms of misuse imply two categories of potentially worrisome users: those who are not competent to analyze, interpret, and communicate the findings, and those who would use the findings for allegedly deplorable purposes.

The issue of misuse raises the following questions:

- Is the potential misuse of health data—again, presuming these data are fully anonymized—any more dangerous or inimical to the public good than the misuse of any other kind of data? If so, why?
- What is the rationale for restricting data use to users with specific credentials? Who should decide what credentials are needed? What policies or procedures could be put in place to widen access to data while adequately mitigating the potential for error or misuse?
- Are there categories of data users for whom access to anonymized data should be virtually absolute? For example, should agencies that are part of the publicly financed health-care system—regional health authorities, governments, hospitals, home care programs—have blanket authorization to use such data? Where users are employees, they can be governed by policies and sanctions that powerfully reinforce responsible use. It is not clear why the advancement of the public interest requires any distinction between government and other public sector agencies over which government has control. In any case, reasons should be articulated; policy should not derive solely from past practices and power.
- Should different rules be in place for private sector access to anonymized health data? If so, what is the rationale? Is it better that private sector research and activity be informed by (at least some of) the same data used to inform public sector decisions, or by different data?

Objections That Dare Not Speak Their Names

As noted above, sometimes privacy concerns are genuine, while in other cases they may be pretexts used to camouflage the real objections to broader data access, use, and reporting. This possibility raises a further series of questions about what drives the privacy arguments put forth by various groups:

- In what circumstances is there a legitimate fear that disclosure of data, even with sound privacy protection, could cause harm to individuals or identifiable groups? Is there a taxonomy or catalogue of such instances and, if so, what are their common characteristics? Can the concerns be addressed without compromising all data access?

- To what extent are providers' concerns about being measured and judged the real rationale for their objecting to assembling, analyzing, and reporting on health information?

- To what extent is antipathy to wider data access, use, and reporting based on concerns about evidence-based findings supplanting opinion, anecdote, and tradition as bases for decision-making—thereby enhancing transparency and accountability?

- To what extent are claims to or policies that create differential access to information based on protection of privileged position rather than protection of substantive merit and the public interest? Is there an underlying fear of democratizing data and, if so, on whose part, on what basis, and to what end?

Using Privacy Protection to Address Other Problems

It is important to protect privacy, and many concerns about privacy are serious and legitimate. Privacy is in one sense an intrinsic good: the right to be left alone, or to keep information about oneself to oneself, is a core value in liberal democracies.

One can elevate privacy to a right, in which case it does not need to be defended on instrumental grounds. However, this right is not absolute in the context of health information because it has long been established that, on occasion, legitimate claims to privacy must yield to a greater good.[8] Moreover, it matters that medicare is a universal public system that creates an obligation for its funders and providers to manage it well, which in turn requires data about the people it serves. In the case of anonymized data, a utilitarian calculus seems appropriate: What is the ratio of benefits to costs (of all types) inherent in using the data, and is the ratio acceptable?

The violation of privacy can have consequences ranging from deadly serious to utterly benign: blackmail is quite different from junk mail. Since health and health care are in some aspects unique, it is worth examining why some violations cause harm, and what the remedies might be. Here are some questions that need to be addressed:

How and in what circumstances can we expect a privacy violation to cause real harm? Why does harm result? Does there have to be a specific author of the harm or is the violation in itself harmful?

Where discrimination against individuals or groups is a predictable consequence of data use and reporting, is the privacy violation the real problem, or the consequent discrimination? Some "privacy" concerns cannot be made invisible—for example, the appearance of characteristic lesions in people with AIDS, or seizures in people with epilepsy, or the physiognomy of people with Down syndrome. For them, privacy is unavailable. In these cases, we do not deplore the absence of privacy; instead, we rightly deplore the attitude and actions of the discriminators. This is not an argument to deny those fortunate enough to have an invisible condition their continued privacy; it is to suggest that the adverse consequences are due not to the lack of privacy, but to discrimination. Furthermore, we should not allow a legitimate preoccupation with privacy to diminish efforts to address the root cause of the harm, which is discrimination.

To what extent is protection of privacy conflated with concerns about the misuse or misunderstanding of data? What are other possible measures to minimize the risk of misinterpretation? It is generally understood that the search for truth (or progress, or a solution to a problem) flourishes where many people freely explore its dimensions, advance propositions, and test them against competing notions. There are always missteps and blind alleys along the way, but these are the progeny of uncertainty and openness and in many cases essential steps in the journey. In other words, free inquiry by many people using the same data is in itself a self-correcting mechanism by which even the most entrenched accepted "truths"—the Ptolemaic universe, the non-bacterial causes of stomach ulcers—are eventually superseded. In science, including health science, all truths are contingent and, in theory, falsifiable by new observations or new data. There is good reason to expect that wider access to and broader use of data will lead to earlier detection and correction of errors. This is not to deny the potential harm caused by misuse or misunderstanding of data; it is to balance that harm against the enormous benefits that accrue from a broadly dispersed and open search for truth that thrives in an open information environment.

To what extent are arguments for restricted use based on concerns that multiple explorations may challenge existing policy and practice, unsettle communities of practice, or raise doubts about firmly held preferences and values? That change is often difficult to manage is a small price to pay for the good that comes from abandoning obsolete practices and embracing new insights. How much objection to the use of data is based on providers' fears that exposing certain truths will cause embarrassment, negative judgment, and reduced autonomy? To the extent that these fears are a cause of antipathy toward a more open health information culture, surely the most effective and durable approach is to address them directly, rather than camouflage the anxieties in the language of privacy and misuse.

BEYOND THEORY: LOOKING AT THE TRACK RECORD ON DATA USE

It is easy to construct scenarios of harm-causing privacy violation and data misuse of various types. There can be no definitive rejoinder to theoretical harms; as long as they are logically coherent, they will be persuasive to some. For every dazzling encryption there is the prospect of a master decoder. Fortunately, health information use is not a new phenomenon, and there is experience to instruct us on the following questions:

- What kinds of data security violations have taken place historically, and which of them have actually caused harm to individuals? What proportion of these violations resulted from carelessness and/ or failure to follow established policy (e.g., encrypting files, using passwords, not transferring data from secure sites to laptops)?
- Where has anonymization not sufficiently protected privacy? What have we learned from these experiences and how have protections evolved to reduce the chance that they will happen again?
- What is the role of penalties, sanctions, and other measures in deterring data security violations?
- Are expressed concerns about privacy and data security violations commensurate with historical experience and the actual harms experienced? If the perception of risk and probability of harm is inaccurate, what would be the most effective way to communicate the actual situation?

There have been many reports of sloppy data security—laptops left in taxicabs with hard drives full of data without password protection, paper records blowing about in alleyways, and failure to follow established policies. These are indefensible transgressions that rightly raise media and public concerns. Notably, though, it seems impossible to find the catalogue of actual harms resulting from these violations. The person who steals the laptop left in an unlocked car is not interested in the data, but in fencing the computer. Citizens are not lurking beside dumpsters in the hope that a carelessly disposed paper medical record will furnish them with information to use against an individual. Very few people have any motive to learn anything about an identifiable individual's health condition.

Some do—for example, in some cases, insurance companies or employers. There are laws governing non-consenting access to such information, and there are non-discrimination provisions in human rights codes that should be powerful deterrents to misuse. Many insurers require accurate disclosure of relevant health information as a condition of underwriting a policy. Some insurers are prohibited from risk selection.[9] None of these

realities is an excuse for being blasé about consent and ironclad protection of privacy. But nor should the theoretical possibility of potentially
sinister use have undue influence over the development of the health
information culture and policies governing data use.

Information Is Power

To accept uncritically that advocacy of a restrictive data access policy
is based exclusively on concern for public and patient welfare is to be
oblivious to the realities of power, hierarchy, privilege, resource allocation, and professional identities. It is difficult to begin a conversation
that raises the spectre of ulterior motive, but avoidance merely conceals
an important reality.

Information is the great leveller: where performance is transparent,
power shifts from autonomous practitioners to peers, managers, govern-
ors, and ultimately service recipients and their families. The information
revolution has already begun to redress the huge asymmetry of information between health-care providers and everyone else in the system. This
is and should be seen as an advance not only by the public and their
agents, but by practitioners as well. Working smarter is invariably better
than working in the dark. Teamwork and engagement of individuals
more fully and in a more evidence-oriented way in their own health and
care are advances possible only in a highly developed health information culture. Information and disclosure are powerful tools for improvement, and for demonstrating rather than simply assuming excellence.
Transparency and revelation mark a cultural shift, and cultural change
inevitably encounters resistance.

STRATEGIES FOR MOVING FORWARD

What is to be done? In particular, what steps need to be taken to ensure
that a historic opportunity does not pass Canada by? It will take a multi-
pronged, systematic effort to secure Canada's health information future.
There is important work to be done on three fronts:

- developing a more knowledgeable and information-oriented culture
  at all levels;
- reducing the risks of ethical and security violations that—regardless
  of their actual impact—might compromise public support; and
- designing information systems and access provisions that maximize
  the returns on the investments in health information technology.

Effecting cultural change requires broad-based engagement and advocacy
supported by policy. Such change originates in a deeply felt dissatisfaction
with the status quo and a sense of urgency about the need for reform.

Health and health care are infinitely complex, layered with politics and fraught with uncertainty. Changing the information culture has proven difficult, and the way forward is by no means clear. The following set of proposals envisions a diverse set of initiatives on the part of many actors. Some are more practical than others, and the shortest way to success would be a unified resolve among governments to promote an open information culture and enshrine key principles and processes in legislation. Only an undeterrable optimist would hold much hope for such a definitive step in the short term, which suggests it is prudent to keep all avenues open for exploration.

The proposals here are intended more as food for thought than carefully crafted and tested recommendations. They are a menu of options to consider, and if a reasonable number find takers, some momentum may develop. While suggestions about which organizations might take the lead are attached to each proposal, the issues must be aired and resolved at multiple levels. Individual voices matter, and where opinions differ, there must be opportunities for debate and processes for making decisions.

In most cases it would be wise to build in opportunities for broader, non-token public engagement. Although most of the precise work and development of options will inevitably fall to experts and insiders, whatever is ultimately recommended should be shared in deep deliberative processes with the public (polling based on simple questions, implausible hypotheticals, or limited choices are especially unlikely to yield anything valuable).

Fostering Cultural Change

1. Establish partnerships to articulate and promote the principle that health information is a public asset whose joint stewards are governments, health organizations, and providers united by a commitment to using health information to advance the public interest.
   Lead responsibility: Canadian Institutes for Health Research (CIHR), Canadian Health Services Research Foundation (CHSRF), Canadian Institute for Health Information (CIHI), Statistics Canada, Canada Health Infoway

2. Encourage governments to promote a culture of information use and application in their public statements (e.g., throne speeches, budget documents, white papers) and policies.
   Lead responsibility: CIHR, CHSRF, CIHI, Statistics Canada, provincial granting agencies, Canada Health Infoway

3. Develop a sustained strategy for engaging the media and the public on the importance of using health information widely and often to advance the public interest.
   Lead responsibility: a broad partnership of granting agencies, universities, and health-care agencies, with CIHR/CHSRF taking the lead

4. Establish standing committees, permanent forums, and/or other mechanisms whereby governments, health-care organizations, professions, data repositories, and researchers regularly convene to discuss and develop information use goals and policies.
    Lead responsibility: a broad partnership including research granting agencies and quality councils, with regional health authorities taking the lead

5. Create opportunities for health professionals to develop and work in a culture that embraces the importance of using administrative and clinical data for surveillance and research purposes.
    Lead responsibility: academic health sciences centres, CIHR, CHSRF, provincial granting agencies

6. Promote and support the principles and strategies discussed at the broadly attended 2005 and 2007 Montebello and Kananaskis summits, and particularly the importance of designing the EHR and EMR to support extensive analytical use at all levels.
    Lead responsibility: CIHR, CHSRF, CIHI, Canada Health Infoway

Ensuring Ethical Data Use

7. Develop national standards and guidelines for the use of administrative and clinical data for surveillance and research to ensure privacy, confidentiality, and security.
    Lead responsibility: Tri-Council Agencies in partnership with Statistics Canada and existing data repositories

8. Develop a consistent approach to interpreting Canada's privacy legislation in relation to the use of administrative and clinical data for surveillance and research purposes.
    Lead responsibility: national and provincial privacy commissioners in consultation with health-care leaders

9. Develop and promote a consensus position on principles governing access to and the use of anonymized, person-specific, and identifiable person-specific health information respectively for non-clinical purposes, to form the basis for policies and practices on data access and use.
    Lead responsibility: Tri-Council Agencies in consultation with privacy commissioners, CIHI, governments, health-care organizations, researchers

10. Develop a program to increase the consistency with which research ethics boards interpret and apply principles and evaluative criteria governing access to data.
    Lead responsibility: Tri-Council Agencies

11. Strengthen commitments to data security, including standardized and mandatory protocols for researchers and other data users, various levels of sanctions for inappropriate use, and strategies for minimizing the potential impact of inadvertent lapses.
    Lead responsibility: Tri-Council Agencies, Statistics Canada, major data repositories

Information Systems Design, Policy, and Practice

12. Promote principles and policies that define clinicians, managers, health organizations, governments, and researchers as legitimate and interdependent partners in producing, analyzing, and reporting on health information.
    Lead responsibility: governments, professional organizations, health-care agencies

13. Encourage governments to develop their overall health information technology and systems plans to be compatible with and supportive of a progressive culture of research, analysis, accountability, and quality improvement.
    Lead responsibility: CIHR, CHSRF, CIHI, provincial granting agencies, health-care organizations, Canada Health Infoway

14. Engage governments to commit to ensuring that investment in the EHR and EMR is tied to developing common data standards, interoperability, and linkability.
    Lead responsibility: health-care organizations, CIHI, Statistics Canada, Canada Health Infoway

15. Develop opportunities to educate undergraduate and apprenticing health professional students about the need for and importance of health information use at all levels.
    Lead responsibility: academic health sciences centres, CIHR, CHSRF, provincial granting agencies

It will take a great deal of commitment by many people and organizations to create a principled, pragmatic, and advanced health information culture in Canada. Articulating the case, addressing concerns, dealing with unstated but competing agendas, and reshaping the vocabulary as well as expectations are hard and persistent work. The Canadian environment remains fragile, and a clear and honest debate is frustrated by the presence of subtexts and the absence of data-driven practice. Some access and usage issues are genuinely complicated, and some cases are hard. But just as hard cases make bad law, thorny data use cases make bad information access policy. A generally open and facilitating set of policies and practices does not preclude special vigilance in certain cases. Exceptions should be treated as exceptions. There is nothing wrong with raising concerns, exploring hypothetical cases, and identifying potential harms. The error is to focus too much on abstractions and low-probability scenarios and too little on context and the enormous harm that takes place every day because we do not use information enough, or well.

NOTES

1. Whether these views are expressed fully and openly is another matter. It is a socially desirable response to promote the use of health information and evidence-informed decision-making. The debates have not been fully resolved partly because the issues have not been directly and fully engaged. It is a breath of fresh air when papers such as Ouellet's in this collection are commendable for their clarity in revealing how organized medicine has a different view of data stewardship, access, and use than most other constituencies.
2. There are of course variations on these themes, and the vocabulary is richly diverse.
3. C. Schoen, R. Osborn, P.T. Huynh, M. Doty, J. Peugh, and K. Zapert, "On the Front Lines of Care: Primary Care Doctors' Office Systems, Experiences, and Views in Seven Countries," *Health Affairs (Millwood)* 25, no. 6 (2006): 555-71.
4. This is not hyperbole. A failure to prevent complications of a chronic disease will result in more physician visits, more interventions, and greater use of system resources. As a result, everyone involved will get paid more.
5. S. Clarke and J. Oakley, "Informed Consent and Surgeons' Performance," *Journal of Medical Philosophy* 29, no.1 (2004): 11-35; S.F. Marasco, J.E. Ibrahimand, and J. Oakley, "Public Disclosure of Surgeon-Specific Report Cards: Current Status of the Debate," *ANZ Journal of Surgery* 75, no.11 (2005): 1000-1004.
6. There is a distinction between partial person-specific data—for example, person X has a diagnosis of Type 2 diabetes—and complete and fully linked data about person X. The risks of identifiability generally rise with comprehensiveness, but to what extent will vary.
7. For example, only an extreme democrat would argue that a strongly held public opinion that building codes were too strict or expensive should govern how the bridge is built rather than technical expertise.
8. Examples include publicly visible quarantining of infected persons, and the duty to disclose communicable disease status to those with whom one has or contemplates intimate contact.
9. For example, sickness funds in a number of European countries, and insurers of groups of employees.

INDEX

CONTRIBUTORS

WENDY ARMSTRONG is an independent investigative researcher and long-time consumer advocate. For over 20 years she has monitored and researched the growth of new applications of information technologies and how these applications are changing relationships in both the private marketplace and public spaces. She is the former chair of the provincial Presidents' Council of the Consumers' Association of Canada and served as president and executive director of the Alberta Chapter from 1993 to 1998. Wendy's 2000 report for the Consumers' Association, *The Consumer Experience with Cataract Surgery and Private Clinics in Alberta: Canada's Canary in the Mine Shaft*, led to new regulation of these clinics and was cited by the dissenting judges in *R v. Chaoulli*. Her past committee work includes the Public Advisory Committee of the Law Commission of Canada, the Alberta Clinical Practice Guidelines Program, and the National Privacy Group on Health Information. Wendy is currently affiliated with PharmaWatch, the Alberta Consumers' Association, and Women and Health Protection.

ROGER CHAFE is the director of pediatric research and an assistant professor in the Faculty of Medicine of Memorial University of Newfoundland. He is also an adjunct professor in Dalhousie University's School of Health Services Administration and a member of the editorial board of *Healthcare Policy*. Previously, he was a CIHR/CHSRF post-doctoral fellow in the Department of Health Policy, Management and Evaluation at the University of Toronto and the Cancer Services and Policy Research Unit of Cancer Care Ontario; and a post-doctoral research associate of the Comparative Program on Health and Society at Munk Centre for International Studies. He is the author of *Allocating Health Care Resources in Canada: A Comparison of Nine Case Studies* and numerous articles and reports. He holds a PhD in medicine and an MA in philosophy from Memorial University.

LAUREL CHALLACOMBE is manager of research and evaluation at CATIE (Canadian AIDS Treatment Information Exchange). Laurel has worked in the field of HIV for over ten years and has held a variety of positions in both provincial and regional organizations, working in research and knowledge transfer and exchange. She holds a master's in health science in epidemiology.

MEGAN EDMISTON is an articling student at a Toronto law firm. While in law school, she was a research assistant at Canadian Institutes of Health Research's (CIHR) Institute of Health Services and Policy Research. She holds a JD from Queen's Faculty of Law and a BA from McGill University.

MARK FISHER has worked in the HIV/AIDS field since 1992, developing information technology solutions initially in the area of laboratory testing. Mark developed a database for the National Serological Reference Laboratory in Australia for HIV and HCV testing and surveillance. In 1995 he migrated to Canada and developed a similar database for the Provincial Public Health Laboratory, which performed all of the HIV testing in Ontario and expanded to other areas of serological testing. Mark has been involved with the Ontario HIV Treatment Network (OHTN) since 1999 in an ex officio capacity. In 2005 he joined the OHTN as director of information technology and has been involved in such initiatives as providing clinical management systems to HIV primary care doctors, a technology refresh for AIDS service organizations, technological infrastructure for the OHTN including the COHORT study, and supporting partners with their technology requirements. Current projects include OCHART and OCASE and the new initiative PHA Tools.

COLLEEN M. FLOOD is a Canada Research Chair in Health Law and Policy and was scientific director of the CIHR Institute for Health Services and Policy Research from 2006 to 2010. She is also associate professor in the Faculty of Law and cross-appointed to the School of Public Policy and the Department of Health Policy Management and Evaluation at the University of Toronto. She is the author of *International Health Care Reform: A Legal, Economic and Political Analysis* (Routledge, 2000) and the editor of *Access to Justice, Access to Care: The Legal Debate over Private Health Insurance* (University of Toronto Press, 2005, co-edited with Kent Roach and Lorne Sossin), *Just Medicare: What's In, What's Out, How We Decide* (University of Toronto Press, 2006), *Canadian Health Law and Policy*, 3rd edition (LexisNexis, 2007, co-edited with Jocelyn Downie and Timothy Caulfield), *Administrative Law in Context* (Emond Montgomery, 2008, co-edited with Lorne Sossin), and *Exploring Social Insurance: Can a Dose of Europe Cure Canadian Health Care Finance?* (McGill-Queen's University Press, 2008, co-edited with Mark Stabile and Carolyn Tuohy).

ANDREA S. GERSHON is a respirologist at Sunnybrook Health Sciences Centre and a scientist at the Institute for Clinical Evaluative Sciences. She is also a clinician scientist within the Division of Respirology, Department of Medicine, University of Toronto. Andrea's current research interests include investigating health outcomes, health services, and drug safety and effectiveness in individuals with respiratory disease. She holds a medical degree from the University of Toronto, where she trained in general internal medicine and respirology, and also completed a master's of science in clinical epidemiology.

ELAINE GIBSON is associate professor at the Schulich School of Law and associate director of the Health Law Institute at Dalhousie University. Her areas of expertise include health law, public health, medical malpractice, privacy law, patient safety, and torts. Elaine's current research interests include issues surrounding the privacy and confidentiality of health information, focusing on the uses of information in the areas of health research and public health surveillance. She has served on both the CIHR-IHSP Research Advisory Board and the CIHR Institute Advisory Board Ethics Designates Committee. Elaine is co-editor (with Jocelyn Downie) of *Health Law at the Supreme Court of Canada* (Toronto: Irwin Law, 2007). She holds an LLB from the University of Saskatchewan and an LLM from the University of Toronto.

MELISSA HUDSON is a senior advisor in the City of Toronto's Risk Management and Information Security division. Her areas of expertise include privacy and information security, with a focus on health-care privacy and e-health security. She currently conducts privacy impact assessments and threat risk assessments on the City's enterprise information systems. Previously, she was a senior privacy analyst at Cancer Care Ontario. Melissa is a Certified Information Privacy Professional/Canada (CIPP/C) and a Certified Information Systems Security Professional (CISSP). She holds an MA in political science from Stanford University.

ALAN KATZ is associate professor and director of research in the Department of Family Medicine at the University of Manitoba. He is a past chair of the Health Research Ethics Board in the Faculty of Medicine and is a senior researcher and associate director for research at the Manitoba Centre for Health Policy. Previously, he worked in rural Saskatchewan and at a community clinic in Winnipeg. His research interests are focused on primary care delivery, including quality of care indicators, knowledge translation, and disease prevention. He received his medical training at the University of Cape Town in South Africa.

DAVID KERRY has more than 15 years of experience as a research coordinator and data manager in the fields of HIV/AIDS and cancer research.

He has held a variety of positions in the development, implementation, and management of several health research databases.

Patricia Kosseim has been general counsel of the Office of the Privacy Commissioner of Canada (OPC) since January 2005. She oversees the Legal Services, Policy and Parliamentary Affairs Branch which provides strategic legal and policy advice on a broad range of complex privacy issues; represents the OPC before courts and parliamentary committees; and develops innovative legal and policy approaches for dealing with emerging privacy issues in collaboration with relevant stakeholders across multiple jurisdictions and sectors. Prior to joining the OPC, Patricia spent five years building up and leading the Ethics Office of the then newly created Canadian Institutes of Health Research. She has also worked with Genome Canada and Canada Health Infoway, and spent over six years with a large national law firm in Montreal. Patricia holds a master's in medical law and ethics from King's College, University of London (UK), as well as an LLB and a BCom from McGill University.

Steven Lewis is the president of Access Consulting and an adjunct professor in both the Department of Community Health Sciences at the University of Calgary and the Faculty of Health Sciences at Simon Fraser University. He is a health policy consultant and health services researcher. His interests include ethical issues such as distributive justice in health and health care, comparative health policy, and health services quality and utilization. Prior to resuming a full-time consulting practice in Saskatoon, Lewis headed a health-research granting agency and spent seven years as chief executive officer of the Health Services Utilization and Research Commission in Saskatchewan. He has served on a number of boards and committees, including the Canadian Institutes of Health Research's Governing Council, the Saskatchewan Health Quality Council, and the Health Council of Canada. He co-edited the first five annual Canadian Institute for Health Information *Health Care in Canada* reports, and has written extensively on how to strengthen medicare. He is also a member of the editorial board of *Open Medicine* and an associate editor of the *Journal of Health Services Research and Policy*.

Lisa M. Lix is associate professor and centennial chair at the School of Public Health at the University of Saskatchewan. She is also an associate member in the Department of Mathematics and Statistics and in the Department of Community Health and Epidemiology. Her research interests include case ascertainment methods for administrative health data, quality of secondary data, analysis of repeated measures/longitudinal data, and multivariate statistics. Lisa collaborates widely on projects about population health and the association between chronic disease and quality of life. She has served on the Board of the Statistical

Society of Canada since 2005 and holds the designation of Professional Statistician. She holds a PhD (interdisciplinary) from the University of Manitoba.

William W. Lowrance is a health research policy and ethics consultant. He has recently focused on the use of health information and biospecimens in research. He has prepared reports for the Nuffield Trust, the US National Human Genome Research Institute, the UK Medical Research Council, and the Wellcome Trust. He also chaired the Interim Advisory Group on Ethics and Governance during the start-up of UK Biobank. William is currently completing a book with the working title *Privacy, Confidentiality, and Health Research.*

Carol Major is a consultant/advisor for the Ontario HIV Treatment Network, a community-based organization committed to improving the quality of life of people with HIV, and is the technical consultant for the Ontario HIV Point of Care Testing Program. She was formerly the head of the HIV Laboratory for the Ontario Ministry of Health and Long-Term Care and has also served as chair of the Virology Committee of the Quality Management Program – Laboratory Services and as an assessor for the Ontario Laboratory Accreditation program. Carol continues to be involved in international HIV capacity development and is a founding member of the Canadian HIV International Program, a multidisciplinary organization committed to HIV capacity development in resource-poor settings.

Patricia Martens is a professor in the Faculty of Medicine at the University of Manitoba, and the director of the Manitoba Centre for Health Policy, an internationally acclaimed research centre for population health through the use of population-based health and social services administrative databases. She received the prestigious 2005 CIHR Knowledge Translation Award for Regional Impact for her work with Manitoba's Regional Health Authorities and the Department of Health (in a research collaboration with *The Need To Know* Team). Her research interests include studies on health status, inequities, healthcare use patterns of rural and northern residents, child health, and the health of Aboriginal people. She holds a CIHR/PHAC Applied Public Health Chair (2008–2013), and received the 2010 YM/YWCA Woman of Distinction for Health and Wellness. Dr. Martens has spoken at over 300 national and international conferences, and published over 200 articles.

Kim McGrail is an assistant professor at the University of British Columbia, associate director of the UBC Centre for Health Services and Policy Research, and a senior researcher with Statistics Canada. Kim's current research interests include variations in health-care services' use and outcomes, understanding health care as a determinant of health, comparative health policy, and the development of health information and technology to improve evidence and practice. She has collaborated with provincial and federal policy- and decision-makers, including the BC Ministry of Health Services, the Health Council of Canada, and the Canadian Institute for Health Information. Kim was the 2009–10 Commonwealth Fund Harkness Associate in Health Care Policy and Practice. She holds a PhD in health care and epidemiology from the University of British Columbia, and a master's in public health from the University of Michigan.

DALE MCMURCHY is an independent health-care consultant with experience in international, academic, private sector and governmental organizations, and expertise in health system and policy research, health financing and economics, policy, and planning with an emphasis on public health and primary health care. Her recent experience includes the evaluation of Ontario's Family Health Teams and, prior to that, the Primary Care Reform pilots, Ontario's Nurse Practitioner Initiative, Telehealth Ontario, and the Public Health Agency of Canada's programs targeted toward at-risk pregnant women and preschool children. She also managed HealthInsider, a semi-annual national health survey of 2,500 Canadians. At the time of writing, Dale was a senior consultant to the scientific director of Canadian Institutes of Health Research's (CIHR) Institute of Health Services and Policy Research. She is a member of the CIHR HIV / AIDS Research Advisory Committee, and served on the board of the Canadian Association for Health Services and Policy Research.

PEGGY MILLSON is an associate professor in the Dalla Lana School of Public Health at the University of Toronto. Since 1987, Peggy has been principal investigator or co-investigator for 38 research studies related to HIV and more recently hepatitis C, including studies of prevention, harm reduction, HIV in prisons, partner notification, psychosocial aspects of living with HIV for women, HIV care for marginalized populations, and costs of HIV in Ontario. She is the research consultant and scientific writer for two best practice documents created by the Provincial Infectious Disease Advisory Committee for the Ontario Ministry of Health and Long-Term Care: best practices for public health management of sexually transmitted diseases (including HIV), and best practices for public health management of hepatitis C. Peggy has an MD and specialty training in community medicine / public health, both from the University of Toronto.

KAMINI MILNES is director of cancer informatics for Cancer Care Ontario (CCO). She leads the cancer-related information management and business intelligence activities of CCO including data collection, standards, and quality; reporting and analytics; and development of a person-centred enterprise data warehouse for cancer. Her current areas of focus include implementing synoptic pathology reporting, automating the electronic collection of collaborative staging data, and supporting the implementation of an integrated cancer screening strategy. Previously, she was director of decision support and utilization management at Sunnybrook Health Sciences Centre. She holds a BSc (honours) in microbiology and immunology from McGill University and an MBA in health system management from McMaster University.

ROBERT OUELLET has nearly 20 years' experience working in both public and private health-care sectors. He launched and ran Canada's first private CT scan clinic in 1987 and Laval's first private MRI clinic. He currently provides radiology and management services at the five clinics he runs, and radiology services at the L.H.-Lafontaine Hospital. He previously worked in the radiology departments of the Trois-Rivières Regional Medical Hospital, the Saint-Marie Pavilion, the Saint-Joseph Hospital in La Tuque, the L.H.-Lafontaine Hospital in Montreal, the Centre hospitalier ambulatoire régional de Laval, and the Cité de la Santé de Laval (where he also served as head of the department). Robert serves as a board member of the Canadian Medical Association and has served as president of the Quebec Medical Association, as an imagery consultant on the Laval integrated network information system, and as an advisor on a Canada Health Infoway committee.

DOROTHY PRINGLE is professor emeritus at the University of Toronto where she was dean of nursing from 1988–1999. Since 1999 she has served as the executive lead of Health Outcomes for Better Information and Care (HOBIC), an Ontario Ministry of Health and Long-Term Care initiative to integrate a set of nursing-sensitive patient outcomes that are electronically assessed by nurses across Ontario health-care facilities. She has five honorary degrees, is a recipient of the Jeanne Mance Award from the Canadian Nurses Association for lifetime contributions to nursing, and was invested as an officer of the Order of Canada in 2008. She was the inaugural chair of the Institute Advisory Board of the CIHR Institute of Aging. Her research has focused on the well-being of family caregivers of individuals with dementia and on the quality of daily life of cognitively impaired older people.

SEAN B. ROURKE is currently scientist and director of research for the Mental Health Service at St. Michael's Hospital, and associate professor of psychiatry at the University of Toronto. In these roles, Sean has built an internationally recognized research program focusing on the neurobehavioural complications associated with HIV. Since 2004 he has also been the scientific and executive director of the Ontario HIV Treatment Network (OHTN), where he has been instrumental in developing and implementing the OHTN's strategic plan to move research evidence into action, and to establish the OHTN as a leading organization for HIV research and knowledge transfer in Canada. In 2009, he became the director for the CIHR Centre for REACH in HIV/AIDS and Universities Without Walls, both national initiatives to build capacity in population health and health services, and to help train the next generation of HIV researchers in Canada. Sean received his PhD in clinical psychology with a specialization in clinical neuropsychology from the University of California at San Diego in 1995.

PAMELA SPENCER is vice-president of corporate services, and general counsel and chief privacy officer at Cancer Care Ontario (CCO). She manages a diverse portfolio at CCO including legal, procurement, facilities and leasing, privacy, and enterprise risk management. Pamela also serves as corporate secretary to the CCO Board of Directors. Prior to joining CCO in 2003, she practised corporate commercial law, specializing in the health sector, at Fraser Milner Casgrain LLP. Pamela is a Certified Health Law Specialist, Law Society of Upper Canada; former chair of the Ontario Bar Association, Health Law Executive; and former chair of the Law Society of Upper Canada, Health Law Specialist Certification Committee. She has written and lectured widely on many aspects of health law and health privacy. She holds a law degree from Osgoode Hall Law School, as well as a bachelor in social sciences from the University of Ottawa and a master's in health science in the Health Administration/Collaborative Program in Bioethics from the University of Toronto.

TERRENCE SULLIVAN is the independent chair of the board of the Canadian Agency for Drugs and Technologies in Health. He is also the chair of the board of the Ontario Agency for Health Protection and Promotion. He has worked at Cancer Care Ontario since 2001, including seven years as president and chief executive officer. Terry is the founding president of the Institute for Work and Health, and has played senior roles in the Ontario ministries of Health, Cabinet Office, and Intergovernmental Affairs. He served as assistant deputy minister, Constitutional Affairs and Federal Provincial Relations, during the Charlottetown negotiations and for two successive first ministers of Ontario as executive director of the Premier's Council on Health Strategy, including a period as deputy minister (1991). Terry is the author/editor of seven recent books, over 100 papers, and dozens of reports on occupational health, health policy, and cancer control. He holds faculty appointments at the University of Toronto and is an associate scientist at St. Michael's Hospital in Toronto.

SIMON B. SUTCLIFFE graduated with honours from St Bartholomew's Hospital, London, in 1970. His training has encompassed internal medicine, scientific research, and medical and radiation oncology in the United Kingdom, South Africa, the United States, and Canada. He has held appointments as a clinical oncologist at St Bartholomew's Hospital, Princess Margaret Hospital, and the BC Cancer Agency; as a senior scientist at the Ontario Cancer Institute and the BC Cancer Agency; and as vice president, oncology programs, and president and CEO at the Princess Margaret Hospital/Ontario Cancer Institute and BC Cancer Agency (1979 through 2009). Simon currently chairs the boards of the Canadian Partnership Against Cancer, and the Institute for Health Services Sustainability. He is president of the International Cancer Control Congress Association and the International Network for Cancer Treatment and Research – Canada branch, and a senior advisor to the Terry Fox Research Institute. Simon was awarded the Queen Elizabeth 50th Jubilee Gold Medal in 2003, and the Terry Fox Award (of the BC Medical Association) in 2009 for his lifetime services to cancer control.

ROBYN TAMBLYN is a professor in the Departments of Medicine, and Epidemiology and Biostatistics in the Faculty of Medicine at McGill University. She also holds a position as medical scientist at the McGill University Health Centre Research Institute. Robyn directs a CIHR-funded team that investigates the use of e-health technologies to support integrated care for chronic disease. She also leads initiatives to optimize drug and chronic disease management and enhance the early uptake of evidence into primary care practice, the Medical Office of the 21st Century (MOXXI). Robyn is the scientific director of the Clinical and Health Informatics Research Group at McGill, where she led the development of IRIS-Quebec and the Informatics Innovation Laboratory. Robyn holds a PhD in epidemiology from McGill University, as well as a BSc in nursing and an MSc in epidemiology from McMaster University. She is also a James McGill chair.

DARIEN TAYLOR is director of program delivery at CATIE (Canadian AIDS Treatment Information Exchange) and has been living with and working in the field of HIV for approximately 20 years. Her work focuses on knowledge translation and exchange activities, which have made research findings available in plain language to members of the HIV community. She has represented the HIV community's research needs and interests to policy-makers and researchers, and helped to move HIV research into action. Darien was an editor of an early women's HIV publication, *Positive Women: Voices of Women Living with AIDS*. She was very involved in the activist organization AIDS ACTION NOW! and in the early 1990s founded Voices of Positive Women, an Ontario-based organization for women living with HIV. She has also served as scientific officer for the Canadian Institute for HIV Research's Community-Based Research Merit Review Committee.

BRYAN THOMAS is a research associate / research manager with the Faculty of Law, University of Toronto. His research interests include Canadian constitutional law, liberal theory, and health law and policy. Bryan holds an SJD from the University of Toronto and an MA in philosophy from Dalhousie.

JACK V. TU is a senior scientist at the Institute for Clinical Evaluative Sciences (ICES) in Toronto and is head of the Cardiovascular and Diagnostic Imaging research program at ICES. In addition, he holds a Canada Research Chair in Health Services Research Tier I and is professor of medicine, health policy, and management and evaluation at the University of Toronto. He is an attending physician in cardiology (Schulich Heart Program) at Sunnybrook Health Sciences Centre. He is also the team leader of the Canadian Cardiovascular Outcomes Research Team, a group of over 30 of Canada's leading cardiac outcomes researchers, who are conducting a number of innovative projects on access to quality cardiac care in Canada. Jack holds an MD from the University of Western Ontario, an MSc in clinical epidemiology from the University of Toronto, and a PhD in health policy from Harvard University.

DON WILLISON is senior scientist in the Surveillance and Epidemiology Division of the Ontario Agency for Health Protection and Promotion in Toronto. He has part-time faculty positions in the Department of Clinical Epidemiology and Biostatistics at McMaster University and at the Dalla Lana School of Public Health at the University of Toronto. A key focus of his research is in the area of governance over the use of personal health information (PHI) and biological samples for health research. He has investigated research ethics board policies over use of PHI for research, the notification practices of academic health-care facilities regarding use of PHI for research, and public attitudes toward alternatives to traditional project-specific consent for use of their PHI for health research. He is also engaged in developing innovative approaches to the streamlining of the research ethics review process.

Queen's Policy Studies
Recent Publications

The Queen's Policy Studies Series is dedicated to the exploration of major public policy issues that confront governments and society in Canada and other nations.

Manuscript submission. We are pleased to consider new book proposals and manuscripts. Preliminary enquiries are welcome. A subvention is normally required for the publication of an academic book. Please direct questions or proposals to the Publications Unit by email at spspress@queensu.ca, or visit our website at: www.queensu.ca/sps/books, or contact us by phone at (613) 533-2192.

Our books are available from good bookstores everywhere, including the Queen's University bookstore (http://www.campusbookstore.com/). McGill-Queen's University Press is the exclusive world representative and distributor of books in the series. A full catalogue and ordering information may be found on their web site (http://mqup.mcgill.ca/).

School of Policy Studies

Making the Case: Using Case Studies for Teaching and Knowledge Management in Public Administration, Andrew Graham, 2011. Paper ISBN 978-1-55339-302-3

Canada's Isotope Crisis: What Next? Jatin Nathwani and Donald Wallace (eds.), 2010. Paper ISBN 978-1-55339-283-5 Cloth ISBN 978-1-55339-284-2

Pursuing Higher Education in Canada: Economic, Social, and Policy Dimensions, Ross Finnie, Marc Frenette, Richard E. Mueller, and Arthur Sweetman (eds.), 2010. Paper ISBN 978-1-55339-277-4 Cloth ISBN 978-1-55339-278-1

Canadian Immigration: Economic Evidence for a Dynamic Policy Environment, Ted McDonald, Elizabeth Ruddick, Arthur Sweetman, and Christopher Worswick (eds.), 2010. Paper ISBN 978-1-55339-281-1 Cloth ISBN 978-1-55339-282-8

Taking Stock: Research on Teaching and Learning in Higher Education, Julia Christensen Hughes and Joy Mighty (eds.), 2010. Paper ISBN 978-1-55339-271-2 Cloth ISBN 978-1-55339-272-9

Architects and Innovators: Building the Department of Foreign Affairs and International Trade, 1909–2009/Architectes et innovateurs : le développement du ministère des Affaires étrangères et du Commerce international,de 1909 à 2009, Greg Donaghy and Kim Richard Nossal (eds.), 2009. Paper ISBN 978-1-55339-269-9 Cloth ISBN 978-1-55339-270-5

Academic Transformation: The Forces Reshaping Higher Education in Ontario, Ian D. Clark, Greg Moran, Michael L. Skolnik, and David Trick, 2009. Paper ISBN 978-1-55339-238-5 Cloth ISBN 978-1-55339-265-1

The New Federal Policy Agenda and the Voluntary Sector: On the Cutting Edge, Rachel Laforest (ed.), 2009. Paper ISBN 978-1-55339-132-6

Measuring What Matters in Peace Operations and Crisis Management, Sarah Jane Meharg, 2009. Paper ISBN 978-1-55339-228-6 Cloth ISBN 978-1-55339-229-3

International Migration and the Governance of Religious Diversity, Paul Bramadat and Matthias Koenig (eds.), 2009. Paper ISBN 978-1-55339-266-8 Cloth ISBN 978-1-55339-267-5

Who Goes? Who Stays? What Matters? Accessing and Persisting in Post-Secondary Education in Canada, Ross Finnie, Richard E. Mueller, Arthur Sweetman, and Alex Usher (eds.), 2008. Paper ISBN 978-1-55339-221-7 Cloth ISBN 978-1-55339-222-4

Economic Transitions with Chinese Characteristics: Thirty Years of Reform and Opening Up,
Arthur Sweetman and Jun Zhang (eds.), 2009.
Paper ISBN 978-1-55339-225-5 Cloth ISBN 978-1-55339-226-2

Economic Transitions with Chinese Characteristics: Social Change During Thirty Years of Reform, Arthur Sweetman and Jun Zhang (eds.), 2009.
Paper ISBN 978-1-55339-234-7 Cloth ISBN 978-1-55339-235-4

Dear Gladys: Letters from Over There, Gladys Osmond (Gilbert Penney ed.), 2009.
Paper ISBN 978-1-55339-223-1

Immigration and Integration in Canada in the Twenty-first Century, John Biles,
Meyer Burstein, and James Frideres (eds.), 2008.
Paper ISBN 978-1-55339-216-3 Cloth ISBN 978-1-55339-217-0

Robert Stanfield's Canada, Richard Clippingdale, 2008. Cloth ISBN 978-1-55339-218-7

Exploring Social Insurance: Can a Dose of Europe Cure Canadian Health Care Finance?
Colleen Flood, Mark Stabile, and Carolyn Tuohy (eds.), 2008.
Paper ISBN 978-1-55339-136-4 Cloth ISBN 978-1-55339-213-2

Canada in NORAD, 1957–2007: A History, Joseph T. Jockel, 2007.
Paper ISBN 978-1-55339-134-0 Cloth ISBN 978-1-55339-135-7

Canadian Public-Sector Financial Management, Andrew Graham, 2007.
Paper ISBN 978-1-55339-120-3 Cloth ISBN 978-1-55339-121-0

Emerging Approaches to Chronic Disease Management in Primary Health Care,
John Dorland and Mary Ann McColl (eds.), 2007.
Paper ISBN 978-1-55339-130-2 Cloth ISBN 978-1-55339-131-9

Fulfilling Potential, Creating Success: Perspectives on Human Capital Development,
Garnett Picot, Ron Saunders and Arthur Sweetman (eds.), 2007.
Paper ISBN 978-1-55339-127-2 Cloth ISBN 978-1-55339-128-9

Reinventing Canadian Defence Procurement: A View from the Inside, Alan S. Williams, 2006.
Paper ISBN 0-9781693-0-1 (Published in association with Breakout Educational Network)

SARS in Context: Memory, History, Policy, Jacalyn Duffin and Arthur Sweetman (eds.),
2006. Paper ISBN 978-0-7735-3194-9 Cloth ISBN 978-0-7735-3193-2
(Published in association with McGill-Queen's University Press)

Dreamland: How Canada's Pretend Foreign Policy has Undermined Sovereignty,
Roy Rempel, 2006. Paper ISBN 1-55339-118-7 Cloth ISBN 1-55339-119-5
(Published in association with Breakout Educational Network)

Canadian and Mexican Security in the New North America: Challenges and Prospects,
Jordi Díez (ed.), 2006. Paper ISBN 978-1-55339-123-4 Cloth ISBN 978-1-55339-122-7

Global Networks and Local Linkages: The Paradox of Cluster Development in an Open Economy, David A. Wolfe and Matthew Lucas (eds.), 2005.
Paper ISBN 1-55339-047-4 Cloth ISBN 1-55339-048-2

Choice of Force: Special Operations for Canada, David Last and Bernd Horn (eds.), 2005.
Paper ISBN 1-55339-044-X Cloth ISBN 1-55339-045-8

Centre for the Study of Democracy

Jimmy and Rosalynn Carter: A Canadian Tribute, Arthur Milnes (ed.), 2011.
Paper ISBN 978-1-55339-300-9 Cloth ISBN 978-1-55339-301-6

Unrevised and Unrepented II: Debating Speeches and Others By the Right Honourable Arthur Meighen, Arthur Milnes (ed.), 2011. Paper ISBN 978-1-55339-296-5
Cloth ISBN 978-1-55339-297-2

The Authentic Voice of Canada: R.B. Bennett's Speeches in the House of Lords, 1941-1947, Christopher McCreery and Arthur Milnes (eds.), 2009.
Paper ISBN 978-1-55339-275-0 Cloth ISBN 978-1-55339-276-7

Age of the Offered Hand: The Cross-Border Partnership Between President George H.W. Bush and Prime-Minister Brian Mulroney, A Documentary History, James McGrath and Arthur Milnes (eds.), 2009. Paper ISBN 978-1-55339-232-3
Cloth ISBN 978-1-55339-233-0

In Roosevelt's Bright Shadow: Presidential Addresses About Canada from Taft to Obama in Honour of FDR's 1938 Speech at Queen's University, Christopher McCreery and Arthur Milnes (eds.), 2009. Paper ISBN 978-1-55339-230-9 Cloth ISBN 978-1-55339-231-6

Politics of Purpose, 40th Anniversary Edition, The Right Honourable John N. Turner 17th Prime Minister of Canada, Elizabeth McIninch and Arthur Milnes (eds.), 2009.
Paper ISBN 978-1-55339-227-9 Cloth ISBN 978-1-55339-224-8

Bridging the Divide: Religious Dialogue and Universal Ethics, Papers for The InterAction Council, Thomas S. Axworthy (ed.), 2008. Paper ISBN 978-1-55339-219-4
Cloth ISBN 978-1-55339-220-0

Institute of Intergovernmental Relations

Canada: The State of the Federation 2009, vol. 22, *Carbon Pricing and Environmental Federalism,* Thomas J. Courchene and John R. Allan (eds.), 2010.
Paper ISBN 978-1-55339-196-8 Cloth ISBN 978-1-55339-197-5

Canada: The State of the Federation 2008, vol. 21, *Open Federalism and the Spending Power,* Thomas J. Courchene, John R. Allan, and Hoi Kong (eds.), forthcoming.
Paper ISBN 978-1-55339-194-4

The Democratic Dilemma: Reforming the Canadian Senate, Jennifer Smith (ed.), 2009.
Paper ISBN 978-1-55339-190-6

Canada: The State of the Federation 2006/07, vol. 20, *Transitions – Fiscal and Political Federalism in an Era of Change,* John R. Allan, Thomas J. Courchene, and Christian Leuprecht (eds.), 2009. Paper ISBN 978-1-55339-189-0 Cloth ISBN 978-1-55339-191-3

Comparing Federal Systems, Third Edition, Ronald L. Watts, 2008.
Paper ISBN 978-1-55339-188-3

Canada: The State of the Federation 2005, vol. 19, *Quebec and Canada in the New Century – New Dynamics, New Opportunities,* Michael Murphy (ed.), 2007.
Paper ISBN 978-1-55339-018-3 Cloth ISBN 978-1-55339-017-6

Spheres of Governance: Comparative Studies of Cities in Multilevel Governance Systems, Harvey Lazar and Christian Leuprecht (eds.), 2007. Paper ISBN 978-1-55339-019-0
Cloth ISBN 978-1-55339-129-6

Canada: The State of the Federation 2004, vol. 18, *Municipal-Federal-Provincial Relations in Canada,* Robert Young and Christian Leuprecht (eds.), 2006.
Paper ISBN 1-55339-015-6 Cloth ISBN 1-55339-016-4

Canadian Fiscal Arrangements: What Works, What Might Work Better, Harvey Lazar (ed.), 2005. Paper ISBN 1-55339-012-1 Cloth ISBN 1-55339-013-X

Canada: The State of the Federation 2003, vol. 17, *Reconfiguring Aboriginal-State Relations,* Michael Murphy (ed.), 2005. Paper ISBN 1-55339-010-5 Cloth ISBN 1-55339-011-3

Queen's Centre for International Relations

Security Operations in the 21st Century: Canadian Perspectives on the Comprehensive Approach, Michael Rostek and Peter Gizewski (eds.), 2011. Paper ISBN 978-1-55339-351-1

Europe Without Soldiers? Recruitment and Retention across the Armed Forces of Europe, Tibor Szvircsev Tresch and Christian Leuprecht (eds.), 2010.
Paper ISBN 978-1-55339-246-0 Cloth ISBN 978-1-55339-247-7

Mission Critical: Smaller Democracies' Role in Global Stability Operations, Christian Leuprecht, Jodok Troy, and David Last (eds.), 2010. Paper ISBN 978-1-55339-244-6

The Afghanistan Challenge: Hard Realities and Strategic Choices, Hans-Georg Ehrhart and Charles Pentland (eds.), 2009. Paper ISBN 978-1-55339-241-5

John Deutsch Institute for the Study of Economic Policy

The 2009 Federal Budget: Challenge, Response and Retrospect, Charles M. Beach, Bev Dahlby and Paul A.R. Hobson (eds.), 2010. Paper ISBN 978-1-55339-165-4
Cloth ISBN 978-1-55339-166-1

Discount Rates for the Evaluation of Public Private Partnerships, David F. Burgess and Glenn P. Jenkins (eds.), 2010. Paper ISBN 978-1-55339-163-0 Cloth ISBN 978-1-55339-164-7

Retirement Policy Issues in Canada, Michael G. Abbott, Charles M. Beach, Robin W. Boadway, and James G. MacKinnon (eds.), 2009.
Paper ISBN 978-1-55339-161-6 Cloth ISBN 978-1-55339-162-3

The 2006 Federal Budget: Rethinking Fiscal Priorities, Charles M. Beach, Michael Smart, and Thomas A. Wilson (eds.), 2007. Paper ISBN 978-1-55339-125-8
Cloth ISBN 978-1-55339-126-6

Health Services Restructuring in Canada: New Evidence and New Directions, Charles M. Beach, Richard P. Chaykowksi, Sam Shortt, France St-Hilaire, and Arthur Sweetman (eds.), 2006. Paper ISBN 978-1-55339-076-3
Cloth ISBN 978-1-55339-075-6

A Challenge for Higher Education in Ontario, Charles M. Beach (ed.), 2005.
Paper ISBN 1-55339-074-1 Cloth ISBN 1-55339-073-3

Current Directions in Financial Regulation, Frank Milne and Edwin H. Neave (eds.), Policy Forum Series no. 40, 2005. Paper ISBN 1-55339-072-5 Cloth ISBN 1-55339-071-7

Higher Education in Canada, Charles M. Beach, Robin W. Boadway, and R. Marvin McInnis (eds.), 2005. Paper ISBN 1-55339-070-9 Cloth ISBN 1-55339-069-5
